"A compelling book with provocative details of a city's response to lost innocence; whether justice was delivered or denied, Corey Mitchell presents a solid case that hope for healing never fades."—**Joyce King**

"*Murdered Innocents* is not a book you will read and forget. On this journey through a botched investigation, questionable interrogations and the eight-year ordeal of the victims' families, Mitchell raises questions about the pursuit of justice that will haunt you for a long time to come."—**Diane Fanning**

"Corey Mitchell takes us right inside the search for justice— a disturbingly long and convoluted search at that. A haunting and thought-provoking book."—**Sue Russell**

"Corey Mitchell proves that he is the leading voice of true crime with *Murdered Innocents,* a complex, frightening, and frustrating tale of Texas Terror."—**Dennis McDougal**

Dead and Buried:

"A front seat on a roller coaster of terror."—Dennis McDougal

"Some of the most up-close, incisive true-crime coverage in a long time."—**Poppy Z. Brite**

"A powerful and frightening book. It is not to be missed."
—**Dana Holliday,** coauthor of *Zodiac of Death*

Also by Corey Mitchell*

Dead and Buried
Murdered Innocents
Evil Eyes
Pure Murder
Savage Son

*Available from Kensington Publishing Corp.

STRANGLER

COREY
MITCHELL

PINNACLE BOOKS
Kensington Publishing Corp.
http://www.kensingtonbooks.com

PINNACLE BOOKS are published by

Kensington Publishing Corp.
119 West 40th Street
New York, NY 10018

All Kensington Titles, Imprints, and Distributed Lines are available at special quantity discounts for bulk purchases for sales promotions, premiums, fund-raising, and educational or institutional use. Special book excerpts or customized printings can also be created to fit specific needs. For details, write or phone the office of the Kensington special sales manager: Kensington Publishing Corp., 119 West 40th Street, New York, NY 10018, attn: Special Sales Department, Phone: 1-800-221-2647.

Pinnacle and the P logo Reg. U.S. Pat. & TM Off.

ISBN-13: 978-0-7860-4262-3
ISBN-10: 0-7860-4262-1
First Kensington Mass Market Edition: September 2007

eISBN-13: 978-0-7860-4263-0
eISBN-10: 0-7860-4263-X
Kensington Electronic Edition: February 2018

10 9 8 7 6 5 4 3

Printed in the United States of America

For Emma Mitchell,
with love and respect,
Daddy

One may understand the cosmos, but never the ego; the self is more distant than any star.

—Gilbert Keith Chesterton

PROLOGUE

Friday, July 14, 1995, noon,
KPRC Channel 2 Newsroom,
Houston, Texas.

"There's a serial killer out there."

The male voice on the other end of the "Bat Phone" spoke calmly. Twenty-three-year-old Barbara Magana, morning assignment editor for NBC television news affiliate KPRC, listened to her end of the telephone with only half an ear. Her job was to monitor the police scanner and answer phone calls for any possible stories and then assign them to reporters to air on the evening news at six.

While many of her coworkers left for lunch, Magana had answered the Bat Phone, which was used as an emergency tip line. Everyone who called the tip line claimed his or her call was urgent. Usually they weren't. Most of the time they were simply reporting an automobile accident or a purse snatching, all too common occurrences in the fourth-largest city in the United States.

The Bat Phone also received its fair share of wack jobs.

At first, Magana only partially listened to the caller.

Another nutcase she assumed. "How do you know?" she responded.

"I'm going to tell you where you can find a body," the man replied rather nonchalantly.

"Tell me where I can find the body," Magana requested in an almost sarcastic tone.

The caller, however, did not hesitate. He began to describe a location just north of Houston, near the George (H. W.) Bush Intercontinental Airport.

Magana patiently wrote down the directions, but did not understand where one of the streets was located.

"Richey Road in Pasadena?" Magana inquired.

The man had been referring to the Richey Road off Interstate 45 (I-45) in North Houston. The caller was getting tired of Magana's inability to take dictation and let his frustration be known. "No, listen to me. I'm going to tell you exactly where it is." He was adamant that she do everything perfectly.

After the man snapped at Magana, her demeanor visibly changed. She realized this was not some fruitcake after all. She was on the phone with someone who knew where a murdered corpse lay.

The man proceeded to give Magana a precise description of the location of the body. "Take I-45 until you hit the Richey Road exit. Turn right and head up until you come upon Northview Park Drive and turn left. Go all the way to the end of Northview Park, where you will come to a dead-end sign. You will find the body lying in some tall grass. Some tall weeds."

Magana instinctively reached for her Houston Key Map guide to find the location. She used one on her job all the time.

The caller eerily informed her, "Don't go for your Key Map. You won't find it. It's a brand-new subdivision. It's not on a Key Map yet."

Magana was completely freaked out. Is he watching me? she thought. She also started to wonder if the caller was more than just a witness.

"You can use your chopper to find her," said the caller, referring to the Channel 2 News helicopter, which was often used for live coverage. "She's lying faceup and your chopper should be able to spot her rather easily."

Determined not to let this man get off the telephone, Magana asked, "What can you tell me about the victim?"

"Her name is Ruby," began the caller. "She was born on May eleventh. She is wearing several gold rings on her fingers. She is fifteen years old."

Magana wrote furiously as the man recited the information. Sensing that he was wrapping up the conversation, she boldly decided to ply him with one final question.

"Am I talking to the killer?"

There was only silence punctuated by short drawn breaths on the other end of the phone.

"Am I talking to the killer?" Magana asked again.

Again, a breath. And then a small laugh. The phone went dead.

Magana hung up the Bat Phone and glanced up at the newsroom clock: 12:37 P.M. She had spoken to the alleged killer for thirty-seven minutes. She logged the call in the company book and then kicked it into high gear. She started by looking up the address of the alleged body dump. In her mind Magana kept thinking of nearby Pasadena, but she eliminated that thought from her head and focused on North Houston. She was able to pinpoint the location as just outside the city limits. She then picked up a different phone and notified the sheriff's department of a tip about a possible murder victim.

* * *

Friday, July 14, 1995, 2:35 P.M.,
17000 block of Northview Park Drive.

Harris County Sheriff's Department (HCSD) Homicide Division detective William "Bill" Valerio arrived at the dead end of an industrial-area concrete road. He was the one who fielded the tip call from Barbara Magana. Northview Park Drive is located just east of Interstate 45 and south of Richey Road. At the time, the area was considered to be a "light industrial area." It is currently home to a typical American big-box urban sprawl with a Lowe's and generic chain restaurants, like Chili's and T.G.I. Friday's.

Instead of immediately rushing to the location provided to him by Magana, Valerio opted to hold back. He believed that people who call in tips for dead bodies oftentimes may hang around the scene and attempt to interject themselves into the investigation. He had a feeling that would be the case here, so he drove around the area looking for a male between the ages of thirty and forty, probably white, possibly Hispanic. It was easy work. There was practically no vehicle traffic in the area and absolutely no foot traffic.

Detective Valerio was joined at the scene by Harris County Sheriff's detectives Roger Wedgeworth and Bill Taber. The three men began their search in a field at the dead end of Northview Park. It was covered in dense thornbushes making it nearly impossible to even walk through, much less search. They glanced at one another and concluded that no one would be able to successfully dump a body in that particular area.

The officers then decided to search the three dead-end streets off Northview Park. The first street, Northtrace Drive, is located on the west side of the field they had just searched. They found nothing.

The second street, Willow Drive, is located on the north side of Northview Park. Again, they found nothing.

The officers got back into their cars and headed over to Northview Park Drive, off Richey Road. At the end of the wide concrete road, Detective Valerio exited his cruiser and made his way over to the nearby field overgrown with tall green grass, acutely aware of the oppressive heat that had marked this unreasonably hot summer, even for the notoriously scorching Houston.

Taber and Wedgeworth pulled their vehicle up next to Valerio's. Taber headed toward the west side of the street while Valerio checked the east side.

The familiar, acrid smell caught Detective Taber's attention.

"Valerio, get over here!" Taber hollered. Valerio sidled up to the edge of the field. He noticed that the green grass was blotted with a large twenty-foot-long pathway of dead brown grass. At the upper portion of the dead grass path was an image that would forever be etched in the mind of the thirteen-year veteran detective. It was the severely decomposed body of a human being. It appeared as if a scarecrow had been blown off its perch by a tornado, its clothes and hat ripped off in the process, revealing nothing but the skeletal remains.

As Valerio stepped closer to the body, combating the stench and controlling his gag reflex, he noticed a full head of black hair, almost like a wig, atop a human skull. The skull was not completely shorn of all its flesh. It appeared as if the skull were wearing a Leatherface mask from *The Texas Chainsaw Massacre*. It was a grayish tan color. Bits of the skull peeked out at certain points. The victim's eyeballs were missing and the ears were halfway chewed off. Valerio turned his head away and gathered his senses. When he turned back to the corpse, he looked closer at the neck. There appeared to be some type of yellow nylon rope, like a boat-docking rope, twisted around it. The ends of the rope had been purposefully melted to prevent fraying. Inserted within the rope was what appeared to be two pieces of a broken blue toothbrush handle. The end with the bristles was positioned directly below the area of the ligature. The entire contraption had the rudimentary appearance of a crude tourniquet.

Valerio stepped back to inspect more of the body. He noticed that the entire rib cage was exposed and that a black, mucouslike liquid encased the body like a chicken in mole sauce. The leg bones were also completely stripped of flesh and covered in the black liquid. Strangely enough, the flesh on the skeleton's feet was still relatively intact.

The arms of the victim were similar. Large portions of exposed bone peered out from in between shards of tan flesh. The hands of the victim, however, seemed to be wearing Ed Geinish flesh gloves.

The entire pelvic region was also flesh-free and covered in the same black fluid.

It was completely contorted, lying on its left side with the head hyperextended backward.

As the detectives and Crime Scene Unit (CSU) specialists processed the scene, several patrol officers approached and questioned any looky-lous who may have wandered nearby the scene. Detective Valerio surmised that the killer might stop by to witness the police assessing his or her handiwork.

The body lay directly in the flight path from the majority of departing airplanes, as if the killer wanted the pilots of those planes to spot the body. In between engine roars Valerio was able to confer with one of the officers about a missing person who might fit the description of the corpse before them.

Sixteen-year-old Dana Sanchez had gone missing eight days earlier. Her physical description matched that of the corpse, from the long black hair to the jewelry that still adorned the body.

Valerio first had his assistants track down the family of Ruby Ambriz, a young Hispanic girl who had been reported missing, but the girl's father informed them that he had heard from his daughter the night before.

With the missing Ruby ruled out, Valerio concluded the body belonged to Dana Sanchez, and later, after conferring with Houston Homicide detectives, it was suggested that Sanchez was probably the third serial-killing victim in three years. The previous two victims were twenty-one-year-old Maria del Carmen Estrada and nine-year-old Diana Rebollar. All three were attractive, diminutive Hispanic girls, with long, straight black hair.

Part I

CARMEN

Ego non baptizo te in nomine patris, sed in nomine diaboli!

—Herman Melville

(Translation:) "I baptize thee, not in the name of the father, but in the name of the devil!"

CHAPTER 1

In 1990, there were purportedly 12 million illegal immigrants in the United States, the vast majority of which came to America for economic reasons, taking some of the lowest-paid jobs to help their families back home.

It was under these conditions that Maria Carmen del Estrada followed her father, Felipe Estrada Santana, from Cuernavaca, Mexico, to Houston, Texas. Estrada, known to her friends and family as Carmen, or Carmelita, grew up in the city of Lerdo, in the state of Coahuila, along with several brothers and sisters and numerous cousins. However, in 1991, she and several of these family members decided to pursue the so-called American Dream. So, she emigrated to Houston and moved into a tiny apartment in the Shady Villa complex, along with her father, her brother Guadalupe Estrada, her cousin Remigio Estrada, and another cousin, Andrea Miranda. Carmen was the only female in the apartment.

In 1991, Houston, dubbed the "Murder Capital of the World" during the 1970s and 1980s, was awfully close to regaining that title yet again. The Houston Police Department (HPD) reported 608 homicide victims, with 84 percent of them male, 16 percent female. In addition, the HCSD reported 102 homicides, with 84 percent male and 16 percent female.

The men in Carmen Estrada's family were very protective of her. A very beautiful young lady, she was petite, standing only five feet one inch and weighing 104 pounds, and looked much younger than her twenty-one years. She had long, thick, straight black hair that billowed down to the middle of her back and was always well-kempt, and her smooth olive complexion was offset by beautiful almond-shaped dark brown eyes and red Cupid's-bow lips.

Carmen was determined to make a better life for her and her family, and to accomplish her goal, she arduously worked two jobs. She babysat a neighborhood four-year-old boy, who suffered from diabetes, in a nearby apartment complex from 7:00 A.M. to 4:30 P.M., and then went directly to her night job working as a maid on a night shift crew for an office-building cleaning company.

Carmen's best friend was a young woman named Rosa Agreda, who originally migrated from Mexico City to the United States in 1985, under the same conditions as Carmen, and even attended school in the United States. Rosa, though, dropped out before ninth grade, and by the time Carmen met Agreda, Rosa had two children, both of whom were conceived and born in the United States.

Carmen was introduced to Rosa by her father, who said he had been friends with Rosa's grandmother back in Mexico.

And it was actually Rosa who referred Carmen to Janice Travis, the mother of the young boy with diabetes, after Agreda, who had taken care of the little boy, got a job as a leasing agent that paid more money.

Carmen was usually the first passenger on the #72 Westview bus, which she took every day to her babysitting job, according to the bus driver, Patrick Bolger.

Bolger always attempted to engage her in small talk, but she would demur only offering him a smile, paying her bus fare, and quietly ambling toward her seat. Over time, Carmen loosened up around Bolger and began reciprocating "Hellos" and "Have a nice days," albeit in Spanish. She never spoke to any of the passengers on the bus.

Rosa recalled Carmen as painfully shy. And the fact that she did not speak any English did not make things any easier for her. She almost never dated. Even when Roas would introduce Carmen to one of her friends, Carmen would *maybe* say "Hello" but would then recoil and not participate in the conversation.

Carmen's bus routine was pretty indicative of her social existence. She spent the majority of her time with her friend Rosa under some professional circumstance. The women had a daily routine: Carmen would go to Rosa's for breakfast before 7:00 A.M., then she would help out with the kids. Afterward, the ladies would head over to Mrs. Travis's apartment, which was less than a mile away. Rosa would act as an interpreter between Carmen and Janice, and then she would take off for her leasing job. The two young women would meet back at Rosa's for lunch, return to their jobs, and then return to Rosa's for dinner after work. Rosa referred to their time together as "our world, just us two."

Needless to say, Carmen had very little spare time for socializing. She did, however, meet a nice young Hispanic man named Jesus Torres de la Cruz, whom she began to date around December 1991. The couple led a very chaste relationship. Carmen believed in the sanctity of purity and informed Jesus that she would not have a sexual relationship with him until they were married. Jesus had no problem with her request, especially since the couple had begun to make wedding plans.

CHAPTER 2

Thursday, April 16, 1992, before 7:00 A.M.

Metro bus driver Patrick Bolger was concerned. The young man counted on Carmen Estrada's presence at her bus stop every Wednesday morning. On this day, however, she was a no-show. He actually waited at the corner for five minutes to see if she would appear. *Maybe she slept in late today* or *Maybe she's sick,* he thought. Bolger finally threw the bus into gear and slowly pulled out into the street. He glanced over at his side-view mirror for one last check, but did not spot his favorite passenger.

CHAPTER 3

Thursday, April 16, 1992, 10:30 A.M.,
Dairy Queen Restaurant Drive-thru,
6707 Westview Drive,
Houston, Texas.

Douglas Jackson wheeled his old beater into the Dairy Queen drive-thru. He and his coworker, Isaac Houston, had been bagging diapers on a local assembly line. The men had only worked three hours of a long twelve-hour workday, yet they were already famished. So, as was Jackson's daily routine, the two men took an early lunch at Dairy Queen, the world-famous fast-food ice cream and hamburger joint that Texas claimed as its creation. (Though, it originally did open in 1940, in Joliet, Illinois.)

After the two men placed their orders, Jackson threw his car into drive and pulled forward to the restaurant window, where the food was served piping hot.

Again, Jackson shifted his car into drive and slowly pulled forward. After only a few feet, he was forced to turn left, as there was a wooden fence to the right and a chain-link fence in front of him, but something caught Jackson's eye next to the concrete back wall of the Dairy Queen.

It was a half-naked body of a young woman.

Houston was staring at the girl's dead body, his mouth agape. Jackson looked back at the girl, but instead of stopping, he hit the gas pedal and took off.

They drove on, speechless.

CHAPTER 4

Thursday, April 16, 1992, 10:35 A.M.,
Dairy Queen Restaurant Drive-thru.

Robert Levy II backed his large Mrs. Baird's Bread
truck to the rear of the Dairy Queen restaurant. Levy was
a deliveryman for the bread giant, whose day began at
5:00 A.M. and sometimes lasted until 3:00 P.M., and the
Westview Drive Dairy Queen was one of his several stops.

The drive-thru exit shares space with the back door to
the restaurant, and Levy was forced to wait while an old
beater pulled around and exited the parking lot. Once
the back area was clear, he pulled the big bread truck
toward the back door. When he checked his driver's-side
mirror, he spotted something unusual—something too
big to roll over. He depressed the brakes and shifted into
park. The truck was mere inches from the object.

Levy climbed out of the cab of his truck to see what was
blocking his path. What he originally thought was a large
trash bag turned out to be the corpse of a young woman.

According to Levy, the body lay face first on the asphalt, right forearm tucked under right hip, and only a
few inches from a small hallway that led to the delivery

door at the back of the restaurant. Her left arm stretched forward above her head as if she were swimming the butterfly with one arm. Her legs were daintily crossed at the ankles. She wore a bright, short-sleeved silk blouse, with pink orchids and green-and-yellow plant patterns, which appeared to have been pushed or pulled up to the middle of her back; one-half of a white bra, which had been sliced down the middle between the cups, peeked out from underneath the left side of her blouse. The upper portion of her body lay directly below a yellow metal gutter drain.

She wore a pair of rainbow-colored cotton panties that appeared to have been torn in haste on the left side and dark tan pantyhose which had been pulled down to midthigh. Her panties were also rolled down and were intertwined with her pantyhose. The young woman's well-shaped bottom was exposed for the whole world to see.

Levy scooted past the body, onto the concrete back-door hallway, and began to bang on the large metal door at the back of the restaurant. The Dairy Queen manager came out back to see what all the fuss was about.

"Call the police," Levy barked.

The manager locked eyes with Levy, then followed the deliveryman's glance toward the dead body.

This was not the usual morning delivery.

CHAPTER 5

Thursday, April 16, 1992, 11:30 A.M.,
Dairy Queen Restaurant Drive-thru.

Sergeant Stuart "Hal" Kennedy, nineteen-year veteran of the Houston Police Department, and ten-year veteran of the Homicide Division, received the call at the downtown police headquarters at 1200 Travis Street. Kennedy and his partner, Sergeant Rick Massey, took almost thirty minutes to drive out to the Spring Branch location. Upon arrival, the sergeants were greeted by a uniformed patrol officer and a couple members of the Crime Scene Unit.

After conferring with the first responders, Kennedy and Massey walked around to the back of the store to look at the dead body. Based on the position of the body, Kennedy determined that she had probably been killed elsewhere and dumped behind the restaurant like a discarded hamburger wrapper. Kennedy also believed that the killer probably pulled her out of the driver's-side door, based on her position.

He also noted that he saw neither slacks nor a skirt near the body, and quickly determined that the young woman was probably a victim of sexual assault.

Sergeant Kennedy asked the medical examiner on the scene to turn the body over for a closer inspection. The young woman's right front side was covered in gravel from the asphalt parking lot, but amidst the gravel, the sergeant noticed something unusual on her left breast, surrounding her areola. It appeared to him that there were human bite marks.

Kennedy skimmed over the victim's neck area, where strangely the victim still wore a gold chain, but it was covered in long, thick black hair. He moved up toward her face. Her eyes were partially open, and her tongue had swollen up in her mouth and was partially distended beyond her lips. Her lips were also swollen and bloody, and had turned copper black. The cut was on the right side of her mouth and extended at least one-half inch outward. Blood from the cut acted as an adhesive to her long black hair and held it intact on her right cheek.

Sergeant Kennedy made sure that all of the evidence on the victim's body was properly recovered for any possible DNA specimen and she was swabbed in the usual areas conspicuously associated with sexual assault. He also later made sure the medical examiners clipped Estrada's fingernails to check for any possible skin scrapings that she may have picked up in case she defended herself against her attacker.

Kennedy was almost done with the perusal of Houston's latest casualty when he again looked at the young lady's neck. It almost went unnoticed a second time. Just above the gold necklace, Kennedy noticed a line across the victim's neck. It appeared as if she also wore a thin choker necklace.

It was a tiny, thin white rope cord. Kennedy lifted her head slightly to follow the path of the cord. The cord had been twisted tightly around her throat and knotted together on the right side of the back of her neck. These were not knots from tying one's shoes. These were a series of overhand square knots. Enclosed within the cord and the girl's hair was a small wooden dowel, which measured almost two inches in length and appeared to have been used as a tightening mechanism.

Kennedy had found the killer's weapon of choice, but it was the first time he had ever seen such a device used on a human. The detective, born in Wharton, Texas, had seen it used on horses. It was called a "twitch," a device used by ranchers to keep horses in line. It works by placing a rope in the mouth of the horse and slipping in a wooden piece and twisting it down. The end result is that the animal will move in whichever direction the rancher wants because it is at the rancher's mercy. By placing the twitch on her throat, the killer insured that his victim would not fight back. The girl's killer had to be one sick individual.

CHAPTER 6

Sergeant Kennedy spent the next few hours tending to the Dairy Queen crime scene. He interviewed all of the employees of the restaurant and no one had any idea who the girl was, nor had they seen any suspicious activity. There was also no video camera on the premises.

Some of the employees, however, were able to give a description of a vehicle that had used the drive-thru window at the approximate time that the body may have been dumped. They described the vehicle as a beige or tan four-door 1981 Pontiac Catalina. Also, they were able to give a description of the driver as a white male in his late thirties or early forties, short light-brown hair, and a mustache. The man wore dark-blue work pants and a short-sleeved button-down white shirt. He appeared to be medium weight and height.

The area surrounding the Dairy Queen is predominantly Hispanic. Practically no one in the area speaks English. To deal with this obstacle, Kennedy summoned the "Chicano Squad"—a group of Spanish-speaking police officers who focused on gangs. Once the Chicano Squad arrived, Kennedy ordered them to canvass the area and interview as many residents as possible.

Though most information collected proved to be fruit-less, Kennedy turned the crime scene over to the capable hands of the Chicano Squad and then returned to police headquarters.

It wasn't until nearly 10:00 P.M. that a determination was made as to who the dead girl was.

Sergeant Kennedy was approached by a group of Hispanics led by a distraught-looking man. The older gentleman clutched several photographs in his hand. He heard about the murder of a young woman and was worried because his daughter had not come home from work that evening.

The older gentleman, Felipe Estrada Santana, handed a photograph of his daughter, Carmen Estrada, to Sergeant Kennedy.

Right away, Kennedy knew he was standing before the father of the dead young woman.

CHAPTER 7

Thursday, April 16, 1992, 3:05 P.M.,
Office of the Medical Examiner of Harris County,
Joseph A. Jachimczyk Forensic Center,
1885 Old Spanish Trail,
Houston, Texas.

Deputy Chief Medical Examiner Aurelio Espinola stared at the corpse of Maria del Carmen Estrada. He began the clinical procedure with an external observation of the victim's body. Carmen measured only five-one and weighed in at 104 pounds. He noted that she had long, dark brown hair that measured approximately ten inches long from her scalp.

Her brown eyes matched her hair color. The whites of her eyes, however, were covered with tiny red dots known as petechiae, which are caused by a constriction to the air passage by some form of outside pressure. There were also signs of petechiae on the left side of Carmen's face and neck.

As Espinola continued his observation, he noticed a simple piece of white nylon string that only measured an eighth of an inch and was tied around her neck and knotted on the right side. The string was somewhat loose on her neck.

Espinola lifted up Estrada's long hair off the back of her neck to take a closer look. He saw that the string had been knotted very tight at the back of her neck. A small piece of wood that measured $3\frac{1}{8}$ inches in length by $\frac{3}{8}$ inches in diameter was inserted into the string. The wood appeared to be used as a tightening tool and both the wood and the string were intertwined with Carmen's hair. Dr. Espinola was able to separate the items from her hair and remove the ligature from around her neck. He noted that the impression left by the weapon measured a quarter inch in width.

Dr. Espinola directed his attention to Carmen's upper torso and chest area. He glanced at her left breast and determined that the abrasions first seen by Sergeant Kennedy were probably, in fact, bite marks from human teeth. The medical examiner also noted that there was blood in Carmen's vulva and vagina, as well as a contusion on the vagina in the "seven o'clock position."

After finishing up the external observation of Carmen Estrada, Dr. Espinola began the internal investigation. After opening up the twenty-one-year-old young woman's body, one which had been breathing and functioning just fine less than ten hours earlier, Dr. Espinola dictated that most everything inside Carmen seemed normal.

Except, of course, her throat and neck area.

There were several hemorrhages underneath where the ligature covered her light brown skin. Petechial hemorrhages were also found on her larynx and vocal cords. Also, her hyoid bone remained intact. The hyoid bone is oftentimes snapped when a person chokes someone to death with their hands. There was, however, slight hemorrhaging of the soft tissues that surrounded her hyoid bone.

Dr. Espinola's conclusion as to the cause of death for Carmen Estrada was fairly obvious: "asphyxia due to ligature strangulation."

CHAPTER 8

Saturday, April 18, 1992,
Houston, Texas.

Sergeant Kennedy was feeling a bit overwhelmed with the Carmen Estrada case and enlisted the assistance of HPD sergeant Jim Ramsey. Kennedy asked Ramsey to take Estrada's daily route to work, be it by bus or on foot, so he could question the young woman's neighbors.

Kennedy thought one possibility may have been that Estrada had been abducted while walking to work or while waiting for her bus. So, Ramsey also knocked on several hundred residents' doors along her route to see if anyone saw anything. Unfortunately, he struck out.

Kennedy also had members of the Chicano Squad create flyers with Estrada's photo and plaster them all over the Spring Branch area. The Chicano Squad also contacted the local Spanish-speaking media to help spread the word requesting information about the murder. This lit a fuse, and the police department received hundreds of calls in regard to the murder. Unfortunately, as is usually the case, almost all of them came from crackpots or vengeful boyfriends or girlfriends.

The police, however, had no choice but to look into each and every single lead for fear of leaving the appropriate stone unturned.

Sergeant Kennedy also enlisted the help of Sergeant Bill Dunn, from the HPD Sex Crimes Unit (SCU), whom Kennedy asked to try and find any similar cases to the Estrada murder. Unfortunately, despite Sergeant Kennedy and his staff sifting through hundreds of cases, they could not come up with anything in regard to Carmen Estrada.

But one benefit of requesting help from Sex Crimes was that Sergeant Dunn was able to have suspects come in and give up DNA samples to see if he could match the DNA recovered from under Carmen's fingernails and the semen allegedly discovered in Carmen's mouth. No matching DNA samples turned up, but Kennedy and Dunn were able to rule out certain suspects.

Sergeant Kennedy then contacted the Houston Chapter of Crime Stoppers for their assistance. Crime Stoppers, a crime-fighting organization that offers money to potential witnesses if their information leads to the arrest and conviction of criminal suspects, broadcasted information on the local media, but again, they received several tips that turned out to be worthless.

Despite the efforts of Sergeant Hal Kennedy, all roads led to dead ends in the case that came to be known as the "Dairy Queen Girl Murder."

Part II

DIANA

The ego is not master in its own house.

—Sigmund Freud

CHAPTER 9

Sunday, August 7, 1994, noon,
6600 block of North Main Street,
Houston, Texas.

Diana Rebollar stepped outside the front door of her family's home in the area known as The Heights and into the sweltering lunchtime heat of Houston, Texas. The Heights area sandwiched in between two major freeways—the North Loop West (Loop 610) and Interstate 10 (I-10)—was considered to be a calm, family-oriented neighborhood, conveniently located only five minutes north of downtown Houston. It is comprised of several medium-sized Victorian-era homes, as well as Craftsman bungalows, with numerous parks that dot the landscape and many streets that are kept cool by lush sweeping trees. The Heights has sometimes been called "the Mayberry RFD of Houston."

Diana's family lived in the front half of a duplex in a very modest-sized area of less than one thousand square feet. Tight quarters for a large family composed of parents, stepparents, grandmothers, cousins, brothers, sisters, stepbrothers, and stepsisters.

Diana was a very sweet, yet serious little girl. Born in Guerrero, Mexico, on September 3, 1984, she was the first child of Virginia and Rujilio Rebollar. She was followed the next year by brother Rosario, and the year after that by another brother, Rujilio Jr., whom everyone would call "Jose."

When Diana was only three years old, her father was murdered in the streets of Nuevo, Mexico. Not long thereafter, Diana would take to caring for her brothers and would often help her mother with household chores. Virginia described Diana as very "motherly."

Diana had aspirations of becoming a teacher one day. Even as a child she liked to "teach class" whenever there were guests over. She would have her company sit in chairs while she stood in front of the kitchen wall and wipe board and pretend to be in front of a chalkboard. After her lessons for the day she would send the guests away with homework.

Diana herself was a stellar student. She was easily self-motivated and very studious. She made straight A's in all her classes and the teachers adored her. She was looking forward to her upcoming tenth birthday and starting fourth grade at nearby Burrus Elementary School.

So, without a care in the world, the nine-year-old girl bounced down the three maroon concrete steps that had two house numbers and the name Steele spelled out in metal letters and numerals.

Her aunt Hermina Piedra had given her a $5 bill and asked her to fetch some sugar so they could sweeten their watermelon drinks. It only required walking two blocks, up north on Main Street to the Wing Fong grocery store, a task Diana had successfully undertaken several times throughout the summer. No one thought anything of sending the bilingual girl out on her own into their quaint, predominantly Hispanic neighborhood. And whether she was purchasing groceries or selling Chiclets at the C & F Drive Inn, a nearby watering hole, Diana was always safe and responsible.

Diana was dressed in blue flower shorts, a black Halloween T-shirt which had press-on patches of a bright orange pumpkin and a black cat on the chest, and a purple bat on the upper right area of the shirt near the sleeve. She wore her long brown hair braided in a ponytail, held up with an elastic band with medium-sized plastic baubles. Two tiny specks of gold dotted the bottoms of her earlobes.

As Diana stepped off the porch, she angled right onto the cracked cement sidewalk and headed north. The Wing Fong grocery store was located on the corner of Twenty-ninth Street and Main Street, right next to the freeway. Her round-trip, if she didn't dillydally, should have taken no longer than five to ten minutes.

It was not unusual for Diana's mother not to be aware of where her oldest daughter was—always having her hands full with the younger children.

Still, Virginia was very proud of her beautiful daughter. As a single mother, she had come to America from Mexico by herself to provide a better life for Diana and the rest of her family.

One year after Virginia emigrated, she sent for Diana. It was also at this time that she met the man who would become her new husband. His name was Jose Salazar, and he had a son named Jose Trinidad Salazar Jr., who was now four years old. Eventually Virginia and Jose were able to send for Rosario and Rujilio Jr. to come live with them in Houston, and in the spring of 1990, Virginia and Jose had a daughter of their own, Olga Nellie.

Virginia entrusted Diana with all of the younger children. She knew her oldest daughter was smart and responsible and could easily handle her younger brothers and sisters.

Sometime between 12:20 and 12:30 P.M., Virginia realized that Diana had not returned with the sugar. She placed her youngest daughter, Olga, in her swing, and went out the same front door to search for Diana. She followed her daughter's path down the sidewalk to the Wing Fong grocery store. She did not spot her coming back, so she went into the store. A small shop, it did not take long for her to scan the entire area.

Diana was nowhere to be found.

Virginia began to get concerned as she rushed out of the store, crossed west on Main Street, and walked down the opposite sidewalk back to her home. She became even more anxious as she passed a house where an older woman had recently been murdered and her dead body had been left on her own front porch—on the opposite side of the street from her own home. By the time she reached her stoop, Virginia was frantic. She ran inside to find her husband.

"Diana has not come home from the store! We need to call the police, now!" she screamed to him in Spanish. Jose did not hesitate as he picked up the telephone and dialed 911.

Houston police officer Fin Fahy knocked on the Salazars' front door. The three-year veteran worked in the Missing Persons Division. Before he joined the Houston Police Department, Fahy was a member of the United States Navy and had been deployed on assault craft units throughout Southeast Asia. But on this day, Fahy's most important skill was his fluency in Spanish, so he could speak with Diana Rebollar's family.

Virginia answered the front door and hurried the

officer into her home. Officer Fahy could see the tears streaming down Mrs. Salazar's face.

"Our daughter did not come home," Virginia cried.

Fahy knew he needed to move quickly so he began a search inside the Salazar home. Oftentimes, children under ten years of age who are believed to be missing can actually be located within their own residence playing hide-and-seek. Officer Fahy and his fellow officers looked in closets, in bathrooms, in bedrooms, underneath beds, and found no sign of Diana. Their next objective was to search the immediate outside perimeter of the home. They checked the backyard, behind bushes, and in the duplex garage, but again, found nothing.

The Missing Persons search team determined she was not on the premises, so they expanded their search to head north along Diana's path to the Wing Fong grocery store. One of the officers was able to confirm with a store employee that Diana had been inside the store, purchased the sugar, and left the store to return home.

The officers left the store and began to canvass the neighborhood. They were further able to determine that Diana was spotted leaving the store, crossing Twenty-ninth Street, heading south on the sidewalk, and up to the C & F Drive Inn. From that point on, only one block away from her home, no one could recall seeing Diana Rebollar.

Officer Fahy reconvened his crew and contacted police department headquarters for more backup. Houston police officers, as well as more Missing Persons detectives, were on their way. A determined Fahy even put in a request for a helicopter to scan from the skies.

The Salazars somehow managed to pull themselves out of their despair and quickly put together a Missing Persons flyer for Diana. A local businessman offered the use of his copy machine to make multiple copies of the flyer, and some of Diana's young friends helped in distributing the leaflets around the neighborhood.

At approximately 5:00 P.M., the Salazars received a terrifying phone call. A family friend of the Salazars', and the mother of a young boy who was a classmate of Diana's at Burrus Elementary School, believed she saw Diana in a gray car along with three men near her home. The little girl they believed to be Diana looked very scared. The Salazars feared the worst.

Unfortunately, neither helicopter nor flyers were able to do the trick. Officer Fahy and others canvassed The Heights area for almost twelve hours. No one was able to locate Diana.

CHAPTER 10

Monday, August 8, 1994, 12:15 A.M.,
1440 North Loop West,
Houston, Texas.

Ian Biel was a simple man. Well, boy, really. The eighteen-year-old had dropped out of school at Navarro Junior College, in Waco, Texas, and moved back home to Houston, where he scored work as a security guard for Hamm Security Services—the semi-graveyard shift, from 10:00 P.M. to 4:00 A.M. He was responsible for checking up on several buildings all over the city, every night. Some buildings he would simply drive by in his white Mazda pickup truck and survey the scene to make sure there were no vagrants hanging around urinating on the buildings or vandalizing the area. Other buildings he would survey, then get out of his truck with a flashlight and walk around the building. Still other buildings he would drive around, walk around, and then enter the building, where he would also check on specific suites.

It was an easy job, but he got to wear a uniform and strap on a gun, which he felt restored a little bit of the dignity he lost by having to move back home.

This particular night, Biel had been on his route for a couple hours. As usual, things were pretty uneventful, which was the way he liked it. At just after midnight he found himself at an abandoned three-story office building located at 1440 North Loop West, also known as Loop 610.

Biel was creeped out by the building. First of all, it was located next door to the private, larger-than-it-looks, Adath Emeth Jewish Cemetery. The entire area had an eerie, off-kilter ambience to it. That, combined with the unsavory element that tended to populate the area at night— specifically, prostitutes who allegedly worked out of the Western Inn Hotel located next door and took their tricks behind the building for blow jobs, crackheads who used it to hide out and spark up, and intoxicated homeless people—did not excite Biel. Since it had so much potential for trouble, the security guard was required to get out of his truck, cover the perimeter, and take a peek inside.

Not fun.

Unbeknownst to Biel, the abandoned office building was located only two miles from the Spring Branch Dairy Queen, where Carmen Estrada's body was found less than two years earlier.

Biel pulled off the Loop 610 feeder road and into the building parking lot up a steep incline. He drove slowly in front of the building, shining his flashlight as he passed. He then made his way to the large parking lot in the back of the building, where he turned right. This was the area where he usually found the aforementioned trespassers engaging in unsavory activities and he would have to run them off. On this night he did not see anything out of the ordinary, so he continued to drive along the back side of the building until he came to the driveway area in the back southwest corner.

As he turned the corner to the right, he spotted what looked like a skinny black woman lying on the ground.

Biel assumed it was one of the area prostitutes who may have been beaten up by one of her customers. Biel stopped his car and exited, walked up to the seemingly unconscious person, stopped about three feet away, and drew his revolver. He was not sure if the trick may still be lurking in the shadows nearby. Once he determined that no one was in the vicinity, he radioed for help. First he called 911; then he called his boss.

Upon further examination of the body, he realized that emergency services were not going to be able to help this person. She was already dead.

The first patrol officers on the scene were Art Mejia and Steve Castro. They were soon joined by an ambulance and also members of the local television media. Officers Mejia and Castro took control and kept the cameramen far away from the body. After cordoning off the area, the patrol officers followed correct department protocol and made a call to Homicide.

Homicide detective Robert E. "Bob" King was awoken from his peaceful slumber at 12:48 A.M., Monday, August 8, 1994, by the incessant, high-pitched ringing of his home telephone. The forty-one-year-old detective was a seventeen-year police force veteran, who transferred from Special Weapons and Tactics (SWAT) to Homicide nearly two years earlier.

King started out on patrol on the evening shift. He then switched over to the night shift, where he focused on accidents, which he did for less than one year. He then returned to patrol at the central patrol station for the night shift, where he worked until January 1, 1988.

After eleven years of patrol he then transferred to SWAT, where he worked for 4½ years.

On September 12, 1992, he transferred to the Homicide

Division of the Houston Police Department. Homicide was definitely his favorite assignment.

Detective King had worked on a few high-profile cases, including the case of Michael Durwood Griffith, a former Harris County sheriff who was charged and convicted of killing Deborah McCormick in her flower shop. King and fellow detective Hal Kennedy's successful police work was chronicled in Bill Cox's *Shop of Horrors* (Kensington/Pinnacle, 1998).

King was handsome and clean-cut, but most important, he was all business. He answered the call, darted up, and headed out the door toward the crime scene.

King pulled his vehicle into the front entrance of the vacant office building at 1440 North Loop. He was instantly approached by Officers Mejia and Castro, who informed the detective that they believed the body might be that of a little girl from the neighborhood that had gone missing the day before. Detective King absorbed everything and walked toward the area where the girl's body lay. When he came upon the little girl's naked body, he did not flinch. He kept his steely reserve in check. The sight before him would have turned a weaker man into a quivering bowl of jelly—a response no one would have mocked.

King looked down at the tiny, half-naked body of nine-year-old Diana Rebollar. Her body lay in a near-fetal position on the asphalt of the service driveway entrance at the back of the vacant building. She lay approximately four feet from the ramp that was used to tow heavy items into the building. Her head, which pointed north, lay on its right cheek with the majority of it in the asphalt area of the driveway and the top portion in a patch of grass located between the driveway and a sidewalk next to the building.

Diana looked like a skinny brown capital letter *R*. The tiny little girl lay on her right side with her right arm sticking out to the west, pointing toward the cemetery. Her left arm pointed down and was draped over her left leg, just below the knee and above her thin thigh. Her legs were almost at a 90-degree angle from her trunk. Her right leg slightly extended out in front of her left leg, with her left arm dividing the two. Her entire body was rigid due to rigor mortis.

Officer King could plainly see that Diana's bottom and genital regions were completely exposed, for the corpse wore no shorts, pants, panties, or skirt. He also very obviously saw that blood had cascaded from the virginal nine-year-old little girl's hairless vagina. Four large dried-up blood streaks desecrated her right upper thigh just below her bottom. To make matters worse, there were feces smeared on the little girl's left butt cheek, as well as a two-inch stool protruding from her anus.

The little girl was so scared she had literally shit herself.

It was obvious to everyone at the scene that the little girl had been raped vaginally, as well as anally.

Detective King, unmoved and undeterred, noticed that her black T-shirt had been pushed up above her chest area exposing her nonexistent prepubescent breasts and nearly all the way up her back. The detective noted what appeared to be a large amount of dried vomit on her right sleeve from the shoulder to the bottom of the short sleeve.

King also noticed that the color of the girl's skin was mottled, and that she had been covered in ant bites. The detective had no idea her body had been out in the sweltering, oppressive Houston heat, but it appeared as if a large portion of her chest, stomach, and back had been severely burned from the sun's persistent rays. Further still, the little girl appeared to have been practically devoured by Texas fire ants.

The color had drained from the little girl's face so that

most of it was a ghostly white. Her eyes and lips, however, had turned almost black, as if she had on tons and tons of black eyeliner and lipstick, of which she wore none.

When asked how he felt looking at the body of Diana Rebollar, King stated, "It didn't affect me that much. It did not. I mean, because it's just another murder."

Just as Detective King finished his cursory inspection of the body, the paramedics arrived on the scene. As one of the technicians moved Diana's stiff corpse, her long brown hair shifted off her tiny neck. It was then that King saw the ligature for the first time. He described it as "an olive drab nylon cord" that "had been tightened around her neck with a bamboo stick," which rested on the left side of her throat toward the front of her body. He did not get a good look at it, since they were moving the body; however, he could tell that the cord appeared to have been tightened into her skin very deeply. Detective King also assumed that the cord and bamboo stick worked in concert so the killer could tighten the cord around the victim's neck or loosen it as he or she pleased.

Unbeknownst to King, the tourniquet setup was almost identical to the one used on Carmen Estrada two years earlier.

Monday, August 8, 1994, 5:00 A.M.,
6600 block of North Main Street,
Houston, Texas.

Houston Police Department captain Richard Holland spoke with Bob King about Diana Rebollar. He wanted his detective to notify the little girl's parents before the news was splashed all over the Monday-morning local television broadcasts.

Detective King knocked on the Salazars' front door

well before the sun rose. No one was asleep inside the duplex. The family had been on pins and needles throughout the evening. Jose Salazar opened the door quickly, and Detective King walked inside the small home. He looked around to see if he could spot Virginia Salazar. He did not want to break the news in front of her. Once he realized that the fragile mother was not in the front room, he pulled Mr. Salazar aside.

"Mr. Salazar, I'm sorry to tell you, we found your daughter's dead body just a few hours ago," said King, trying to muster up as much sympathy as the all-business detective was capable of showing.

CHAPTER 11

On Monday evening Detective King received a solid tip that he believed might help crack the case. According to Heights-area resident Diego Dehoyos, he and his best friend, Ernesto "Ernie" Perez, decided to head out to Kemah, a coastal fishing town on the way to Galveston, to pick up some fish for a Sunday cookout. It was the same day that Diana Rebollar went missing.

The two men hopped into Perez's pickup truck and drove north on Main Street at approximately the same time Rebollar would have returned from the Wing Fong grocery store. They took their time driving and headed for the entrance ramp to the freeway. As Perez drove past the C & F Drive Inn, Dehoyos spotted something highly unusual—a white man stuffing a rolled-up carpet into the back of a van. The man's vehicle was parked in the gravel parking lot next to the lounge. Dehoyos saw the man struggle as he threw the carpet into the back of the van.

"Now that's what it would look like if somebody was getting kidnapped," Dehoyos offhandedly remarked to his pal. Perez nodded in agreement, but kept on driving. Dehoyos naturally assumed it must have been someone moving. Perez drove on and Dehoyos looked back at his passenger-side mirror. He caught a glimpse of the van and made a note of the color—beige. He did not give it a second thought.

At least, not until the following day.

On Monday, Perez stopped over at Dehoyos's house. Dehoyos did not feel well so he called in sick for work. Perez knocked on Dehoyos's door and let himself in. He walked back and found his friend in bed.

Perez skipped any pleasantries. "Hey, did you hear about the little girl that got kidnapped?" Perez had heard on the news the night before about the disappearance of Diana Rebollar.

"Don't you remember what I told you that's what it would look like if somebody got kidnapped?" Dehoyos asked.

Perez nodded affirmatively and then asked Dehoyos if he could use his telephone to contact Crime Stoppers.

Eventually the police were called out to Dehoyos's home. They asked the two men to take a look at various photographs of vans to see if they could spot one similar to the one they saw near the C & F Drive Inn. Dehoyos was able to pick out a similar-looking van.

There was another suspect—someone who was at the scene of the crime when Bob King arrived. "A homeless guy," King recalled, "Hyman Dale Luster. He was just in that parking lot and there was a grassy space, kind of a curved area. He had set a sheet down there and was drinking a beer and he had seen the body. He had been in jail Saturday night and got out of jail Sunday morning and so he walked from the central police jail up to his digs, up around Airline and the North Loop. Around Airline and Thirty-third."

Apparently, Luster brought some friends with him. "He walks up there with a box of kittens he's taking care of. He went up to a convenience store and some people give him a couple of bucks and he'd get a beer for himself and a little food for the kittens. So, he goes walking back there and he sees that body and he thought it was a grown woman. Then he finished his beer and he walked back. He went to a store and bought some more beer. He went to a pay phone outside the store at Airline and North Loop." King marveled as he told the story.

"Of course, he's crazy. And he thought he was being watched, so he did not use the phone, but a police car drove by on the Loop and he waved at them." King laughed. "And it went on by, of course. So he walked into the Western Inn and into the lobby. He walked just a few paces in there and there was a girl behind the desk, and I think he mouthed 'Call 911' and then he just walked out. He walked back there and sat behind that office building. The security guard says 'Well, I found this body and there he is sitting over there.' So, I threw him in my car and I retraced all of his steps for the night and we got hair and blood and saliva from him."

King continued to recount suspects.

"The biggest tip was this." King laid it out. "There were two little boys and a little girl riding their bikes—this is fifty minutes before Rebollar was snatched. These are like little cousins, little kiddos, riding their bikes.

"A man in a tan van, a solid tan van. They were riding their bikes in front of a house with a big driveway. He drove by them and he looked over where a yard sale was going on at a house. The kids, they're looking at him drive by. And he's looking over them. He smiles. He's wearing wraparound sunglasses. Blond hair. He keeps going." King paused. "He passes the yard sale and keeps going. One of the little boys says to the other, 'I bet he makes the block and goes to the yard sale.' Right about that time the two little boys ride their bikes off to chase a dog. The little girl sees her cousin riding her bike down the street. She rides her bike over and they both start riding their bikes in circles. Now the mother of the little girl, Marilou Mirales, is sitting on the top of the stairs on the phone talking to her niece. And the guy does make the block." King continued, "Now he drives by just past the little girls, and he pulls over to the side of the road and he parks. There's no reason for him to park there because this is like a fenced-off vacant lot with nothing there. He got out and walked to the back of the van. One of the little girls had her hair bobbed off short and the other one had a long ponytail and he concentrated on the girl with the long hair and he smiled and he said 'Hi' and then he went to the back of the van and started to open the door."

King continued, "Well, now Marilou is talking to her niece on the phone and she says, 'That's strange. This guy just pulled up his van, he parked, and he's looking at the kids, and I wonder what he's doing.' Her niece said, 'Wake up, Marilou, he's gonna snatch those kids.'

"At that point, Marilou took one step down the steps and he's standing at the back of the van, saw her, shut the door, got back in the van, and he drove off." King stated that Mirales described the man as a white male in his early thirties with blond hair pulled back into a ponytail. Blond eyebrows, fair complexion, white T-shirt tucked into blue jeans and work boots. He was slim, trim. He wasn't unneat. Clean shaven, everything. He has this solid tan van and he drives off fifty minutes before she is snatched.

"Marilou's aunt, Hope El Campo, called in that day," King remembered. "The desk people wrote the message down on one of those little phone chits and they put it on my desk, and my desk was so buried with paperwork, I didn't find it. But they [Marilou and Hope] went to the house where Rebollar lived and said, 'Hey, you need to tell the police I think we may have seen the guy who snatched your girl just before he did it. 'Cause he almost snatched one of our girls,'" King continued. "They kept calling back and it was like Wednesday before I got the message. So, I went out and talked to those folks. Got Marilou in for a composite drawing of the suspect and this blond guy with the ponytail and Marilou spotted a van just like the one she saw. She got the license plate number, told us about it."

King added, "Rick Maxey went out to that guy's house and just took pictures of it. It was a solid tan van. Chevy, Ford, Dodge, they all make the same kind of van. They look exactly the same. This solid tan van. Butterscotch-colored. So we had that.

"Then Diego Dehoyos gave us a composite drawing of the van he saw. Now, the van he saw was a tan van with, like, a brick red stripe all the way around it. We were sure that these people had seen the guy and they had a better look at the van," King said about Marilou Mirales and the kids on the bikes. "A longtime look at the van. They just didn't see it in passing. We put out the composite of this blond guy and the look-alike picture of the tan van to the news, thinking that was the right one. We never showed the news the van with the stripe on it that Diego Dehoyos saw; however, we passed copies of that composite around to Central Patrol, which patrols inside the Loop here and North Shepherd Patrol, which patrols outside the Loop.

"At first, the leads were hot and heavy, and when we would go to investigate a person, a man, we would try to get his cooperation. We might say, 'Hey, would you give us consent to search your vehicle? To search your house? Give us hair, blood, and saliva samples?' And to a man, they all did," King declared, somewhat amazed.

"One guy called about himself. He calls in—apparently, on the news broadcast with the composite drawing of the blond guy, we must have said we wanted to interview this guy as a witness, and this guy calls in and says, 'Looks just like me and what's it about?'" King could not believe it.

"I said, man, this guy, I think he probably thought his neighbors were gonna call in because he had been arrested and charged with indecency with a child and he worked as a maintenance man in an apartment and he was watching the Hispanic kids a little too close and they made him go work at another apartment. He was a pack rat too. Floor to ceiling. Newspapers in boxes. I found a complete motorcycle in his linen closet. Standing upright on end. We got all kinds of weirdos."

But that was not the end of the line when it came to suspects.

"And then we got regular guys that people called in because they might look like the composite and might live over there," King continued. "We had this one guy whose ex-wife said, 'You've got the wrong guy. He's the nicest man you'd ever want to meet and he would never do anything like that.' And he was a nice guy."

King even had members of the media calling him with tips. "Years later, Randy Wallace, from channel 26, calls in about some guy who was arrested and charged with molesting some little girls in the neighborhood where he lived, off the Hardy Toll Road. Long blond hair and I spent a lot of time with that guy and he was in jail. I had Marilou and the kids come out and try to spot him in a lineup and they couldn't," King added. "Talked to [the suspect] after the lineup and he says, 'You're trying to nab me for something I didn't do. You need to talk to my lawyer.' Well, I did talk to his lawyer. His lawyer was a real nice guy and the lawyer said he would talk to him. That lawyer talked to him and came to my office on a Sunday and wanted to know why I was going after his client. So, I laid it all out for him. I showed him the composite drawing, the pictures of the van. I laid out the whole case to him. 'I don't think my guy did it, but I'll talk to him and get back with you.' And then he got back with me and he says, 'He didn't do it. He just didn't do it.'"

King lamented the wasted opportunities.

"I spent a lot of time on that guy. I spent a lot of time on several guys. A bunch of guys. And then there were one hundred forty guys whose names came up through various ways." King shook his head. "There might be some news reports about some girl getting killed somewhere and some blond guy did it. Not [on] all of those did we get hair, blood, and saliva. Some of them we never talked to, we never met. Some of them we could clear out by [the] timeline because he was in jail during this one. . . .

"I had Diana Rebollar's picture always where I could see it," recalled Bob King. "I had a box, I had several boxes. . . . I had the 'Favorite Suspects' box. Those are guys like the blond guy that Randy Wallace from channel 26 called me about or other really good ones. Really favorite guys, we had twenty," King said. "You can approach these guys and [say], 'Your name has come up and may I tell you why your name has come up?'

"You talk to them and say, 'Look, okay. If it's not you, then we need to eliminate you as a suspect. Can we search your car? Can we search your house? Will you come down to the police station with us and we're gonna get some hair samples from you?' Back then, it was blood and saliva, all three back then. Now it's just the buccal swab. And those men did supply all of those things."

King spoke of an international plot in the case. "One lead stayed down in Mexico," King stated. "They kill each other left and right down there. They have family vendettas. It came in through Univision. They say Diana Rebollar was killed in retaliation for the murder of some rival family from their home state. We got with Diana's mother and she confirmed that there were deaths on both sides of this family rival," King recalled.

"The tipster said the guy that killed Diana is living and working in Houston now and we went out and found him. Had Chicano Squad come out. He didn't speak any English. Put him on a polygraph and he passed, and I remember Cecil Vasquez interviewed the guy and said, 'I'm not getting any bad vibes from this guy. I don't think he did it.' Basically, we ruled that guy out."

And on it went.

CHAPTER 12

Monday, August 8, 1994, 8:55 A.M.,
Office of the Medical Examiner of Harris County,
Joseph A. Jachimczyk Forensic Center,
1885 Old Spanish Trail,
Houston, Texas.

Dr. Harminder Narula had the unenviable task of performing the autopsy on young Diana Rebollar. Dr. Narula observed the physical condition of the nine-year-old little girl. Diana measured four feet eleven inches and weighed only sixty pounds. The once-beautiful little girl was now a tragic sight. Her body was still in a state of general fixed rigidity, so she remained in the fetal position at the beginning of the examination. She was also in an unfixed state of lividity and had purple spiderweb-like spots of ecchymosis under the pleura, all across her chest and face, known as Tardieu's spots. Her body was having epidermal slippage and her skin was sliding off, which left patches of white circles on her face the size of silver dollars.

Furthermore, the ant bites that resembled a witch's nose warts that marred her inner thighs, buttocks, lower back, chest, face, and eyelids had swollen well beyond normal size.

Dr. Narula even had to clear away several live ants that were crawling on Diana's body.

The medical examiner proceeded to examine the little girl's head. As typically occurs after death, her lips had darkened. He then mentioned that there was a ligature in place around her neck with a wooden stick on her left side. Dr. Narula described the string ligature as green and approximately an eighth of an inch in width. When he removed the ligature, he noted that the impression left in the little girl's neck was also an eighth of an inch wide. It completely encircled her throat and neck and was almost perfectly horizontal.

Interestingly, as in the Carmen Estrada postmortem, there appeared to be an abrasion over the areola and nipple of the young girl's right breast. No determination was made as to whether or not it was caused by human teeth.

The doctor then observed the young girl's genitalia. He noted that there were several abrasions on the vagina and a one-eighth-inch laceration on the vaginal wall. Also, there were abrasions on the anus. She also had abrasions on her inner thighs consistent with sexual assault.

Once done with the external examination, Dr. Narula prepared to examine Diana Rebollar from the inside. After completing the Y incision on her chest and removing the chest plate, the doctor determined that she had otherwise been a very healthy little girl.

But once her neck and throat were opened up, Dr. Narula denoted soft tissue hemorrhaging of the neck, where the ligature had been in place.

Interestingly, no sperm was found from the swabs applied to Diana's vagina, anus, and mouth.

CHAPTER 13

To try to determine who killed Diana Rebollar, police officers even looked into another murder in the neighborhood that occurred one year before. Eighty-three-year-old Lillian Wimberly, who lived only two blocks away from Diana on Main Street, was discovered dead in the entryway to her home on the morning of June 7, 1993. She had been beaten to death. Unfortunately, her killer had never been found. Some people in the neighborhood could not help but think that the person who killed Wimberly may have also killed Diana.

"This is not just happening to just this family," declared Salazar family friend Andrea Rey to the *Houston Chronicle*. "This community is a family and we've all got to bond together to stop this." Rey, who volunteered on behalf of a victims' rights group, spoke about other murder cases that occurred in the area. She mentioned the brutal double rape and murder of fourteen-year-old Jennifer Ertman and sixteen-year-old Eizabeth Peña at T. C. Jester Park, only one mile away from where Rebollar's body was discovered. The teenage girls were murdered in June 1993 as well. Two teenage boys had been arrested and convicted for their murders, while three more awaited trial.

"These people need help," Rey said of the Salazars. "They're not alone." The family would hopefully receive some support through a memorial fund established by Texas Commerce Bank. The goal was to help the family raise money so they could give their daughter a proper funeral service and burial.

CHAPTER 14

Tuesday, August 9, 1994,
Houston, Texas.

Another goal of the memorial fund was to help raise money to fly Diana's grandmother and seven-year-old brother to Texas from southern Mexico so they could attend Diana's funeral. City of Houston Mayor's Office Crime Victims Assistance director Andy Kahan was also on board to assist the Salazars with the funeral arrangements and flight plans. Kahan was able to secure two free flights, generously provided by AeroMexico. The family was not having as much luck raising money for Diana's funeral until United States attorney general Janet Reno intervened on behalf of Diana's family.

Wednesday, August 10, 1994,
Houston, Texas.

Meanwhile, the Houston Police Department called in the HPD helicopter to scan nearby building rooftops for the bag of sugar Diana had purchased at the Wing Fong grocery store, in case her killer might have tossed it aside. Despite spending over an hour in the sky, the helicopter pilots and police officers were not able to locate the bag of sugar.

CHAPTER 15

Thursday, August 11, 1994, 10:00 A.M.,
Our Lady of Guadalupe Church,
2400 block of Navigation Boulevard,
Houston, Texas.

Dozens of people milled about outside Our Lady of Guadalupe Church, a tiny Catholic Church that Diana Rebollar's family attended. Unfortunately, this time they were there to mourn the loss of their beloved daughter. They were joined by friends, neighbors, and many people they did not even know. More than two hundred people showed up to pay their last respects and to offer their condolences to Virginia and Jose Salazar.

The Reverend Jose Gonzales, a visiting priest from Mexico, led the Mass. As Reverend Gonzales stood near Diana Rebollar's tiny white casket, he begged the parishioners to help stop the cycle of violence.

Next up to speak was Houston city councilman Felix Fraga, who also bemoaned the state of violence in the country's fourth-largest city. He spoke to the audience about how Diana's family had uprooted themselves to escape the ever-present violence in their home country of Mexico—violence that took Diana's young father, Rujilio Rebollar Sr.

"All of us should feel the pain," Fraga proposed to the audience in regard to young Diana. "We shouldn't permit this. We should draw the line now. If this doesn't do it, we're a lot worse off than I thought we were."

After the ceremony several people spoke with reporter Pam Easton. One of Diana's best friends was eleven-year-old Laura Donjuan. The young lady appeared to be in a daze over the loss of her closest companion. "I keep thinking she's alive. We used to jump in her bed and talk about things in school. She was a very good student. I miss her a lot."

Andrea Rey spoke about the impact on her neighborhood. She was not going to take it sitting down. "We have a murderer or murderers loose in our community. We want justice and we won't be happy or satisfied until we have [it]."

Several people in attendance did not know Diana Rebollar. Many were parents who had brought their young children in hopes of teaching them a lesson. Richard Sister cried as he listened to the warnings. He held his ten-year-old daughter, Courtney, close by his side.

"Now do you see why Daddy don't want you to play outside?" he questioned his daughter between tears.

"I don't want to go out by myself ever again," his daughter sobbed.

Despite their fears, the reality of violent crime in Houston was quite different from the perception. The number of murders in Houston had actually decreased steadily each year since 1991 when the Houston Police Department reported 608 homicides. In 1992, the total was 465. In 1993, it was 446, and in 1994, it dropped down to 375 people murdered. In addition, the reported number of rapes also marginally declined each year. In

1991, the number was 1,213; in 1992, it was 1,169; in 1993, it was 1,109; in 1994, it was 931.

In addition to lower homicide and rape numbers, the amount of kidnappings had also decreased annually.

Most acknowledged authorities credited President Bill Clinton's commitment to crime prevention, which included an additional hundred thousand police officers nationwide, including several in Houston.

If one were to believe the American news media, you would think that our country is crawling with crazed killers, rapists, and kidnappers on almost every square inch of real estate. You may also believe that the vast majority of the bad guys are all evil strangers lurking behind bushes waiting to jump out and attack every innocent, decent, and defenseless person out there. The reality, when it comes to crime in the United States, is that the vast majority of murders, rapes, and kidnappings occur within the family.

Dr. Mark Warr, professor of criminology at the University of Texas at Austin, likes to say, "You kill the ones you love." The majority of people who commit these heinous crimes are usually brothers, sisters, fathers, mothers, sons, daughters, aunts, uncles, grandparents, neighbors, coworkers, and best friends.

Furthermore, news media has completely distorted the perception of crime in our country. Despite the fact that the murder rates have dropped steadily for the past thirty years (except during President George W. Bush's tenure), the television news media increased its murder coverage by over 600 percent. As a result, people who get their news from television believe that it is a far scarier world than it has ever been, when the reality is, it has actually gotten much better. Barry Glassner, USC professor and author of *The Culture of Fear,* claims the reason for this deceptive coverage is to keep viewers at home so they will watch more television commercials and order more consumer products. As a result, they will be too afraid to venture out into the big, bad, mean, cruel world.

But the murder of Diana Rebollar confirmed and even exacerbated the fears of Houston residents.

At the funeral Richard Sister also brought along his other daughter and wife.

"This has really touched me," the concerned father tearfully informed the *Houston Chronicle*. "Before, they didn't understand why I didn't want them to go out and play outside. I'm scared that something will happen to them."

Victims' rights advocate Andy Kahan was appalled by the implications of such a crime. "You can't send your kid to the store? That says something about society," he stated, intensity rising in his voice. "This is a situation that no one should have to go through."

Kahan glanced over to the grave site where Diana Rebollar's tiny little body would be permanently laid to rest inside her tiny white casket. He saw a small boy standing beside her grave. It was one of Diana's cousins, nine-year-old Oscar Villegas. Kahan could see the boy as he looked at his cousin's casket and uttered the question, "Why her?"

Kahan reiterated the need to never forget the victim. "The worst mistake people can make is to shrug their shoulders."

Indifference was not acceptable.

CHAPTER 16

One person who would not be indifferent was Homicide detective Bob King. The detective, along with Detective D. D. Shirley, decided they needed the media's help to track down the blond man who was reportedly seen at the scene of the crime.

"There are thousands of people out there who match this composite," Detective Shirley informed the media, "and thousands of vans that look like this van. We're trying to narrow our scope a little bit." Shirley also stressed that the individual in question was not a suspect, just a witness. "We're asking people in Houston if they know someone who looks like this, and who owns or has access to a van like this, to call us."

The Houston Police Department Homicide Division geared up for an influx of phone calls. Several extra detectives were brought in that night to help answer the tip lines. Unfortunately, the phones barely rang. Only twelve calls were received and none of them were helpful.

* * *

Monday, August 15, 1994,
Houston, Texas.

An antigang group called Parents Ganging Up On Gangs aided the police, informing the local media that it had raised $1,000 to add to the standard $1,000 reward from Crime Stoppers.

Echoing the concerns of Andy Kahan, Heights resident Ernestine Pina-Sandavol, in a letter to the editor at the *Houston Chronicle*, which was printed on August 21, 1994, wrote: "As we unwantingly hear the cries of Diana's mother, many of us can agree this isn't enough. The devastating, brutal crimes committed to this precious child Diana are grotesque. The sick-minded are among us and have no regard for their family or our families. I suspect their malicious plan is to lock us in our homes. Well, we're not ready to give them the key. Let us assure Diana's family that this is a heinous crime we refuse to just read about. Diana reminds us all of our children, our hopes, our future."

Part III

DANA

For if only a single substance exists, then either, I must be this substance, and consequently I must be God (but this contradicts my dependency); or else I am an accident.
—Immanuel Kant

CHAPTER 17

Cesar and Fidelina Sanchez moved from Mexico to Houston, Texas, in early 1979 while eighteen-year-old Fidelina was pregnant with her first child. The Sanchez family, like Carmen Estrada's parents and Diana Rebollar's mother, had left Mexico to create a better life for themselves in the United States. They believed that America could provide a better opportunity for the family they intended to raise. Dana Lizette Sanchez was born in Houston on May 11, 1979.

In 1988, when Dana was nine, her parents gave birth to a baby brother named Cesar Jr., and then in 1993, they brought baby Ivan into the family. Dana began to feel the strain in the family's tiny apartment. The complex was littered with several teenage kids hanging out with their bicycles and skateboards trying to look tough and intimidating, but it was hard for a young teenage girl to remain inside, sharing such small cramped quarters with a screaming baby.

While in seventh grade at Black Middle School, Dana often sat by herself. One day, another seventh grader,

Dianna Zambrana, saw Dana sitting alone. She felt sorry for her so she walked up and said "Hello." Soon thereafter, Dana and Dianna were inseparable.

As a teenager, Dana was a good student. She and Dianna attended Waltrip High School, where both girls were involved in the Second Platoon, A Company—ROTC. According to her mother, Dana wanted to become a doctor—a pediatrician, more specifically. Unfortunately, since the family did not have much money, Dana knew she would have to take a nonlinear route to get to medical school. She informed her mother that she wanted to go into the U.S. Navy first and have them pay for her college education. Dana hoped she would make it as a successful doctor so she could buy a nice car and a big house for her parents, who had very little in way of material possessions.

Over time Dana seemed to get along with most everyone. She was often described as having an outgoing personality, while others described her as quiet. Either way, she seemed to have lots of friends.

Unfortunately, she was having trouble with her parents. They fought often with Dana about her boyfriend, Michael Castillo. So, Dana eventually moved out of her parents' apartment and into an apartment with Dianna and Dianna's brother, John, on Cavalcade Street.

CHAPTER 18

Thursday, July 6, 1995, 5:00 P.M.,
600 block of Cavalcade Street,
Houston, Texas.

Dana and Dianna had been living with Dianna's brother, John, for one week. It was to be a temporary fix for the girls. They did not have intentions of staying long.

Dianna had a busy evening ahead of her. She was planning a birthday party for her nephew, and she and Dana were going to stop by the nearby shopping mall and buy some clothes for themselves and a gift for her nephew.

Dianna arrived back at John's apartment around 5:00 P.M. Dana was already there. Dianna walked into the bedroom and saw her best friend combing her long, thick, dark brown hair. Dana was dressed for the evening. She wore white coveralls over a brown-and-white-striped bodysuit. Her feet sported black Nike low-tops and she carried a black purse that looked like a mini backpack.

Dana told her best friend that she was not going to be able to go shopping with her. She had, instead, made other plans. First she needed to pick up her paycheck from the company where she worked as a receptionist that summer. Then her boyfriend Michael Castillo's mother was going to pick her up and take her back to his house on Greenyard Drive, which was almost fifteen miles away from the apartment.

Dianna, disappointed, left without saying a word to Dana. It would be the last time she would ever see her best friend.

Not much is known about Dana Sanchez's last hours. Apparently, she was spotted approximately one mile away from her apartment at Airline Drive and Interstate 45 at a pay phone in front of a Mr. Quick convenience store at 7:00 P.M. She never did meet up with Michael Castillo's mother, nor did she make it to his house. She also never called her best friend, like she normally would.

No one—not her family or her best friend—had a clue where Dana Sanchez had disappeared.

Friday, July 7, 1995,
4000 block of Watonga Boulevard,
Houston, Texas.

Fidelina Sanchez, Dana's mother, insisted that her daughter was not the type of girl who would accept a ride from a stranger—not even if she needed a ride to get to her boyfriend's house. She was too careful.

Fidelina was worried sick over the disappearance of her daughter. She tried everything she could think of to locate her. She contacted all of Dana's friends that she knew. She created flyers with her daughter's photo and distributed them everywhere and she drove in circles looking for her daughter.

Her search lasted for eight days.

Friday, July 14, 1995, 2:35 P.M.,
17000 block of Northview Park Drive,
North of Houston, Texas.

After receiving a call from KPRC's Barbara Magana, Detectives William "Bill" Valerio and Bill Taber, along with Sergeant Roger Wedgeworth, located the severely decomposed corpse of sixteen-year-old Dana Sanchez.

Her remains were dumped off Northview Park Drive, east of I-45 and south of Richey Road.

Friday, July 14, 1995, 9:00 P.M.,
4000 block of Watonga Boulevard,
Houston, Texas.

Detectives Bill Valerio and Bill Taber made the dreaded trip out to Dana Sanchez's parents' apartment, near Waltrip High School. The officers brought with them four different rings that were on the decomposed corpse they discovered earlier that day. The body had two rings on each hand. One ring was a yellow metal band with a center blue stone surrounded by two circles of clear stones. The second was white metal with a clear solitaire-style stone. The third had yellow metal that formed a loop and had a clear stone surrounded by two red stones. The fourth and final ring was made of white metal with a single red stone in the center.

"Mrs. Sanchez, can you please describe to me some of the rings your daughter wears?" Detective Valerio asked Fidelina Sanchez, consciously referring to Dana in the present tense.

Mrs. Sanchez seemed apprehensive as she began to describe a piece of her daughter's jewelry. Detectives Valerio and Taber wanted to know if Mrs. Sanchez had ever seen any of the rings and if they may have belonged to her daughter.

As soon as they showed the rings to Mrs. Sanchez, she broke down and started to sob. She knew right away that they belonged to her beloved daughter. Mrs. Sanchez had been distraught by the fact that she and Dana had not been speaking to one another. It was unfathomable to her that she would never get to see her precious daughter graduate from high school, from college, get married, have babies, and grow old and happy.

Mrs. Sanchez gave the officers further descriptive details about her daughter: that she had never been to a dentist, so her teeth were nasty-looking; that she had a mole on the right side of her cheek; and that she had a crooked left pinkie finger.

CHAPTER 19

Saturday, July 15, 1995, 3:30 P.M.,
Office of the Medical Examiner of Harris County,
Joseph A. Jachimczyk Forensic Center,
1885 Old Spanish Trail,
Houston, Texas.

Deputy Chief Medical Examiner Eduardo Bellas was
set to perform the autopsy on what was left of Dana
Sanchez. The gruesome collection of bones, rope, and
hair was startling even to the seasoned Bellas.

Dana Sanchez was literally a bag of bones. Her total
body weight was now only twenty-five pounds. Dr. Bellas
noted that the majority of her skin had been eaten away
by maggots. There was no skin on her pelvic, neck, head,
chest, and abdominal areas. Additionally, there was no
skin on her face and her eyes were missing. What little
skin remained was in a nearly mummified state, due to
advanced decomposition. However, all of Dana Sanchez's
long thick hair remained intact.

Dr. Bellas spotted a yellow nylon rope tied around the
neck area, which was double knotted on the right side,
and a blue plastic toothbrush near the knot, which he

assumed to be a tourniquet. Dr. Bellas also spotted a black plastic belt in the right side of her hair, which had been knotted once.

Fidelina, Cesar, and the rest of the Sanchez family could no longer take the pain. They moved out of the cramped apartment less than one month after Dana's body was discovered. Mrs. Sanchez stated that the memories in the apartment were too strong and too painful.

CHAPTER 20

Tuesday, September 19, 1995,
12300 block of T. C. Jester Boulevard,
Houston, Texas.

Two months after the discovery of Dana Sanchez's corpse, a cable television lineman called the Houston Police Department. He had just finished reading an article in the *Houston Chronicle* about the murder of Sanchez and it ignited a memory.

The repairman was convinced that he had seen a pile of clothes out in the middle of a grass field that matched those supposedly worn by Dana Sanchez.

The Houston police sent an officer to the location to check it out. Sure enough, the officer discovered clothes that matched the description of those worn by Dana Sanchez. The clothes were collected and sent off to be tested.

Wednesday, September 27, 1995,
Houston, Texas.

More than 2½ months after her daughter's murder, Fidelina Sanchez was still in shock. Not only had she lost her oldest child, but her daughter's killer had not been caught.

"Sometimes I still listen to her," Mrs. Sanchez admitted. "It's hard to believe she is not here with us anymore." Tears streamed down her tired cheeks as Mrs. Sanchez spoke of her daughter.

"The hardest part is trying to explain to her brothers where Dana is," said Mrs. Sanchez. "The two-year-old does not really understand what is going on, only that his sister never comes home."

She continued on that the oldest boy was very close to Dana. "For him, it's just not real. He never says anything, but I have found him writing her. I guess he expects a miracle."

She also mentioned that he now lived in fear. "He's only seven and he's afraid . . . whoever killed his sister will come and get him.

"Not knowing anything makes it so much harder," she pleaded with the local media in hopes of trying to drum up some eyewitnesses who may have had some knowledge as to her daughter's murder.

"I know my daughter," she continued. "She would not have gotten in [a vehicle] with a stranger."

Mrs. Sanchez also feared for the lives of other innocent young women in Houston. "If he could do it to her, he could do it to another girl, that's why anyone, anyone who knows anything, should call.

"She loved children," Mrs. Sanchez went on as a solitary tear ran down her cheek. "She helped me so much with her little brothers. I miss her so much."

CHAPTER 21

Within days of the discovery of Dana Sanchez's decomposed body, the Houston Police Department, the Harris County Sheriff's Department, and the FBI pulled together a task force to work on the murders of Carmen Estrada, Diana Rebollar, and Dana Sanchez. They believed they had a serial killer in their midst.

"I believe it was early September when we formed the task force with the county and the FBI, and our crime analyst people were really geared up for it," Detective Bob King recalled.

Apparently, the task force was not always a well-oiled machine. "The FBI brought in a computer system for them to use to tie in all the leads together. It's called Rapid Start, though it was anything but. It took too long to set up. And ultimately after so much effort all that information was lost. Some kind of computer glitch."

King talked about what happened to the cases he was working on when he was assigned to the task force. "They take us out of the call-up which means we're not getting any new cases while we're assigned to this, which means the other guys are getting more than their fair share.

"In homicide, I was a workaholic," said King. "You can

work twenty-four hours a day, seven days a week up there and never get caught up. If I didn't have to eat and sleep, I'd a done it. I just stayed late every day. I'd work for free overtime like late, late, late.

"When we formed the task force in '95, there was a Hispanic girl who was kidnapped in Southeast Houston and raped by a wrecker driver. I spent a ton of time chasing down this wrecker driver with long brownish blond hair and tattoos of spiderwebs on his elbows and I didn't think he was a good lead. I didn't think he was my guy." King was, however, able to bring the guy in.

"I remember he gives hair, blood, and saliva because he knew he didn't do it. He did kidnap that girl in Southeast Houston. Got sent off for twenty-five years. He was an ex-con anyway. But he wasn't our guy and I didn't feel like he was our guy. It took a lot of time away from [our case]."

King noted that there were plenty more suspects to come.

"There was a guy that killed a little girl in Hockley, in his own neighborhood. Eric Charles Nenno," who was arrested in early March 1995.

King continued, "[Nenno] took her up into his home, sexually molested her, and took her body into his attic. Well, that too was investigated by Harris County. They had a big eighteen-wheeler and they set it up right where the little girl went missing. They set up roadblocks into this little subdivision. Nobody went in or out without having his or her car checked. Nobody. And they started talking to kids in the neighborhood who said, 'Well, that man over there, he did something to a little girl about a year-and-a-half ago.' Nenno had touched a little girl inappropriately as he was repairing her bicycle. A report was made on it, but the parents of the little girl didn't want anything to do with it." King shook his head at the memory.

"So the detectives, including Detective Roger Wedge-worth, went to talk to him at his house. Roger asked the man, 'What kind of person do you think we should be talking to?' Nenno answers, 'A person like me.'

"They had a polygraph set up in that eighteen-wheeler and set him down there and an FBI agent ran a polygraph. Bombed it. He confessed and said, 'She's up in my attic and she's dead.'"

King was hopeful. "So, we wanted to see if Nenno is the guy who did Estrada and Rebollar and I went out there and talked to the county guys and said, 'We have this tourniquet issue. Anything like that?' and they said no. So, I walked through his house and there was nothing there to suggest any tie-ins with the Hispanic girls. That may be the first time they were made aware."

King spoke of the day Dana Sanchez's body was discovered. "The detectives saw the yellow nylon rope, I call it ski rope, and a toothbrush. On that day I happened to be with two witnesses in a dope killing, taking their statements, so I couldn't go out to the scene. But Wayne Wendel went out there and then, the next day, we went to the morgue and looked at the body."

Task force member Sergeant Stuart "Hal" Kennedy was responsible for a crucial task. According to Kennedy, the HPD property room tended to bulge at the seams with evidence from their multitude of cases. Periodically, usually on an annual basis, the property room staff disposes of unwanted or unacknowledged items of evidence to make room for more evidence from newer cases. The staff sends out a form to the various officers and asks if the evidence needs to be held.

Sergeant Kennedy received such a request nearly every year since 1992 in regard to the fingernail clippings of Maria Estrada, but he made sure they preserved the evidence.

He resubmitted DNA samples from suspects each year because there were constant advances being made in DNA technology and he hoped that one day they would find a match.

Unfortunately, nothing turned up for several years.

CHAPTER 22

Monday, November 11, 2002, 10:00 P.M.,
KHOU-TV, Channel 11,
Houston, Texas.

Seven years later, local CBS News affiliate KHOU-TV—Channel 11—aired what would be the first part in an ongoing investigation into the Houston Police Department Crime Lab. The expose was the culmination of a three-month-long investigation conducted by KHOU along with the help of several outside forensic sources. The problems uncovered with the HPD Crime Lab were vast and their conclusions could have had a lasting impact on hundreds of criminal cases.

KHOU's televised report focused on forensic analyses that were conducted by the DNA/Serology Section of the crime lab. The chief complaint was that it took far too long to receive DNA-testing results for criminal cases, thereby leaving several defendants sitting in jail for months on end.

According to the Houston Police Department's own internal-investigation report, the problems with the

crime lab began in the mid-1990s. The basis for the
problems began with silly personal politics in the office,
which led to a severe lack of supervision. The crime lab
"began performing its own restriction fragment length
polymorphism (RFLP) DNA analysis" by May 1992.

At the time James Bolding was the Criminal III supervisor and Dr. Baldev Sharma was one of two Criminalist
II senior bench analysts in the department. The following year Bolding received a promotion to Criminalist IV,
where he oversaw the Trace and DNA/Serology Sections, in addition to the crime lab's Central Evidence Receiving (CER) Unit. Likewise, Dr. Sharma received a
promotion as well to Criminalist III for DNA/Serology.

Things seemed to run smoothly for the next year-and-
a-half until October 1994, when Bolding and Sharma got
into a spat. The two disagreed over the inclusion of a
new analyst in the DNA/Serology Section. According to
Sharma, Bolding took his frustration out on him by low-
ering his evaluation scores the following year. Sharma,
in turn, filed a grievance against Bolding, which led to
a seven-month investigation.

On February 2, 1996, Bolding allegedly struck back at
Sharma by filing a formal complaint against him with
the Internal Affairs Division for "official repression" and
for several cases of misconduct. According to the report,
the bitter feud took its toll on everyone in the DNA/
Serology Section line and spread throughout the entire
crime lab.

Later that year, on October 11, 1996, the *Houston
Chronicle* reported on the case of Lynn Jones, a man
charged with sexual assault. Jones sat in jail for nearly
nine months while awaiting DNA test results from the
HPD Crime Lab that eventually cleared him.

As a result of the report, crime lab chief Donald

Krueger removed Dr. Sharma from his post as the line supervisor for the DNA/Serology Section. Sharma retained his Criminalist III title, but was no longer in charge. The department, however, never found a replacement for Dr. Sharma as the Criminalist III line supervisor.

On September 14, 1999, three years after Dr. Sharma was removed from the supervisory role, six analysts sent a memorandum to HPD chief Clarence O. Bradford. The memo "Restoration Criminalist III Position to Serology/DNA Section" castigated the former supervisor, Sharma, and declared that the years from 1993 to 1996 were a "total disaster" because of his "mismanagement." The analysts informed the chief that it was imperative to fill in the position with one of the top criminalists already in the section.

The following month, on October 20, 1999, several of the analysts met with Chief Bradford about the possibility of installing a line supervisor for the DNA/Serology Section. By all accounts, the meeting was a huge success and, apparently, Chief Bradford gave off a vibe of proactivity to the analysts who collectively described themselves as "euphoric" at the chief's realization.

But their euphoria was short-lived, for Chief Bradford sent out a memo soon thereafter that stated that the "Criminalist III position has been put on hold until sufficient funding is acquired."

Simultaneous to the DNA/Serology Section's difficulties was the dramatic increase in the use of DNA as a forensic tool. The crime lab was missing the boat on this new technology.

Another critical and far more egregious practice was uncovered in the crime lab in the HPD internal investigation report: "drylabbing."

Drylabbing is the act of fabricating forensic analysis. In the HPD Crime Lab, the drylabbing consisted of "controlled substances analysts creating false documentation intended to reflect analytical procedures that were never performed." The report stated that HPD was aware of at least four instances of drylabbing that were committed by two Criminalist I analysts in the Controlled Substances Section between 1998 and 2000. The incidents were detected by a Criminalist III line supervisor.

One instance of drylabbing involved a case against a suspect who allegedly poured an illegal substance into another person's beverage. The analyst misidentified the substance as flunitrazepam, a tranquilizer considered to be a date-rape drug. When the results were passed on to the Criminalist III supervisor, they were double-checked and actually discovered to be clonazepam, possession of which is only a misdemeanor. Instead of actually testing the substance used by the suspect, the analyst used a standard sample of flunitrazepam and those results instead.

In 2000, the same analyst used a report in a separate case from a different analyst that stated the steroid stanozolol was present in a substance. The unrelated results were incorrectly included in the case file and the careless analyst was about to be placed on indefinite suspension, but quit instead.

By December 2002, less than one month after the KHOU-TV News investigative report on the HPD Crime Lab was unveiled, the Houston Police Department decided to place a moratorium on all DNA.

The following October 2003, all toxicological analyses were suspended in the Toxicology Section. That same month, Irma Rios, who had previously worked on the "Austin Yogurt Shop Murders" case back in 1991 (see *Murdered Innocents* by Corey Mitchell, Kensington/ Pinnacle, 2005), was named the new head of the HPD Crime Lab.

It was against this uncertain backdrop that Bob King was faced with a choice, the decision of which had been made for him.

CHAPTER 23

"It was about February of 2003," Bob King recalled, "and Danny Billingsley called Captain Holland, the captain of Homicide, and said, 'I'd like to reform that task force.' He said, 'We have a cold case squad over here now. It's Harry Fikaris and Roger Wedgeworth. I would like for you to send Bob King and maybe John Swaim over here to work out of the Harris County Homicide Office. I'd like to work out all of the leads on these cases that haven't been worked out.'"

King continued, "Not everyone in homicide thought these three cases [the three Hispanic girls] were related. We couldn't prove they were related by DNA. We could only prove they were related by MO. Captain Holland thought they were related, and through the years, I kind of became the keeper of the leads."

King talked about one of the suspects. "The truth be told, Danny Billingsley had a favorite suspect—a Hispanic guy who lived in an apartment complex on Cavalcade, where Dana Sanchez was staying when she disappeared. So, Captain Holland decides to send me and John Swaim over to Harris County Homicide to work out these leads.

"I talked to Roger Wedgeworth and he asked me to

come on over. The Cold Case Unit (CCU) had been kicking over there and they're solving all of these old cases. I got over there and said, 'John and I are supposed to come over here pretty soon. What do you think we'll be doing?' They said, 'Danny's got a favorite suspect and we don't want to go tracking down all of these leads.'" King assumed he knew what they wanted to do.

"We've got a killer DNA lab called Orchid Cellmark out of Dallas," King was told, "and there is this analyst there named Katherine Long, who is just great. We send her evidence and [she] found the old DNA. We don't have any DNA on Dana Sanchez. She was just rawhide and soot. We want the DNA from Estrada and Rebollar to send to Orchid Cellmark. If there is DNA to be found, they'll find it."

"So, I went back and I told Captain Holland and Lieutenant [Greg] Neely this is what they want. Well, it's a lot of evidence to be tested and it all costs money. So, Captain Holland arranged to get the funding for it. This is a months-long process and it's late August or early September before this stuff can be sent and paid for."

Wednesday, October 15, 2003,
Orchid Cellmark,
13900 block of Diplomat Drive,
Farmers Branch, Texas.

According to its Web site, "Orchid Cellmark is one of the oldest and most experienced providers of forensic DNA identity testing services." The company's services have been used by police departments worldwide and in high-profile cases such as O. J. Simpson, JonBenet Ramsey, and the "Green River Killer."

At the behest of Captain Holland, Bob King was able to submit samples, specifically Maria Estrada's fingernail clippings, to Katherine Long for DNA analysis. It did not take long before Long discovered a hit. She forwarded the results to Dr. Dennis Loockerman, the supervisor in charge of the Combined DNA Index System (CODIS) at the Texas Department of Public Safety (DPS), to check for a comparison.

CODIS is a tool created by the FBI that is used to index DNA samples from crime scenes that can be accessed by "federal, state, and local crime labs to exchange and compare DNA profiles electronically, thereby linking crimes to each other and to convicted offenders."

On October 16, 2003, CODIS struck gold. Long received an answer from Dr. Loockerman in short order.

The following morning Long contacted the Houston Police Department and spoke with Captain Holland.

"I was at home," King remembered, "and Captain Holland called."

"Does the name Anthony Allen Shore mean anything?" Holland asked King.

"No," responded the detective confidently. He knew the names of every suspect.

"We're gonna research this guy," Holland informed King. "And we're gonna do it without him knowing we're doing it."

Part IV

TONY

The creative artist seems to be almost the only kind of man that you could never meet on neutral ground. You can only meet him as an artist. He sees nothing objectively because his own ego is always in the foreground of every picture.
                                                            —Raymond Chandler

CHAPTER 24

Anthony "Tony" Allen Shore was born on June 25, 1962, at Ellsworth Air Force Base in Rapid City, South Dakota, to Deanna and Robert Shore. According to Shore, his mother wanted to name him Anthony Steven Shore. His father overruled her because Anthony's initials would have spelled out "ASS," so they changed his middle name to Allen.

Ellsworth Air Force Base was established in 1942 as a training base for B-17 Flying Fortress crews for World War II. Thousands of pilots, navigators, gunners, and radio operators made their way through Ellsworth during the war.

The base was also home to twenty-three squad members who tragically lost their lives in a crash over Newfoundland in March 1953. One of the twenty-three was Brigadier General Robert E. Ellsworth, commander of the Twenty-eighth Strategic Reconnaissance Wing. President Dwight D. Eisenhower dedicated the base in honor of General Ellsworth.

By October 1960, Ellsworth Air Force Base refocused its efforts on the "Space Race," with the establishment of the 850th Strategic Missile Squadron. The focus of the 850th was work on the Titan I Intercontinental ballistic missiles, which arrived in early 1962. The Titan I's lifespan in South Dakota was cut short by that same July; one week after, Tony Shore was born in the base hospital.

The Shore family lived east of the Black Hills National Forest off Highway 16, north of Mount Rushmore National Park.

According to Tony Shore, his mother, Deanna, or "Dea," did not want to have any more children. She and Robert, more informally referred to as "Rob," did, however, have more children: two daughters—Regina, whom they called "Gina," and Laurel.

The Shore family stayed in Rapid City until Tony turned three. Thereafter, they began a perpetual cycle of moving from one city to another as Rob continually received new job offers. The Shore family shuttled back and forth between Oklahoma City, Oklahoma, where Rob's parents lived, and Liberal, Kansas, where they had more family.

The Shore family also followed Rob to New York City for a brief stay. Tony remembered that his mom was always worried about the rats.

The Shore family then moved across the country to Irvine, California, to stay with Dea's parents, Don and Elizabeth Lasley—or "Pappoo" and "Mammoo," as they were affectionately known. Tony described their residence as a "gorgeous home surrounded by orange orchards."

Tony Shore also remembered living in a white house in Fair Oaks, California, when he was four years old. "I recall my little sister—most of my memories involve her. Mom and Dad always were yelling or fighting, it seemed."

He recalled being "attacked savagely" by a giant Saint Bernard dog while living with his father's relatives. He claimed that he carried a severe paranoia of dogs for years as a result.

Used to packing up his bags and heading out to a new city at a very young age, Tony also learned that it was not wise to strike up friendships with the other kids because, sooner or later, he would be moving again.

He also claimed to have a recurring nightmare that haunted him for years. In the nightmare Tony would appear in a field of flowers. "Blue flowers waving in the wind." He described being in the mountains; however, he could not see the peaks of the mountains. It was always a beautiful sunny day.

"I would swoop down through the flowers," he recalled, "as if in a part of the wind or some omnipresence until I came upon a little girl in a blue dress with lots of lace. She would be about three or four years old (maybe five at best). She was divine with curly long blond hair that fell in ringlets around her. She had eyes, as blue as the flowers, that seemed to look right through me."

In Shore's nightmare he saw that the little girl "would be far away and as I would get closer and closer, until I could almost reach out and touch her, I would realize suddenly [that] she looked confused or possibly afraid. And then it would start—the paralyzing cycle of the nightmare that I could not wake up from."

The dream was only beginning. "I would look at her eyes and [their] confusion, and all else would disappear and blackness would set in. It was as if I closed my eyes to escape some imminent evil, and when I would open them, I would be looking up from the bottom of a deep hole in the earth. The smell of dirt [was] overwhelming me. My eyes no more than blinded.

"Filled with terror," Shore continued, "I would look up from this hole and see the sky of clouds passing by. It's still daylight and I could see a few blue flowers near the rim of the hole." Shore dreamed he was stuck in the hole and that a multitude of logs engulfed him.

"I couldn't breathe. This time the black void would last for a few moments as the void would fill up with the face of a man with black long hair and a black beard. He was old, with a long nose and lines in his face, and had dark piercing eyes, and he would start to smile the most evil smile.

"Before I could scream," Tony continued, "I felt like I was swallowing my tongue. I would feel sharp electrical-type shocks and suddenly I was back in the field of blue flowers. Just as abruptly, the fear would disappear and there I was flying over this field."

The hunt for the little girl continued. "Swooping down through the flowers, blowing in the breeze, and I would see her again. Far away at first, but getting closer. I would see the same little girl in a blue dress with blond hair and blue eyes, holding in one hand one of the beautiful blue flowers, and [then] the same identical series of events would repeat over and over and over. [It] would seem like an eternity—hundreds of times."

Tony admitted that the nightmare often made him wet the bed.

He also stated that the nightmare occurred "at some point when I was very sick. [I had] the same recurring nightmare for many years to come . . . usually at times of severe illness and was accompanied at times with shocking pains, like electrical sparks all over my body, but primarily my legs."

Tony would have this dream over and over again throughout his early years.

Anthony Shore continued to be haunted by the nightmare of the old man.

"It wasn't until many years later in life that I finally recognized the face. [I] positively identified the evil old man.

"We were living in Orlando, Florida, at the time. I must have been about twelve years old and I was looking at one of my mom's books, *Czar Nicholas,* and in that book was a picture of the very infamous warlock witch Rasputin."

Grigori Efimovich Rasputin was a Russian mystic who manipulated the Russian czar Nicholas II and his wife, Czarina Alexandra, even claiming he could heal the lame, to garner political power. Eventually Rasputin was assassinated.

"I screamed and damn near swallowed my tongue. It was him!!! Positively.

"Also, ironically, my dad bears an uncanny physical resemblance to Czar Nicholas. In fact, they could be twins."

When Tony was five years old, the Shore family moved to Shawnee, Kansas. Tony claimed this is where he had his first girlfriend and allegedly got into fights with a boy named Scott Beavis. Tony said he had long curly hair, which his mother got rid of and replaced with a severe buzz cut, and which he cited as the first time he received a severe beating at the hands of his mother.

When Tony was six, his second sister, Laurel, or, as he called her, "the unwanted child," was born. He claimed that his parents "did not plan on her and resented her."

It was during this time that the Shore family relocated to Marietta, Georgia. Tony remembered it as a time when his parents continued to scream and fight with each other.

Tony also recalled that his best friend was a little black boy who lived across the street; that he had another friend who was killed; that he had his first crush, on a schoolteacher; that he had a crush on a black girl from school; and that he got into a lot of fights in school.

Somewhere between third grade and fourth grade, Tony's family moved to Alabama. His random thoughts from this era pointed toward a severe internal change. He claimed that he was the "whipping boy" at Fifth Avenue Elementary and that his family lived in a "bad neighborhood." He believed his teacher hated him and he continued to get into fights with other kids frequently. His mother fought with the school to do something about the bullies who picked on her son, but the school was unable to stop them. Tony "hated school" and claimed that he had a "chip on his shoulder" and that he was "always afraid and mad." He also feared for his life, especially after another student was stabbed on the school playground.

Tony was relieved when he was able to return to Irvine, California, to live with his Pappoo and Mammoo. But though he loved it there, something deeper seemed to be transforming inside him. At an incredibly young age he declared that he "stopped believing in God" and that he "felt cursed."

By the fourth grade Tony's family moved yet again, this time to Houston, Texas. He felt like an outcast. He did not remember much of the year he spent there.

The following year the Shores moved to Huntsville, Alabama, where they, according to Tony, lived in a huge mansion. Tony claimed that his sister Gina was diagnosed with schizophrenia the same year and put on Ritalin. She was in third grade.

Tony was in fifth grade and claimed to have an Indian female friend, who was a "major girlfriend." He took judo lessons, guitar lessons, and rode motorcycles. He claimed he was a football star and that he liked shooting his BB gun.

Tony also believed that his father went through severe violent episodes; however, he was vague about the details.

Tony claimed that when he was in sixth grade, a "crazy woman," who lived around the corner, tried to "kidnap Gina." He also claimed that his mother had an affair with a neighbor named Pablo, that she smoked "lots of pot," and that she developed an interest in witchcraft the following summer, between his sixth and seventh grades.

Tony's life continued this way for years. He would fall in love with a beautiful girl. He would get beaten up. He would play music and would get in trouble at school. He claimed he was often left at home to take care of his sisters while his mom was out sleeping around and his dad was traveling—and sleeping around as well. By the time his family moved back to Texas, he had a self-proclaimed "bad attitude."

Eighth grade was a pivotal year in Tony Shore's sexual awakening. In addition to lots of fights and, as he wrote, "being repulsed by noses," Tony "discovered [his] first gay kid." He also had sexual relations for the first time. He claimed that his first carnal experience was with a girl named Cindy at an 8 Days Inn motel. According to Tony, she wore hip-huggers and had the "beginning of breasts." He fell in love and "wished on stars." He and Cindy went at it for three to four days when she suddenly left. Tony was devastated. "Thought I wouldn't survive the heartbreak."

Tony's family moved to League City, Texas, the summer after eighth grade. He recalled that his mom tried to be a housewife, but she was too bored. He also claimed that she got heavier into witchcraft and also took up astrology. The burning of sage to ward off evil spirits was a common occurrence in the Shore household.

Tony also claimed that his mother molested him when he was thirteen or fourteen years old.

"Mostly she would wrestle with me and touch my privates, tickling me or kissing me inappropriately."

Tony added that he was inexperienced when it came to sex and that his mother encouraged him to try masturbation, but he was not too fond of the practice.

"I attempted to masturbate a few times," Tony recalled, "but never successfully ejaculated." He added, "I never grasped, and to this day still don't understand, how anyone could get all that excited over a greasy palm or a two-dimensional piece of paper with a picture on it.

"By this time," he continued, "I was pretty much disgusted by my mother and her ideas about masturbating, that I never got past the notion that this activity was gross and kinda disgusting. The few times I tried, I always had a heavy feeling of shame and disgust."

Dea Shore denied ever molesting her oldest child. Everyone else in the Shore family denied that such behavior ever existed.

"My first intercourse was with a friend of my mother's," Shore claimed, conveniently forgetting Cindy from the 8 Days Inn. "She was twenty-nine and I was fifteen." Tony, the stud, then claimed that he had two girls on the side named Patty and Christina, each of whom had boyfriends. Tony said he had sex with each girl "as often as possible" and also engaged in several ménage à trois trysts with the two girls.

"I was very sexually active," Tony proclaimed. "From day one I would say I had sex four to five times a week. Sometimes two or three times the same day and occasionally with multiple partners."

Tony did not see anything unusual about his sex life. "I never thought of it as deviant. I thought more of sex as recreational fun."

Tony also stated that by this time his dad had several

girlfriends all over the place and that his mom "started seeing Dad's friends."

The alleged "unusual behavior" in the Shore household was what, Tony Shore claimed, drove him to seek companionship of a different sort. He loved music and became enthralled with musical instruments.

Tony's love for music showed itself at a very early age. Shore claimed to remember that he had musical memories as far back as the age of three when he "was watching these long hairs called the Beatles on *Ed Sullivan* and wanting to be a rock-and-roll guitar player star."

Another memory was his strong desire to own a guitar. Tony claimed that he bugged his father continuously until he finally relented and bought him one from a garage sale for $5. "I begged and begged relentlessly for a guitar till my dad finally gave in one day."

Tony was a natural, quickly teaching himself to play several children's songs such as "Twinkle, Twinkle, Little Star," "Mary Had a Little Lamb," and some Christmas songs as well.

"My parents, mainly Mom, were very impressed to [discover] I had musical aptitude," recalled Shore.

The guitar was Tony's preferred musical weapon of choice. His mother enjoyed piano music and encouraged her husband to purchase one for the family. Rob Shore bought an inexpensive upright piano from a local garage sale. Tony had no interest in playing the piano but "was forced to take lessons." This resulted in one of Tony's first displays of aversion to authority. "My piano teacher was an old hag and wouldn't let me play what I wanted to. Instead, I was forced to play what was written on the page of music. Play note for note what is written. This leaves very little room for artistic interpretation."

At the age of five Tony was battling it out with his elders. "My piano teacher and I went head-to-head often." Tony begrudgingly played music her way, but "much to her dismay, I would learn [the songs] her way, then interpret them and play them the way I thought they should sound."

Shore's memory of his musical background was strikingly clear. "I specifically remember playing 'The Battle Hymn of the Republic.' I could play what was written fine, but refused because it sucked. I would play it my way and change it to something else." Shore's ego knew no bounds. "I liked it so much better my way. I was convinced the composer [Julia Ward Howe] was an idiot."

Shore reveled in his rebelliousness. "At the recital, everyone was amazed at my insolence but very pleased with the version *I* played nonetheless.

"I was more of a composer than a player," he recalled, "and failed to recognize the value of classical knowledge as a foundation for what I was trying so hard to accomplish. Besides . . . I wanted to play guitar anyway, not piano."

Tony could, in fact, play almost any musical instrument he picked up. The musical prodigy could grab an instrument he had never played before, listen to a song he had never heard before, and play the entire song within ten minutes. Whether it was heavy metal, salsa, jazz, or classical, it did not matter.

Tony played trombone in the school band (and was "damn good," by his own estimation) and bass guitar for his band on the side. He also dated the clarinet and flute player from the school band named Nadine. He claimed that Nadine was his "second major sexual encounter."

Tony also continued to get into trouble. He claimed he did not drink or smoke, but he definitely got bored. He and one of his friends, Rusty, would allegedly go out and steal Rusty's father's boat and take it out for a spin on Clear Lake.

Tony experienced what he called "the Big Event," which changed his life forever, when his dad came one day to pick him up from band practice instead of his mom. Apparently, Rob and Dea had split and Tony was going to be shipped back out to California to live with his aunt and uncle. He was excited because, as he said, "my mother had quit bothering me, so, in my mind, life was good and I had a huge ego."

During that summer he claimed to have discovered the Hare Krishna religion and vegetarianism.

While in Irvine, California, Tony also ran into a childhood sweetheart. According to Shore, she was now a dropout, into drugs and rock and roll, and "would have nothing to do with me; however, I still had a major crush on her."

Tony continued down the wrong path while in California. He started running with a jock named Elton. He even slept with a friend's "crazy sister." He was also stealing guns and breaking into apartment duplexes.

He got into trouble as a teenager, including, or so he said, involvement in the possible murder of a homeless man. He also developed a penchant for stalking and harassing pretty young girls.

Tony soon moved again and this time ended up attending Del Campo High School. While there, he signed up for drama classes and played the lead role in "The Frog Prince." He also met several young fellow students/musicians. He claimed that sex and smoking pot were the order of the day and that he and his buddy Chris would regularly steal Chris's mom's Matador.

But Tony still had a penchant for music and enough initiative to form a band called Foxfire, with Eric Wheeler on drums, Randy Wheeler on saxophone, a guy named Mike on guitar, Chuck Woake on bass guitar, and

Tony on keyboards and trombone. He also played his Fender Rhodes '73 vintage guitar.

Tony was the youngest member of Foxfire and supposedly the most inexperienced when it came to women. He stated that he once hooked up with a beautiful young girl from the Philippines. The two went to make out and Tony "got a little breast action." He then made the "fatal mistake of going back and telling my friends." Once the girl found out he blabbed, she blew him off.

But Tony bragged that he always had a girlfriend or a nymphomaniac sex partner to keep him occupied.

During this time Tony's mother held a job at Denny's, where she met a man named Jon Teel, who, according to Tony, was this "great songwriter" and also a recent ex-convict.

Tony claimed that he was forced to walk two miles every day with his trombone and schoolbooks in tow and that his mom would come home from work late at night and smoke pot and drink wine with him.

Tony also acted in several plays. His band allegedly opened up for the female-fronted rock band Heart, one of the biggest musical acts at the time. He believed he was on his way to becoming a rock star.

Tony's junior year in high school, however, turned out to be a disaster. He dropped out of high school, and then his band broke up. Soon thereafter, he applied for and was granted emancipation from his mother, and then he signed up for and attended American River Junior College. He also took on two jobs, one working at Denny's and the other working for Rueben's Planthouse.

Tony also claimed that he met a young girl named Vicki, with whom he fell in love and got engaged to on his eighteenth birthday. Vicki was from a religious family and did not believe in premarital sex, so Tony allegedly continued his trysts with his ménage à trois buddies, Patty and Christina.

"I didn't mind at the time," Tony recalled, "because I was in love with Vicki and my sexual needs were still regularly met by Patty, Christina, and whoever else I might know or meet on the side that was willing."

During this time Dea Shore remarried. Tony did not like his stepfather and even accused the man of pulling a gun on him. He decided to get away and moved to a commune in Auburn, where he found Jesus. He later moved into a house with a friend, where they ran out of money and eventually ate all their meals from a fifty-pound bag of rice.

Tony packed his bags one more time and headed back to Texas, with a goal to get his father to pay for his college tuition.

CHAPTER 25

Rob Shore's memory of his marriage to Dea is slightly fuzzy. Same goes for his recollection of raising his children. He spent the majority of his kids' formative years traveling and working. The family was constantly uprooted as Rob's expertise in computers provided him with ample job opportunities, since he was one of only a handful of people at that time who worked with computers. He described the computers he worked on as the kind that were so huge they took up an entire office room.

But Rob would be the first to admit that he was not much of a father. He believed Dea was much better suited for parenthood than he was.

"Dea was a good mother," Rob recalled much later. "I'm not positive she was, I just felt like she would be better for them than I would have been.

"We didn't ever really seem to have any trouble with the kids that I can recall. We weren't called into school for anything."

* * *

The adult Anthony Shore told a slightly different story about his upbringing.

Shore claimed that his parents met at a bar. Allegedly, Dea was roommates with a young woman by the name of Jan Russo. Dea and Jan used to go out to bars with Rob and his friend Duke Holsworth. Jan and Duke also eventually married each other.

Shore wrote that his mother called his father a "fighter." Apparently, there were several Sioux Indians around the Air Force base and Rob used to get into all kinds of fights with them. Shore claimed his father had a very short temper and would pick a fight with an Indian for no reason whatsoever. Rob was also a Golden Gloves boxing champion, according to his son, so he knew how to use his hands for violence.

In an autobiographical journal that he began to write on his birthday in 1998, Shore claimed to have been told exactly where and how he was conceived. He claimed that his mother told him, often, that she was raped by his father "on someone's lawn."

Shore's earliest memories involve his parents "fighting, yelling, and throwing stuff. I recalled being scared a lot of the time." He also had memories of his sister Gina "as a baby and recall the privilege of holding the baby on occasion."

His sister Gina also claimed that their father was often abusive to Tony. She claimed that Rob Shore would grab "whatever was conveniently able to be picked up, be it a guitar or a belt. . . . My dad has a very bad temper."

In response to this accusation by his own daughter that he threw items at his son, Rob Shore tentatively stated, "I don't remember." He paused briefly. "I don't recall ever doing that. But I don't recall lots of things." He laughed.

Rob Shore claimed that his faulty memory was due to

his focus on work. "I'm very conscientious about how I make my living."

When asked if he believed that Dea may have had any confrontations with his son or the girls, he stated, "Only with Laurel," much later in their relationship. "But I don't recall her having any severe run-ins with Gina or Tony."

Gina backed up Rob Shore's version of how Dea Shore treated the kids. She stated that Dea never even so much as spanked them. Dea's method of discipline consisted of sitting her children down and talking to them about what they did wrong, why it was wrong, and what the kids needed to do to make it right.

Gina also recalled that her father was not the only one in the family with a bad temper. She said she was prone to fits of rage as well.

Young Tony, however, did display his share of deviant behavior. According to Gina, when he was five years old, Tony abducted the neighbor's kitten. Apparently, Tony loved the little creature and wanted it to come live with his family. His sister told him that he couldn't keep the kitten.

"But I want him to come out and play," the young boy pleaded.

"No, Tony. He's not yours. Take him back," Gina ordered.

Tony did not listen. Instead, he went into the kitchen with the kitten in tow, grabbed a sharp knife, and took the kitten back outside. He clutched the defenseless feline by the nape of its furry neck and jammed its face into the dirt of their backyard. He then took the long kitchen knife and pierced the kitten's skull. He pushed so hard on the knife that it slid completely through the animal's skull, past its jaw, pinning it to the ground.

When Dea Shore discovered the bloody and mutilated

kitten, she was mortified. She had no idea why Tony would lash out at the poor creature. She decided that it would be best if Tony received some help. She contacted her church's priest and asked him to come speak to her son.

Tony's unusual behavior, however, did not cease after the meeting with the priest. According to Gina, Tony even lashed out at her one time. Apparently, Tony once pushed a screwdriver through the top of his sister's head. She had no idea why he did it.

By the time Tony entered sixth grade, he and the family packed their bags again. They headed to Florida, where they stayed for the next three years.

"[Tony and I] would go for bicycle rides," Gina recalled, "where he would have me go up and knock on people's doors and have people's daughters come out." These were usually either young friends of Gina's or female classmates of Tony's. Gina stated that Tony liked to "grope them" and that he "tried to kiss them and stuff."

Gina also noticed a pattern of the type of girls that Tony preferred. They were usually skinny, attractive, and had long hair. They were also typically small-framed and not imposing in any way. Gina described these girls as "mousy." She also noted that a lot of the girls tended to look like her.

Tony continued to get Gina to play the bait-and-switch game with the young girls for several years. Eventually, however, Gina had had enough and decided to put an end to Tony's behavior. It happened when Tony sent her out on yet another mission to a friend's house. When Gina knocked on the neighbor's door, one of her teachers opened it. Gina realized that if she was responsible for her teacher's daughter getting groped by her big brother, it would come back to haunt her in some way.

She said, "Tony, I can't do it. I love going to school, and I don't want any kind of problems."

Gina also responded to Tony's claim that their mother practiced witchcraft. According to Gina, Dea Shore believed herself to be a good witch. It was not uncommon for Dea to burn sage in and around their home to ward off any potential evil spirits. Gina claimed that such behavior was culled from her mother's Italian heritage.

CHAPTER 26

By 1983, Tony Shore moved back to Houston, Texas. He was twenty-one years old when he met the love of his life, an older woman by the name of Gina Worley.

Gina Lynn Worley was born in 1959 on Offutt Air Force Base, Nebraska. Her father was a member of the U.S. Air Force for twenty-eight years, so she spent much of her infant and toddler years overseas in such European countries as Austria, Italy, and France. Her family settled in Texas when she was four years old, but the following year they moved to Arkansas.

By 1973, however, Gina's parents divorced and the majority of her family ended up in Houston, Texas. Her father moved there first; then Gina and her mother followed suit.

In high school Gina was definitely not a social butterfly. She described herself as "quiet. Really, really quiet. Bookish." She made good grades but did not have many friends. "Maybe one. I liked to read a lot and keep to myself."

Gina graduated from high school in 1977 and then attended the College of the Mainland in Texas City. But she soon dropped out and enrolled in paralegal school. She eventually earned her paralegal certification and landed a job with a Houston-based attorney.

"I discovered I did not like attorneys," Gina later declared. She especially did not like the fact that the family law attorney she worked for would look up dirt on people. "They're evil."

Gina Worley married a young man named Robert in 1981 when she was twenty-two years old. She said that she "was too young to have any sense." They were divorced in 1982, less than a year later, because "we were both too young and he was an idiot."

She met Tony Shore after Thanksgiving in 1983.

"I was checking the mail in my mailbox and he ran down the stairs all flustered and introduced himself, saying, 'Hi! I'm Tony Shore! I'm the nicest guy you'll ever meet.'" Gina was smitten. "I thought he was charming. He is a charming guy. He was really a nice, open genuine person."

Shore asked her out then and there. The couple spent most of their time together gearing up for the Christmas holiday. He would take Gina in his big Impala, for which he paid $100, to the upscale Galleria in Houston for some serious Christmas shopping. Gina remembered she thought his car was cute with a peace sign sticker in the back window and a rusty scraped-up bumper.

"It had an exhaust leak," Gina remembered, "so [whenever] you drove more than ten minutes, man, you were happy [when] you got there.

"It was really neat when we met. We had almost the same kind of books. At that point in time we were reading things like *Jonathan Livingston Seagull,* those types of books. So, we really hit it off. We really got along."

The young lovebirds wasted no time in tying the knot. They were married on March 25, 1984, just four months after they first met. Gina remembered the ceremony as a quiet, intimate affair. The couple was married by a justice of the peace at the courthouse annex. "Rob Shore was there and my mom and my friend Suzanne. And Tony's stepbrother at the time, Kenny Hanks," Gina recalled. "It was a real small ceremony. I was young and naive, and he was really charming. He was very well-spoken, intelligent, and articulate."

After the wedding the newlyweds traipsed to Sacramento, California, to visit Shore's mother and sister. They stopped first, however, at Newport Beach, California, to visit a friend of Shore's and stay at his condominium on the beach. Gina had a tough time. First she was stung by a jellyfish; then she suffered severe burns from the sun after she fell asleep outside; then she drank the water and caught a stomach virus. Their marriage was off to a rough start.

Gina, however, still had fond memories of her early times with Tony Shore. "Those were the salad days. They were a lot of fun." She talked about his interest in music. "We'd go to a Hilton and find one of the rooms where they kept instruments and Tony would start playing the piano. That is until they caught him," referring to the hotel staff. "He was really good."

Tickling the ivories wasn't the only thing that Shore was good at.

One month after they were married, Gina got pregnant. After they returned from California, the couple moved into The Atrium apartment complex near the airport. Money was tight for the couple, so Gina, who already worked as an administrative assistant for Whataburger, took on a second job of delivering newspapers while she was seven months pregnant.

Their first child, Amber, was born on April 9, 1984. Gina took some time off from work to care for her daughter, but she eventually returned to her job at Whataburger while her husband remained at Southwestern Bell. Gina also maintained her second job delivering newspapers.

"I would be home in time for him to get up and go to work," Gina added, "and to take care of Amber. She was never left alone."

Despite the long work hours and money problems, Tony and Gina got along just fine. "We rarely argued," Gina noted. "Mainly, we would sit around and play role-playing games like Avalon Hill or Titan." Shore did, however, seem to have a problem with Gina's physical appearance after the birth of Amber. "He always called me fat," she stated, "even though I barely weighed one hundred ten pounds." This hurt Gina immensely.

She recalled that when she lived in Arkansas as a young girl, she "was constantly tortured. The new kid, the fat kid, the smart kid, the dork kid, the retard kid. I was sensitive. That was one of the things when I had my own children I forbid them from name calling. No name calling in the house. Call them by their given name or something nice, nothing else."

By the time their second child, Tiffany, was born, on June 5, 1985, Shore had received a promotion to customer representative, which allowed him to work inside the offices of Southwestern Bell. Gina still worked to help out on the financial front and then focused her attention on her daughters when she got home. Shore was not happy with the lack of attention.

"Whenever I had given birth to Tiffany, she was nine pounds nine-and-a-half ounces. There's that period of time where you have stitches and all that and he wanted to have sex. And I'm like, 'No, are you crazy?' He got really mad at me and he forced himself on me. It was very, very, very unforgiving. It was unpleasant." She continued on with the painful memory of the spousal rape. "After that, our sex life was pretty sketchy." She sometimes blamed it on the fact that Shore worked a lot and that she had to take care of both girls. But deep in her heart, she knew it was because he had frightened her. "It was really touch and go after that happened with me."

"I cursed him. I hope you get warts," she told him.

He did.

The very next day.

"He got the most raging case of genital warts and no one could figure out where he got it because I didn't have them! It creeped him out."

After Tiffany was born, Gina noticed something peculiar with Amber. "She didn't like to be held. She wouldn't speak. She wouldn't say 'Mama,' 'Dada,' those types of things. Her first word was 'Tiger.'"

Gina and Tony realized something was different about their daughter, but they could not place their fingers on it. Gina, who described herself as an avid researcher, dove into learning about potential medical issues. Shore, on the other hand, seemed turned off by Amber's behavior. He began to shun her more and more.

Eventually Gina's research led her to conclude that

her daughter might be suffering from a type of autism. "She showed a lot of symptomatic displays of autistic behavior," Gina recalled. "When I would pick her up and try to breast-feed her, she would go all rigid on me. I had no idea that that was a common trait with infantile-autism behavior. She wouldn't scream. She would just get all stiff."

Shore used to say that Gina was "hysterical" with her analysis.

"You just don't live with her," Gina responded.

Gina talked about her daughter's "inappropriate behaviors": "We'd be walking along in the mall, minding our own business," Gina recalled, "and Amber saw a young, statuesque African American woman, very attractive. She had on a long dress that was all in leopard tone. Amber walked up to the woman, lifted her dress up, stuck her head under, and said, 'You're not a guy underneath.'

"You either went crazy or developed a sense of humor." Gina chuckled. "That was my strategy. You develop a sense of humor and Daddio just didn't have one.

"Tony's suggested strategy was to beat the hell out of her," Gina intoned, "but that's just what he *wanted* to do. He never hit either one of them."

Gina tried a slightly different approach that was suggested by some of Amber's doctors. "If she did something inappropriate in public, I would sometimes just ignore it."

Unfortunately, it was often impossible to completely ignore Amber. "One of the things she would do was to pull her hair out, hit herself, throw herself against the wall. Someone came up to me and said, 'I'm gonna report you to CPS [Child Protective Services],'" to which

Gina jokingly asked, "Will they really protect me from my children?"

Gina complained that Shore wanted to be more of a best friend with the girls as opposed to being their father. "He liked to do all the 'uncle' things. He was an 'uncle daddy.' But if anybody got sick or he had to change a diaper, he'd say, 'I'm not gonna do that. I might get something under my nails.' He never changed a diaper, but he did all the pictures, all the arts and crafts. The cool dad. All the fun stuff."

At the same time Shore used to get on Gina about the way she handled the girls. "If you weren't so lenient," he often told their mother, but Gina had no idea what Tony really wanted her to do with them.

Shore apparently was envious of Amber. "Part of it was jealousy," Gina continued, "because she demanded a lot of attention. This is the person who could stay up for seventy-two hours straight, sleep for two, and then go for another seventy-two hours."

But Shore did not deal with "rejection" lightly. "He would ignore her [Amber] and put all of his attention on Tiffany," Gina recalled. "Tiffany was his girl, his baby, his sweetheart. She was the pretty one. She was the fun one. She was the one that he wanted to teach how to play music. He just gave her more.

"We never argued until the day they diagnosed Amber with a form of autism, invasive developmental disorder. She didn't even speak until she was six or seven years old."

According to Gina, Shore blamed her for Amber's alleged autism. "He washed his hands of her," she recalled. "He couldn't stand her. Said that she was a retard. He said really mean things about Amber." Gina was shocked by her husband's response to their firstborn child.

"He had a problem with human frailty. He really despised people who were in some way lesser." Gina described Shore's judgmental behavior that he never displayed while courting her. "People who were not well-groomed, people who were not well-made, people who gained weight—it just put him off." Amber became one of those people in his mind.

"Amber was having all of these behavior problems," Gina said, "and she went to one of these diagnosticians who was one of the best, and she had an EEG [electroencephalogram], and an MRI [magnetic resonance imaging], which showed that it was nothing organic—she didn't have a brain tumor—but she did have the developmental disorder."

Gina recalled how Shore always picked on Amber. "Tony would [call Amber stupid] so she couldn't hear it. Just because a child couldn't hear, she knows what your attitude is. She can sense it."

"No she can't 'cause she's stupid," Shore shot back when Gina told him this.

According to Gina, "the Shore gene is predominant. You look at Robert Shore, Tony, Tony's sister Laurel, Amber, and Tiffany. They all have the same eyes and big heads. That's a Shore trait.

"I said it takes two people to make a baby and everybody on my side of the family is sane! It could be you!" Gina taunted Shore. "It could be your genes."

Needless to say, Tony Shore was not happy.

During this time Tony Shore's escape was a large alternative rock/jazz collective called St. Vitus Dance. Gina described them as "a ten-piece band with the commitment The Commitments never had." Shore played piano and keyboards.

Gina recalled his obsession with perfection. "He practiced enough to drive you insane." She recalled he would play the song "Locomotive Breath" by Jethro Tull over and over on the upright piano in their apartment's living room. "If he made a mistake, he would start over from the very beginning, instead of where he messed up because 'that would be practicing your mistakes.'"

CHAPTER 27

Friday, October 24, 2003, 4:53 P.M.,
Houston Police Department—Sixth Floor—Homicide Division,
Interrogation Room #6,
1200 Travis Street,
Houston, Texas.

Twenty-two-year veteran Todd Miller got the first crack at Tony Shore. Miller had worked in the Homicide Division for nearly twelve years at the time of Shore's arrest. The detective had been at Champion Collision Center earlier that day, along with Officer Robert Farmer and Sergeant Hal Kennedy. When Miller arrived on the scene, Shore was already sitting in the back of Officer Farmer's patrol car. Miller informed Farmer that he would meet him downtown at Homicide.

When Officer Farmer arrived at headquarters with Tony Shore in tow, both men headed up to the sixth floor to the Homicide Division. They were greeted by Miller, who instructed Farmer to remove Shore's handcuffs and to escort the suspect to the interrogation room. Miller removed his gear and placed his weapon in his desk drawer, locked it up, and headed to the interrogation room. The room, which was fourteen feet by nine feet, with blue-green carpet and acoustic foam tiles on the walls, had one door without a lock and a small window.

By the time Miller stepped into the interrogation room with Tony Shore, it was 5:00 P.M. Miller introduced himself and read Shore his rights, which he waived. Miller then asked Shore if he would like something to drink or eat. Shore declined.

Miller informed Shore that he was under the arrest for the murder of Carmen Estrada. The detective went on to explain that Shore's DNA had been found on Estrada's body, but he did not tell him where specifically. He also told Shore the general area where they discovered Estrada's body, but did not pinpoint the location.

According to Detective Miller, he and Shore had a congenial conversation. When they first started out, Shore referred to Miller as Officer Miller. As their discussion progressed, Shore resorted to the more casual, Todd. Miller did not correct him. Instead, he let Shore believe he was in control of the discussion. "Never in all the interviews I've ever conducted [has someone referred to me by my first name]. That's the only time it's ever happened."

During their conversation it came up that Miller and Shore actually knew one another and had even met before. Turned out that Shore's first wife, Gina Worley, was the daughter of Miller's ex-wife's second husband, Floyd Worley. Apparently, Floyd Worley lived in Lake Livingston, Texas, and that is where Miller and Shore had previously met.

Todd and Tony chatted for three hours, until 8:05 P.M. Shore answered every one of Miller's questions and had several of his own, which he inquired of Miller. During that time Shore never confessed to murdering Carmen Estrada.

Miller asked Shore if he needed to make a visit to the restroom and again offered food or drink. Shore declined and Miller excused himself from the interview room. The detective met up with his fellow task force members Sergeant John Swaim, Lieutenant Greg Neely, and Harris County sheriff's deputy Roger Wedgeworth. After the four men discussed the current situation, Miller asked Sergeant Swaim if he wanted to take over the interview. Swaim agreed that he should. They all sensed that Miller was not making any headway in the interview and that a fresh face might loosen Shore's tongue up a little.

At 8:07 P.M., Sergeant John Swaim entered interrogation room #6 and sat down next to Tony Shore. Swaim introduced himself to Shore in a quiet, even voice. The sergeant informed Shore that he, too, would like to talk about the murder of Carmen Estrada. Swaim informed Shore that he would succinctly lay out the evidence they had against him and let him make the next move. Swaim then read Shore his rights, which the suspect waived.

Swaim told Shore that DNA was why they were there. Specifically, Shore's DNA was found underneath Estrada's fingernails.

"Did you know her?" Swaim asked.

"No, I did not know her," Shore calmly replied.

"Do you know how DNA works?"

"Yeah, I know," Shore stated.

"Do you think that we are lying to you about the DNA?" Swaim wondered.

"No, I don't think you're lying. I just have no idea why you would have my DNA."

"How did it get on her?"

"I don't know," Shore proclaimed. "I can't explain that."

The line of questioning continued and Shore continued to deny the allegations. All the while he was calm, cool, and collected. He also looked Swaim directly in the eyes during the entire conversation. According to Swaim, Shore "did not show any of the normal signs, through my experience, of someone who was lying."

Swaim realized two things about Shore. First, he was dealing with one smart individual. Second, he was not sure if Shore was even capable of telling the truth.

Swaim was also surprised when Shore referred to him by his first name. As with Miller, Swaim had rarely ever been called by his first name by a suspect during an interview.

The two men seemed to get along just fine, but Shore was not admitting anything. Swaim assumed that it was going to be a very long night for everyone involved.

At 9:20 P.M., Shore used the restroom, then accepted an offer by Swaim for coffee. But when Swaim exited the interrogation room, he had nothing.

Next up was Deputy Wedgeworth. He entered at 9:25 P.M. and spoke to Shore about the Dana Sanchez murder. He was not able to get a confession out of Shore either. The deputy exited the interrogation room at 10:15 P.M., empty-handed.

The task force members agreed that Miller should go back in the room. Miller noted that Shore seemed a bit more subdued this go-round. He also seemed less eager to ask questions. He did, however, continue to answer every one of Miller's probes. The detective also noted that Shore was still very sharp and he continued to look the officer directly in the eyes.

Miller then laid out several crime scene photos that he removed from a binder. Shore instantly turned his head away from the gruesome pictures; however, he just as quickly turned his head back and began to stare at them.

"C'mon, Tony. Tell me the truth," Miller cajoled. "We know you did all these. We've got the DNA to prove you're the one responsible for all these dead girls."

Shore did not deny the accusations. "Well, I just don't remember," he stated. "I don't remember being there. I don't remember seeing her. I don't remember." Suddenly the cocksureness left his demeanor.

Miller and Shore continued for another ninety minutes when Shore brought up what every detective loves to hear: the hypothetical.

"Let's say, hypothetically, someone were to. . . ." Shore started, but then paused. "No. I'm sorry, Todd. I just don't trust you."

Miller was crushed. He was so close, yet he knew it was not going to happen. He had lost Shore's trust and his suspect was about to clam up.

"Is there someone else you'd rather talk to, Tony? Someone you do trust?" Miller asked.

"I would feel more comfortable with John," Shore referred to Sergeant John Swaim.

"Okay, Tony. Let me go get him for you," Miller offered as he got up and walked out of the interrogation room. Miller found Swaim and let him know that Shore was ready to talk and that he might be ready to spill the beans. Miller was excited, even after nearly seven hours of interviews.

"He wants to talk to you," Miller told Swaim. "He said he wanted to talk hypothetically. You're up."

The time was 11:50 P.M.

Sergeant John Swaim wasted no time getting back into the interrogation room with Shore. Shore looked up at Swaim and the officer greeted him with "What's up, man? What do you want to talk about?"

"Sit down, John," Shore said as he motioned to the opposite chair. "Sit down."

Swaim took his seat and noticed the binder of photographs that Todd Miller had left in the room. Swaim grabbed the binder and then handed it over to Shore.

Shore took the binder, paused, and then looked Swaim directly in the eye and said, "What would you say if I gave you these cases," he directed a glance toward the binder and slightly lifted it up, "and a couple of bonuses?"

Swaim sat up in his chair. "Well, man, that would be great. What's this hypothetical? What were you going to talk about hypothetically?"

"Well, I have this evilness in me." Shore looked exactly the same as he did when he denied everything to Swaim earlier. "I think if I tell you what I've done, it will release that evilness and I will feel better."

"Great," Swaim said. His demeanor did not change either.

"Before I tell you this, can you tell me what I'm going to be charged with?" Shore wanted to know.

"Well, you know, that's something that the district attorney's office decides. I don't decide that. But if you're going to tell me what I think you're going to tell me, then it's a capital murder charge; and that carries, you know . . . two things can happen to you. Either life in prison or the death penalty."

Shore stared at Swaim for several seconds with almost no reaction. He then looked directly into Swaim's eyes and asked, "Does the name Laurie Tremblay mean anything to you?"

The name Laurie Tremblay meant a lot to Sergeant John Swaim.

CHAPTER 28

Friday, September 26, 1986,
Ninfa's Restaurant,
10600 block of Westheimer Road,
Houston, Texas.

Homer Fernandez enjoyed his life. He had a family, a nice house, and a job he loved. He was the manager for his aunt's restaurant on one of the busiest streets in Houston. His aunt was not just any aunt either. She was the incredibly well-known and respected Ninfa Rodriguez Laurenzo, or "Mama Ninfa" as she was known around the city. Mama Ninfa had converted her family's tortilla bakery, which she and her husband had opened in 1949, into a full-fledged TexMex cuisine destination point, located on Navigation Boulevard. They were known for their delicious green sauce and chips, as well as their Tacos ala Ninfa, or tacos al carbon. Mama Ninfa had also been credited with bringing the term "TexMex" into the American lexicon, introducing red and green sauces with chips before a meal, and starting the fajita craze.

The original Ninfa's Restaurant opened in 1973. The success of the first restaurant led to more Ninfa openings across the city. By the early 1980s, there were nine of these restaurants spread across Houston, including two on Westheimer Road, which was one of the most heavily traveled streets in the entire city of Houston. One was near the world-famous Galleria shopping center and one was farther out in the Westchase area.

Homer Fernandez, Ninfa's nephew, was responsible for the Westchase Ninfa's and enjoyed being in charge of such a prestigious restaurant. He loved working for his aunt and providing for his family. His job was to oversee operations of the establishment, which meant making the employee work schedule, payroll, food preparation, and even floor duties while he was there. He also oversaw a team of five managers. Fernandez was smooth, efficient, and hardworking. Almost all of his employees enjoyed working for him and customers loved to chat with him.

Fernandez would sometimes open up the restaurant, which usually meant that he would have to be there bright and early at 7:20 A.M. to unlock the restaurant doors.

When he opened up, he would always park his car in the back of the restaurant because that was where he disarmed the alarm system.

He did so again this morning. Outside it was still somewhat dark, especially since the recent daylight saving time made the morning darkness last just that much longer.

Fernandez pulled into his usual spot, switched off the ignition to kill the engine, and sat in his car for approximately one minute while he fiddled with paperwork. The restaurant is located inside the parking lot of a shopping center that was known as the Kaleidoscope. Since it was so early, there was not one other car in the parking lot.

Once Fernandez gathered his information, he looked out his car window. He was surprised to see another car pull up directly behind the restaurant. This was quite unusual, as the restaurant did not officially open until lunch, so there were never any employees on the premises at this time of morning. Hernandez looked up to see who it was, but the driver did not get out of the car. Hernandez turned his attention back to his paperwork. When he glanced up again, he saw a man outside the parked vehicle standing in between the car and the Dumpster at the back of the restaurant.

The morning glare of the sun prevented Fernandez from getting a close look.

The restaurant manager looked down to the other driver's feet. He was shocked to see a body there. He believed the other driver was staring back at him; however, he could not be certain. Fernandez had dark tint on all of his windows, so it was difficult to make out the driver's expression.

Fernandez was frightened, so he looked back down at his papers. He was afraid he would attract the attention of the driver.

The man by the Dumpster jumped back into his small light-blue vehicle and hightailed it out of the restaurant parking lot. Fernandez could tell the man was white and had dark hair. But that was all he saw.

Fernandez didn't know what to do and panicked. Once he knew the driver had taken off, he turned his attention back to the Dumpster behind his restaurant. He stepped out of his car and headed over to the trash area. As he walked up to the area, he noticed what could only be described as a human pretzel.

A young teenage girl's mangled body lay on her back next to the curb by the Dumpster. Her blue jean Capri-clad legs were splayed out to her left, with her right leg crossing over her left leg at the ankles. She wore a pink interlaced woven shoe on her left foot, but no shoe on

her right. Her left leg, which lay under her right leg, was
bent up at a 115-degree angle, with her knee pointing
toward her left shoulder and the left side of her face.
Her left arm had snaked under her bent left knee and
appeared to be grasping the side of the jeans on her
right leg. The girl's upper half was covered with a short-
sleeved white half-shirt, with an exposed midriff. Lying
in between her stomach and left thigh was her right
shoe. Apparently, the man, who had so deliberately dis-
posed of her body, had almost forgotten one of her
shoes and tossed it on her as he sped off. The girl's right
arm was also extended above her head, with a slight
bend at the elbow, which touched the curb.

Fernandez bent down to take a closer look at the
young blond girl. He noticed that she seemed a little
puffy, especially around the lips, which were discolored,
like sour milk. He also noticed an abrasion underneath
her right nostril, as well as a few scratches on the lower
portion of her right cheek. Her left eye appeared
swollen and purplish. Fernandez also noticed a bright
red contusion that seemed to stretch around her neck
like a coral snake.

He knelt toward the young girl.

"Are you okay?" he asked the dead girl. "Of course
she's not," he muttered aloud. "Stupid."

Fernandez bolted up from the body, unlocked the
back door, disarmed the restaurant security system, and
went into his office. He picked up the phone and, still in
shock, dialed 411.

"Information. What do you want?" the voice on the
other end of the line asked.

Fernandez was confused. He meant to call for help.
"Oh, my goodness," he declared as he realized his mistake.
"I'm sorry." He hung up the phone and slowly dialed 911.

When the emergency operator answered his call,

Fernandez stated, "I want to report a dead body outside of my restaurant." He proceeded to give as many details about the dead girl as he could.

Houston police officers were summoned to the scene and arrived soon thereafter. Fernandez told the officers about the other driver, but added that he did not get a clear look at his face or his vehicle. Fernandez felt bad that he could not provide better information for the officers. He looked toward the body of the young girl. He had no idea who she was, but he felt sorry for her.

The three officers dispatched to the scene at Ninfa's were Jim Ramsey, Larry Boyd Smith, and John Swaim.

Swaim received the call sometime between 7:15 and 7:30 A.M. He arrived on the scene, along with Smith and Ramsey, around 8:40 A.M. Swaim met with a patrol officer, a police supervisor, a sergeant, two paramedics, and a county medical examiner. After conferring with the various personnel involved at the scene, Swaim learned that the girl had been strangled and that her body had only been recently dumped. Swaim also learned that rain fell on the premises at 7:50 A.M. and that a piece of plastic had been placed over the victim's body to preserve any potential evidence.

Swaim approached the still-visibly-shaken Homer Fernandez. He listened as the manager retold the story of discovering the young girl's body.

Swaim then went over to check out the corpse. The plastic had already been removed from the body. As Swaim stepped in, he could see the red abrasions around the girl's neck. Despite the lack of a ligature, everyone at the scene agreed that she died from strangulation.

Swaim took a closer look at the body. He noticed that the young girl had three rings on her left hand and a thin gold watch on her left wrist. She wore a pair of matching earrings that looked like Indian headdresses with tiny crosses attached to the bottoms. She wore a pendant picture holder, with no photograph inside. She also wore two necklaces, one with the letter *L*. Swaim concluded that the young girl probably had not been robbed.

Swaim also noticed some black marks on her denim jeans, but he was unable to identify the marks. Also, the pockets of her pants had not been pulled out. Her shirt had been pushed up above her abdomen and partially covered her neck. The young girl's bra was in place but it was unlatched in the back.

The patrol officers also discovered a purse curled in between her arms. Inside, they were able to find some identification, specifically, a Metro bus pass. The young girl lying before Swaim was fifteen-year-old Laurie Lee Tremblay.

CHAPTER 29

Laurie Tremblay was born on September 17, 1971. Her mother, Katherine Tremblay, turned twenty years old just three days before Laurie was born. Laurie's father left them early on and allegedly never looked back.

Laurie lived with her grandmother in Lake Linden, in the upper peninsula of Michigan, until she was ten years old, because her mother had fallen on hard times. But Laurie loved the open countryside of Lake Linden with its nature trails and beautiful landscapes, and since it was located close to Lake Superior, she was always up for a fishing trip.

When she turned ten, Laurie was able to join her mom. Katherine worked three different jobs to get her daughter down to Houston, Texas, including work at the Ice Capades.

Laurie liked Houston well enough, but she often longed to return to Michigan. She did, however, try to make the best of her time while in Texas. During her preteen years she seemed fairly well adjusted. She did well in school and stayed out of trouble.

By the time high school rolled around, however, things started to change. She grew more despondent;

she became less fond of school and started slacking off in her studies. She started hanging out with a crowd that had a negative influence on her behavior. It all culminated in spring 1986 when Laurie was taken out of Robert E. Lee High School and sent for the following fall semester to an alternative-education institution called the Hope Center for Youth, located on the 4000 block of Yoakum Boulevard, in the central southwest side of Houston.

David Winship, executive director of Hope Center for Youth, described the center as "a private, nonprofit facility for junior and senior high-school students who are emotionally disturbed or delinquent or have experienced behavioral problems." Katherine Tremblay believed that her daughter was not a problem child but just that she underperformed in math and that was why she had to transfer to the Hope Center for Youth.

Laurie started school at the Hope Center on September 2, 1986. Her mother was concerned because she believed her daughter suffered from low self-esteem and would have a hard time making new friends.

But Laurie seemed to make friends. Dr. Gary Blackburn, the director of Hope Center, noted that she seemed popular with her classmates in the short time she was there.

Laurie was an attractive young girl. She stood five feet nine inches and weighed 133 pounds. Her mother described her hair as "dishwater blond" that was very thick and hung down to her shoulders. She had blue eyes and kept herself in good shape.

Other than having to take a Houston Metro bus to school, everything seemed to be working out just fine for Laurie.

CHAPTER 30

Friday, September 26, 1986, 6:30 A.M.,
12700 block of Whittington Boulevard,
Whittfield Apartments,
Houston, Texas.

Katherine and Laurie Tremblay spent the previous evening working together on Laurie's homework. It was the first time the two had fun on such a project. After they finished, Laurie's mom made her daughter a sack lunch that consisted of a bologna sandwich and some pie. Katherine kissed her daughter good night and smiled as Laurie headed off to bed.

The memory helped Katherine Tremblay sleep soundly until the morning. She could hear her daughter getting ready in the bathroom; however, she remained in bed. She then heard a loud *slam!*

Katherine's dreams were generally unpleasant. Her first thought was: *Oh, my God, someone's got her!* She struggled in her hibernation-like state as she worried, *Someone's outside and I can't wake up!* The fear was so overwhelming that Katherine eventually did wake and bolted out of bed. She ran into the kitchen to try and find her daughter.

Laurie was already gone.

Katherine could see that her daughter had taken her lunch sack and purse. She then went outside on the porch, but her daughter was nowhere in sight. She came to her senses and realized that the door slam was just Laurie heading out for the morning to catch the city bus.

Katherine was frustrated that Laurie had to leave so early and she did not like the fact that Laurie had to take the City of Houston's Metro Bus Service to get to school. She was currently at odds with the Houston Independent School District (HISD), since they would not pick her daughter up and take her to Hope Center. Laurie had been forced to walk two miles to get to the HISD bus stop nearest to their apartment. Instead of making that daily trek, Laurie's mother insisted that she take the city bus. Laurie did not disagree.

Laurie started school at the Hope Center for Youth less than a month earlier. She seemed to like the school and her mother sensed that Laurie seemed to be breaking free from her shell—just a bit.

Laurie had left their apartment, walked into the parking lot, and made her way out the front gate, and onto Whittington Boulevard.

According to Katherine Tremblay, Laurie's normal path would have been to walk out of the complex, take a right onto Whittington Boulevard, and head east toward Dairy Ashford Road, where she would take a left and head north. She would walk another quarter mile to the corner of South Dairy Ashford Road and the 12600 block of West Ella Drive, where a rather nondescript bench was located below a Metro bus sign and in front of a mini-strip mall, which included a food mart and a dry cleaner.

When Katherine left to catch Laurie, it was still dark outside.

CHAPTER 31

Saturday, October 25, 2003, 12:08 A.M.,
Houston Police Department,
Interrogation Room #6,
1200 Travis Street,
Houston, Texas.

Sergeant John Swaim could not believe his ears. Somehow, he kept his composure as Shore told him about his first murder. Swaim wanted to be sure to get every last bit of information from Shore's confession, so he turned on his cassette recorder on the table and asked the polite, intelligent man to tell his story.

The following text is the transcript from the actual interrogation of and confession on tape by Anthony Allen Shore in regard to the murder of Laurie Tremblay:

John Swaim (JS): *Alright Tony, I'm gonna turn the tape on right now. This is Sergeant John Swaim, Houston Police Homicide. I'm here in Homicide Division, 1200 Travis Street. I'm talking to Tony Shore.*

Tony Shore (TS): *Anthony—Allen—Shore.*

JS: *Right. Well, what I want to do, first of all, can I call you Tony?*

TS: *That's fine. I just thought you want the record right.*

JS: *Correct. Read you your legal warnings. And they're, uh, 1 to 5.*

Number 1: You have the right to remain silent and not make any statement at all and you know that any statement may be used against you and probably will be used against you at your trial.

Number 2: Any statement you make may be used as evidence against you in court.

Number 3: You have a right to have a lawyer being present and to advise you prior to and during questioning.

Number 4: If you are unable to employ a lawyer you have the right to have a lawyer appointed to advise you prior to and during your questioning.

Number 5: You have the right to terminate this interview at anytime.

Do you understand these warnings?

TS: *Yes, sir. I do.*

JS: *Do you wanna waive these rights and tell me about, talk to me about some cases?*

TS: *Yes, sir.*

JS: *Okay. Let's start with, let's just start with the killing.*

TS: *First is Laurie Ann [actually, Lee] Tremblay.*

JS: *Okay.*

TS: *I was living in Alfred's house at the time. I was working for Southwestern Bell as a marketing representative. Actually, it might have been a service rep at the time. I was in the business office.*

Every morning, I'd be going to work. Every morning this little girl asked me for a cigarette and I couldn't stop laughing. I asked if she needed a ride. Then I gave her a ride. Then, a couple of days went by, she saw me, I gave her a ride again, to school. She had a long freakin' ways from where she had to catch the bus. She was way, way up on Whittington in these apartments.

She and I became more than friends and that's not braggin, it's stating fuckin' facts 'cause I understand she was not of age. And I've also been through a lot of sex offender treatment therapy at this time and I'm starting to understand some of the psychopathology behind my preoccupation. I know it is.

She and I became involved, at least in the sense of two things, I load her bags and I started to give her a ride on a semi-regular basis. Then, one morning, uh, she got to the bus really early, you know, and we got to ride around. There's times I even stopped and we bought kolaches, but we had time to ride around and kick it. And, if they got off of work a little early, it got to be a fairly regular thing giving her a ride.

Then there was, uh, something happened, I don't recall what with her, a couple a weeks there she didn't want a ride. So, I guess she was, decided this was a fucked-up kind of little relationship that's fucking juvenile but, anyway, she decided not to.

JS: *Right.*

TS: *Then one day it was misting rain, she saw me, asked me for a ride and I didn't want her to get more involved in this because it needed stopping. It started off okay and then she was freaked out . . . and I won't deny it I was a sick puppy 'cause I was—*

JS: *What kind of vehicle did you have back then?*

TS: *Cadillac Cimarron. It was light in color. Had a dent in the panel on the driver's side rear door.*

JS: Okay. I was just curious. I'm sorry, go 'head.

TS: So, it got out of hand and she started freakin' out and I begged her, I said, "Please don't." She's like "no."

I freaked out. I don't know what came over me. What kind of sickness. I freaked out.

I had a wife, I had two daughters, living in this reasonably decent house that needed a lot of repairs but it was in a nice neighborhood and all this stuff. And I had a life and I couldn't see it all thrown away. And I freaked out. And, uh, just wanted it to just stop.

Take a cotton cord that time.

JS: Okay.

TS: I remember it was cotton 'cause. . . . I tried to calm her down. She wouldn't calm down. I remember trying to knock her out and I hit her in the back of the head.

JS: Where were y'all at, in your car?

TS: Yeah, in the neighborhood somewhere between Briar Forest and Westheimer. I'm not even sure what streets, cross streets, but if I had to estimate, probably around Wilcrest, maybe, or even further up, maybe . . . I dunno. Somewhere in that ballpark.

JS: Move on.

TS: (Loud sigh)

JS: And then what happened?

TS: I undid her bra. Everything got outta hand. She freaked out. I remember we got into . . . I tried to knock her out because I just really freaked out. It's not right and I just find it hard to talk about.

Took this cotton cord and I tried to make sure she would never, ever tell anybody. Even though I knew that was insane and I knew there was probably no *chance in hell that I wasn't gonna get found out 'cause I was stupid. The number of rides that I had given her, surely somebody seen us together, surely something.*

And the cotton cord broke more than once. It wasn't working. That's all I knew.

JS: *Did you use your hands?*

TS: *I used a cord, a ligature.*

JS: *I know, but did you use your hands on it?*

TS: *I used my hands. I injured my fingers.*

JS: *You did that in the car, is that correct?*

TS: *In the car.*

JS: *And then what after that?*

TS: *I panicked. Daylight came on and I didn't know what to do. And I looked, I mean there was no way to make this go away. I stepped over the line. I knew I was fucked. I needed, this is a, I'm fucked for life and there's nothing I can do to change it.*

JS: *Right.*

TS: *I was sick to my stomach. I even stopped at one point and threw up because I was sick. I had people passing by. I couldn't believe nobody fucking saw shit. Nobody stopped to find out what was going on, anything.*

JS: *Okay.*

TS: *So, I drove up behind the Ninfa's there and I pushed her out of the car. I just wanted to get away from the situation.*

JS: *Mmm, hmm.*

TS: *And I noticed one of her shoes had come off. I picked it up carefully. I think I used the index finger of my*

right hand to pick it up knowing full well I put a
print on it but honestly, at that point, someone's
gonna go look for her . . . and I threw the shoe out.

JS: By her?

TS: Her shoe. Threw 'em off. In the car.

JS: Oh, in the car.

TS: In the car and I pushed her out and her shoes were, I took the shoe, lifted it by my index finger so you will find the print, probably, if you look for it.

JS: Oh.

TS: I threw it out of the car. I remember then I tried to go and accidentally ran over some part of her, I don't know what. There was not, I mean people around the parking lot but there was cars coming and going. There was a car wash or some shit and there was people standing outside and I couldn't believe this.

I was almost in a dream world. I was fucking shot, freaked out, I couldn't think straight.

I remember I was having to go to class, I don't know what kind of class it was. It was off Westpark.

JS: You were talking about her bra was undone?

TS: Yeah.

JS: In the back or in the front?

TS: From the back.

JS: From the back? Okay. Did you take anything from her?

TS: I still had just her school books and that kind of stuff. I didn't take anything else from her.

JS: When you left did you have her property in the car?

TS: Yes, I did.

JS: What was it?

TS: I don't remember. School books, lunch, something. Just some general stuff. Wadded up paper bag.

JS: What happened to that stuff?

TS: Stuck it in a Dumpster somewhere at an apartment complex somewhere.

JS: See, I'm confused. She had a shoe missing, both her shoes were there? You just threw one out, is that right?

TS: I threw one out.

JS: So she had both her shoes there?

TS: Both shoes. One was still on her foot and—

JS: Oh, and one wasn't. I got you now.

TS: That never hit the papers so there's no way I'd know that—

JS: Oh, I know it's true. I know it's true. I was there.

TS: I was sick. I was scared to death. I was paranoid for days. I just knew this was, this was, God, there's no way I could change or have that. I was sick. I didn't want to lose everything. My wife, my kids, my house, and everything and so I tried to put an end to it the best I could that I was in a state of shock for a long time. For months. I promised myself nothing like this would ever, ever, ever, ever happen. Promised, no fucking way.

Then, I had crazy . . . crazy thoughts. I mean I had, I don't know if you call 'em dreams, people talk about voices in their head. I felt like there were voices, almost like my own voice . . . and I'd have fantasy trips which has to do with the preoccupation, which I haven't talked about in sex offender treatment class but I'm aware of it.

And I had these fantasies and I had this one girl that I picked up and I was tying her and—

JS: *Okay. On that case, that's about it?*

TS: *That's all I can remember.*

JS: *It's now about nineteen after midnight.*

Sergeant John Swaim was in a mild state of silent shock, though he did not let on to Tony Shore. Swaim had worked the Laurie Tremblay case on and off for over seventeen years. He had basically written off ever finding the young girl's killer.

CHAPTER 32

September 1986,
Houston Police Department—Homicide Division,
1200 Travis Street,
Houston, Texas.

Seventeen years earlier, John Swaim, Boyd Smith, Jim Ramsey, and Bill Steins began the arduous task of trying to find Laurie Tremblay's killer. Between the four detectives they had decades of police work under their collective belts. Unfortunately, their many years of service could never fully prepare them for the unenviable task of having to inform Laurie's mother of her daughter's death.

Swaim then began the tedious search for Laurie's killer. It was determined from speaking to Katherine Tremblay that Laurie left the house at approximately 6:30 A.M. She would usually walk the half-mile trek to South Dairy Ashford Road and West Ella Drive to catch Metro Bus #53, which would take her in the vicinity of the Hope Center. Metro #53 usually arrived at the bus stop and left with its passengers at 6:41 A.M. every weekday.

Sergeant Swaim had his time frame within which to work. It only lasted for eleven minutes. Swaim's men first appeared at the bus stop to scour the area for clues. They were looking for various items that were determined to be missing from Laurie's person, including a writing tablet, a notebook, and her lunch. They found nothing.

Sergeant Swaim's men also searched Metro #53's route, but again they found nothing. The officers stopped by several businesses that lined Dairy Ashford Road and asked if anyone had seen Laurie Tremblay on the day of her abduction and murder. No one recognized the young girl from a photo they proffered.

Sergeant Swaim's team also conducted a thorough search of the Whittfield Apartments, where Laurie lived, and interviewed several residents of the complex, but to no avail. Still no clues.

In the following days Swaim had an officer return to the bus stop at exactly 6:30 A.M. to interview other bus riders who took the same route as Laurie. They also spoke with the bus driver of Metro #53. Nothing. No one remembered seeing Laurie that day.

A determined Sergeant Swaim continued the investigation by tracking down the trashman responsible for the Dumpster behind Ninfa's, sending officers to the Hope Center to examine the contents of her locker, and interviewing several of her classmates. All proved fruitless.

It appeared as if absolutely no one saw what happened to Laurie Tremblay that day. There also wasn't any evidence pointing to jilted boyfriends or people who may have had ill feelings toward Laurie.

By October 1, 1986, Swaim directed his men to plaster flyers up around Ninfa's, near the Metro bus stop, and up and down Dairy Ashford Road. The flyers had Laurie's picture, the Houston Police Department Homicide Division hotline number, the telephone number for Crime Stoppers, and a plea to call in with information.

It is considered a bad sign when the flyers go up because that usually means detectives don't have a clue.

The flyers did not help. The Homicide Division received numerous tips, which had to be worked on one by one, but none of them led to anything specific or even helpful.

Swaim was flabbergasted. "Nothing is missing and it doesn't appear that she was sexually assaulted," he informed the *Houston Chronicle.* "We don't have any leads or motive in this one. It's scary."

Katherine Tremblay was still in shock. She could not believe that she had to make plans to have her daughter's body shipped in a coffin on a plane to Michigan to be buried. As she ventured forward, she also expressed her dismay and anger toward the investigation into her daughter's death.

"It's like a blind alley," she stated two days after Laurie's murder. "I'm angry, but I have to leave. I have to take care of my daughter. I have to lay her to rest."

The police department was not the only organization with which Katherine Tremblay was frustrated. The Houston Independent School District and their bus service, or lack thereof, was also in her sights. She claimed that HISD refused to pick her daughter up and shuttle her to the Hope Center. As a result, Laurie was forced to use the City of Houston Metro Bus Service. She claimed that had it not been for this fact, Laurie would not have been walking toward the Metro bus stop, would not have been abducted, and would not have been murdered. She was prepared to file a lawsuit against HISD.

"It's just that I have to do something," declared the distraught mother. "I'm considering suing the school district—not for the money, but for the other children. I don't want them to have to go through the same thing."

Katherine Tremblay was disgusted by what she felt was disingenuous treatment from school officials the year prior. "Last year, she had to walk two miles to catch her bus. When I complained, the head of transportation said a lot of kids have to walk a lot farther."

The HISD, however, defended its position. They claimed that Laurie was not qualified for bus service and they were not at fault. "At the time of her death she was not a member of HISD," stated spokesman Claude Cunningham. He added that Laurie had indeed been a student in HISD at one time, until her mother requested that she be transferred to Hope Center, where she began school on September 2, 1986. "She had been one of our students and was in the process of reassignment," Cunningham declared. He added that "once her reassignment procedures had been completed, which included testing and district committee approval, then she would have been eligible for HISD bus services. Unfortunately, she had not yet completed all of the procedures." Laurie had successfully completed her testing; however, she was set to have a hearing for the district approval the same week she was murdered.

Katherine Tremblay did not wind up pursuing the lawsuit against HISD.

Laurie Tremblay's case started to turn cold. Sergeant Swaim and his team had no luck during the ensuing months. At one time they did have a suspect. Swaim's partner, Boyd Smith, played in a band and believed that the garrote used on Laurie Tremblay's neck might have been a guitar string. This conclusion led Swaim and

Smith to suspect that the killer may have been younger, possibly even someone near Laurie's age.

Indeed, they actively pursued one of Laurie's class-mates, who also owned a guitar. The student had given Laurie rides before and had visited her apartment, with-out Katherine Tremblay's knowledge. The young man also drove a car with red carpet similar to a piece of red fabric found in Laurie's shirt pocket.

Swaim and Smith brought the young man in for ques-tioning and grilled him extensively. Swaim believed the kid was somewhat unusual, but, alas, nothing came of it.

By January 1987, Katherine Tremblay had just about given up hope that the Houston Police Department de-tectives were going to be able to solve her daughter's murder. She decided it was time to actively participate.

A divorced woman of modest means, Tremblay of-fered a $2,000 reward for any information that might lead to the whereabouts of her daughter's killer. The money came from Laurie's ninety-four-year-old grandfa-ther. It was his life savings. He had originally given it all to Katherine so she could buy a tombstone for her daughter. Crime Stoppers also offered up some addi-tional money. In addition, Tremblay used $3,000 of her own money to have flyers printed up with the reward information.

"If I can at least know what happened to her," Kather-ine pleaded, "who killed her and why, then maybe I can accept it someday. Then maybe I won't feel so lost."

Tremblay had not done well during the nearly four months since her daughter's murder. "All I have left are the nightmares," she tearfully described. "I see her being strangled. I see her dying. I see myself losing the only thing that ever really mattered to me. And I know I'll never have her back."

She hoped that the reward money would entice someone to come forward and help her regain a little bit of what she had lost.

Over time the grassroots efforts proved unsuccessful—not reward money, not feet pounding the pavement, nothing. To Swaim and Smith's dismay, they were forced to call it a day on the Laurie Tremblay murder.

"We didn't have any new clues," the lead sergeant recalled. "We had worked the clues we did have. We had no information. We covered every base possible."

But a cold case never *completely* goes cold. Otherwise, they would throw them out. "At that point we never put cases away. They're just still in an uncleared case. If some information comes in, we'll work on it."

It would take more than seventeen years for that information to come in.

CHAPTER 33

Saturday, October 25, 2003, 12:21 A.M.,
Houston Police Department,
Interrogation Room #6,
1200 Travis Street,
Houston, Texas.

The following text is the transcript from the actual interrogation of and confession on tape by Anthony Allen Shore in regard to the murder of Maria del Carmen Estrada:

John Swaim (JS): Let's talk.

Tony Shore (TS): Do you wanna know about how it led up to that or do you wanna—

JS: Yes, I wanna know the whole story.

TS: After the first one I tried not to do anything. I was having psychopathology.

JS: Okay.

TS: I know, I'm familiar with that term, I tried to make myself, like never more promise myself that this shit would never happen. There were times when I'd pick

*up girls . . . it was always amazing how people just,
"Yeah, you want a ride?" "Sure." I had some fantasies
in my head but nothing really ever came of it.*

*One girl I picked up once was a prostitute. Noth-
ing happened. I mean just, I didn't pay for anything,
she showed me some stuff.*

One morning, going to work again—

JS: *This when you were working for the phone company
still?*

TS: *Yeah, I was still working for the phone company.*

JS: *Okay.*

TS: *I'm not sure, I think at that time I was still in the
business office but I can't remember, but I was already
moved outside . . . that I'm not positive on. Right in
that timeframe I was changing my position in the
company and I ran across this really, I thought, beautiful young lady and I offered her a ride and she
turned me down. But she was on my way to work
every morning and I was coming up—*

JS: *What, you had seen her several times?*

TS: *A few times. And I was coming up, uh, this street
there, Long, no Wirth maybe. Wirth or some street. I
came up to Westview. A couple of times I'd seen her
and she wouldn't take a ride, but it wasn't uncommon for me to offer—*

JS: *This was a Hispanic girl?*

TS: *Yeah, yeah, yeah.*

JS: *Okay.*

TS: *She told me her name was Carmen and she didn't
take rides from strangers and she didn't speak English. And one morning it was right next to the right
and like the first time after that the weather changed*

and I gave her a ride. This happened over the course of, probably a couple of months.

Became friends with her. I had to bone up on my Spanish so I could flirt with her and stuff. I was fumbling, I said a bunch of shit trying to make a relationship happen.

Once again, I felt . . . it was going places. She was talking about yeah, she wanted to go out. She was studying to be a legal secretary or something. . . . She was also going to school. . . .

. . . And one morning I just, again, things got outta hand. Pulled in behind a Dairy Queen and we . . .

JS: *Down on Westview?*

TS: *Down on Westview and it was going okay. She was open, amenable to . . . a kiss. And when I pushed it further it got outta hand. She freaked out. And similar to the first case I got real paranoid because now this wasn't a consensual thing, this was a fucked-up deal and I got real paranoid. I didn't set out to kill her. That was not my intent.*

JS: *Mmm, hmm.*

TS: *But, it got outta hand.*

JS: *Go ahead, Tony. Just tell me what happened.*

TS: *She just said, "Hey man, not this way. I love you. Not this way. Not here." And I opened her blouse and she was resisting. I had this sick consumption. Not like voices in my head but just driven. I was gonna have her regardless. I don't know what the hell you call it. I tried to understand this.*

And my intention was to have sex with her, initially, and that wasn't happening. She became real violent, but I didn't want her to get out of the car. So,

because I was, at that time I was in the Hyundai
Excel, a little blue Hyundai.

JS: *Mmm, hmm.*

TS: *And uh, car that I bought from my wife. It's her car.*
      And when you lock the door the door handles don't
      open. I locked the door so she couldn't get out. Shit
      didn't go well. And I didn't have sex with her as
      it turned out, but I tried to, but it wasn't gonna
      happen. I remember she had a pair of shoes and she
      had on black shorts. I took them off. And her panty-
      hose, but I didn't take her panties off. I don't know
      why.

    It got outta hand. And she freaked out and I knew
      that this was not, this was, this was gonna be real
      bad and my life was fucked forever. So I panicked and
      once again it just started to become daylight, so to
      avoid discovery, you know, I strangled her because I
      knew that—

JS: *What'd you strangle her with?*

TS: *I wanna say a nylon ligature. Piece of cord. I don't*
      remember.

JS: *Do you remember what type? What color it was or*
      anything?

TS: *No. It might have been white.*

JS: *Okay.*

TS: *I don't know.*

JS: *Did you use a, did you use your hands on this one*
      or use something?

TS: *I wanna say because I had fucked my hands up from*
      the first one I used a piece of wood, a pencil, it might
      have been a pencil. It was something. I don't know,

a paintbrush. Something. Some piece of wood or something that twisted it.

> *Make me in a serious panic, freaking out.*

JS: *Did you take anything from her?*

TS: *Um, her purse and stuff was left in the car. Which I, once again I just, and I don't remember if I left her shorts or if they were in the car or what. I gathered up what I had of her stuff—*

JS: *Mmm, hmm.*

TS: *. . . Found a Dumpster, some apartment complex.*

JS: *Do you remember where it was?*

TS: *No, I don't. I want to say it was a purse. I didn't even go through her stuff, I just got rid of it. Might have been a backpack, might have been a purse. I don't remember. Something.*

JS: *Okay. Now on this one you think it was a white cord and you said like a pencil or a paintbrush or something?*

TS: *Piece of wood. Some kind of piece of wood.*

JS: *I don't know. What's the word? 'Tourniquet' maybe?*

TS: *Yeah.*

JS: *You put it in there and then you twist it?*

TS: *Yeah.*

JS: *Alright, it's now about 12:30 A.M., I'm gonna turn the tape off.*

Detective Bob King recalled John Swaim's interrogation methods.

"He started talking. In the state of Texas it's the detective's choice how he takes a confession," King informed.

"It can be a written confession that the suspect writes out himself or one the detective types out and he signs off on. It can be audiotape or it can be videotaped. It's the detective's choice. John Swaim likes to use the audiotape.

"He didn't have to do it the way he did it," King explained, laughing. "For each murder he stopped, got a new tape, and read the guy his rights again. It was real funny. And Todd Miller and Allen Brown and I are outside watching it on the monitor, going, 'Yes! Yes!' John Swaim goes, 'No. We're gonna talk about this murder on this day and I'm gonna read your rights this time and then when we go to the next murder, we're gonna do it again.' We're all going . . ." He cringed as he recalled the detective's interrogation method.

"You don't have to do it that way." King chuckled at the memory. "You just have to read them their rights one time on tape and they can confess to as many murders as they want to."

CHAPTER 34

Saturday, October 25, 2003, 12:32 A.M.,
Houston Police Department,
Interrogation Room #6,
1200 Travis Street,
Houston, Texas.

Sergeant John Swaim sat down in front of his tape recorder. Tony Shore sat across the table from him. Both men did not seem tired despite the late hour. Swaim continued to get each and every one of Shore's confessions on tape. He proceeded on to another case that no one had any idea Shore was involved in.

The following text is the transcript from the actual interrogation of and confession on tape by Anthony Allen Shore in regard to the 1993 rape of Selma Janske (name changed to protect the innocent):

John Swaim (JS): John Swaim of the Homicide Division here talking to Anthony Allen Shore, correct?

Tony Shore (TS): Yes.

JS: Tony?

TS: *Yes.*

(Swaim proceeded to read Shore his rights.)

JS: *You understand these rights?*

TS: *Yes, sir.*

JS: *You wanna waive these rights and talk to me?*

TS: *Yes, sir.*

JS: *Okay.*

TS: *Talk about another case y'all don't know about.*

JS: *Okay.*

TS: *There's a reason I wanna talk about that.*

JS: *Okay.*

TS: *There was a girl that I'd never seen before, which, once again . . . I had fantasies about her. I had seen her several times.*

JS: *Where was this?*

TS: *[1900 block of] Portsmouth. I don't know for sure that's the right address.*

JS: *Okay.*

TS: *Girl's name is Selma Janske, I know that. J-A-N-S-K-E. I'm guessing she's probably sixteen, seventeen at the time. I'm not really sure how old. She was young. She was attractive. I was a phone man working outdoors, outside plans, and I worked down this street several times.*

I'd seen her coming home and I knew that she was a latchkey kid. Came home from high school or whatever school she was going to and I wanted to put a stop to . . . the taking of life. I didn't want to do this anymore. (Shore's voice quietly trailed off with the last word.)

Hell, I did this, at this time I, it's a sexual union,

had something to do with it. The more I'm thinking, in retrospect, that it's having to do with possession of a person. Making them . . . do . . . things.

So I broke into the house which wasn't easy. The door was unlocked and I waited for her to get there. She got there. I stole twenty dollars off of the dresser, probably her parents' room. She came in and I wanted to prove to myself that I didn't have to . . . take the life. That's the reason why I'm telling you this.

JS: Okay. That's fine.

TS: So I had on—

JS: Now when was, you think, was this?

TS: Probably after . . . I don't remember the timeframe for sure but probably after Diana Rebollar but before Dana Sanchez.

JS: Okay.

TS: Okay. So, I . . . tied her up with electrical cord. And I took, and, the resistance from the violence that I thought that I was going to do this again but I promised myself that I wasn't going to take any more lives no matter what.

As sick and fucked up as it sounds, I really, really, really was trying to get better in a real sick, demented way. I don't discount it. I'm not stupid, but I was trying . . . but I promised myself I wasn't gonna do it and, uh.

In her bedroom, and uh, I told her that I knew how the police would ask her this and that and I told her say that it was a short, fat black man and that if I heard different then I'd come back and take her family out and I made a lot of threats and uh, when I mentioned the family thing she started fighting and kicking. Now her hands were restrained as she started just going berserk. I really didn't know when everybody else would come home or when somebody could show up, I just knew that it got out of hand and I had to make a decision.

JS: At what time? This was when?

TS: Afternoon. Right after school. 4:00, 5:00 o'clock.

JS: Oh, that's right. Right after she got home from school.

TS: So, I thought I had to make a decision. Once again, I started to strangle her and I thought "No, I just can't. I just need to get the fuck out of here." And I left. Thank God.

JS: You take anything?

TS: Naw.

JS: But you didn't, you didn't strangle her at all or you started to—

TS: I started to and I stopped.

JS: Did you have something around her neck to do it?

TS: On this one, no. I think I was gonna use my hands and I just freaked 'cause I promised myself I wasn't gonna do this and all the sudden—like the pathology and the anger and the freaking out. I kept telling myself, "This isn't necessary. This is not. None of it is necessary." So I bolted. I left.

And uh, I walked out, people saw me. There's people walking in the street. Driving by.

JS: Normal business.

TS: Finally walked through the back yard out to the front. I parked my phone truck over on the Whataburger parking lot over at Shepherd and Portsmouth or somewhere in that area. Walked right up to my truck, got rid of my shirt that I had on. Went back to work, scared to death. I was paranoid. I was afraid because I had left somebody as a witness.

Nobody ever came and talked to me. Nobody ever came and arrested me. There was a part of me, I think, that wanted to be caught.

JS: That's what I was fixing to ask you—

TS: I wanted to be stopped so many times. I just wanted this whole thing to end. That's why I'm talking to you now. And I want to make sure that nothing ever happens again.

CHAPTER 35

Thursday, March 25, 1993,
700 block of East Eighteenth Street,
Houston, Texas.

Gina Shore was in for a real surprise on her and Tony's wedding anniversary. "He comes home on our tenth anniversary. We'd gone out to a nice dinner; then we went to IMAX and then we came home and Tony had some champagne, ice, an upright thing, and glasses sitting there," Gina recalled. "We popped and uncorked the champagne. He goes down on one knee and tells me he's been having an affair for months and that he cannot continue to live a lie." Gina was floored by this revelation.

"And he left right there," said Gina, who had been completely blindsided. "I think I just sat there until he left. I was absolutely blown away." Gina described herself as a Pollyanna type who tries to see the best in everyone. "I had not a clue, and now he was gone."

According to Gina, Shore had been having an affair with Elizabeth "Lizz" Martin somewhere between three and six months. To add insult to injury, Lizz was a singer in St. Vitus Dance, Shore's band. "I wrote lyrics for her!" She caustically laughed.

Shore enjoyed talking to Gina about his sexual escapades with Lizz. He told her that his and Lizz's first sexual experience took place on a top of a rice silo.

Bob King later confirmed Shore's predilection for sex in unusual places.

"He had a thing about the Hollywood Cemetery," King recalled with a chuckle. "He loved sarcophagi—those coffins aboveground.

"And he was queer for rice dryers. Like the AR Rice dryers. He loved that shit." King shook his head at the thought. "He was big on creeping around the one off of Studemont they tore down. And there's one on Hempstead Highway that's still there, but it's not a rice dryer anymore. He'd take girls over there and he liked to go creeping around. He just thought they were cool. So I checked to see if there were any bodies found around any of those places and there weren't."

To Gina, that was the first time she thought something was wrong with Tony Shore. "That may be the first glimmer that there was anybody like that underneath the surface. He was a pretty mild-mannered darned guy. He was not prone to shouting, he didn't scream a lot. No jumping up and down. Sure, he got mad on occasion, but . . ."

Gina also recalled that when she and Shore would get into arguments she used to call him "gay. I only did it whenever he would say mean things to me. I do, however, think he's a latent homosexual and that is something, still to this day, that he has to deal with. I do. I do. He had tendencies towards guys. Sexual tendencies. And if he couldn't perform, he'd get mad at me."

Gina added that Shore often gave her too much information after they separated. "He had an enormously big mouth and he loved to talk, especially if it was about himself." He informed her that his relationship with Lizz began to sour almost immediately. "He paid all of her debt, paid for her car to be fixed, made everything good for her, but she left."

During these events Tony Shore was granted custody of Amber and Tiffany.

"They were eight and seven," Gina recalled when speaking about the girls. "I was so irritated. I said, 'If you want to pull this [separation], fine, but can't you just wait until the end of the school year? It's gonna be like two months until the end of the school year and then they'll have summer.'" Apparently, Shore did not care. "Literally, after he walked out on the twenty-fifth [of March], I got up on the following Monday to check the balance on the phone, pay the rent, and he had taken all the money out of our accounts. I had nothing to pay the rent with."

According to Gina, her second ex-husband was remorseless.

"I'm not living here, I'm not gonna pay it," he informed her.

"How can you do this?" Gina queried, dumbfounded. "I'm gonna have to go live with my mother. Yank Amber and Tiffany out of school. You're gonna cause Amber to regress."

"She's already regressed," he said without a lick of concern in his voice for his own daughter.

"I packed everything," Gina recalled. "I packed his stuff. I packed my stuff. I packed their stuff. What I couldn't pack I sold. I preregistered Amber and Tiffany in another school, which they hated."

The separation was hard on Amber. "It's so important for Amber to have that stability. She had to go into a whole new situation. She did indeed regress. It was just nuts." Gina shook her head as she remembered.

"Actually, I gave one of those little fake talks that parents give to children. 'Mommy and Daddy still love you, but Mommy and Daddy aren't getting along,' yadda yadda yadda," Gina continued. "We went to stay with my mom. Tiffany was absolutely bereft. She was daddy's girl."

Tony, Lizz, and her two boys pulled up to Gina's mother's curb in an open-air convertible. "They looked like such the cheery all-American family, and Amber and Tiffany would get in the car and go to AstroWorld and to the zoo and do all these wonderful things."

Gina started feeling like the bad cop in the girls' lives. "When they came home, of course, they had to go to school, they had to do their homework, they had to clean their rooms, they had to sweep, they had their chores. When they get to Dad's, it's fun! They get to meet musicians and have parties!"

The girls began to rebel against their mother. "They decided they would just not do anything I asked them," Gina remembered. "I was trying to find another job and I wasn't working for a while, staying at home with Amber.

"And Tiffany used to say, 'I want my dad! I want my dad! I want my dad!' Finally I just decided that we could always split and I said, 'Tiffany, you can go with your dad and Amber can stay with me.'" Gina did not want to give up her daughter, but she felt it was the right thing to do given her difficult economic situation.

Then Amber informed her mother that "I want to go with my sister wherever she goes. I want to go with my sister."

Tiffany was adamant. "I'm gonna go live with Dad," she informed her mother. "I am."

Gina thought that it probably wouldn't be a bad idea, since Shore lived in a house, had a steady income, and could have Lizz help out with the girls. She felt that it might be good to have Lizz's two boys around to look after them as well. She also knew that Lizz liked to eat good healthy food. Also, her estranged husband would allow the girls to have a dog. All in all, it sounded like the smartest move for everyone, so Gina agreed.

So, when summer rolled around, Amber and Tiffany moved in with their father.

Regina Shore, Tony's sister, claimed that she was not surprised the girls ended up with her brother. She claimed that Tony's wife, Gina, had a drinking problem and couldn't take care of the girls.

Gina Worley Shore adamantly denied any drinking problem. "He spread that around." She then used her daughter Amber as an example for her defense. She stated that Amber said, "I don't remember you ever being drunk or even hearing about that from Dad until after you got a divorce."

Gina declared that this was just another way for Tony Shore to try and exert control over her. She talked about how she was constantly on the go, what with taking the girls to school, church, art classes, and extracurricular activities and that she never had time to have a drink, much less get drunk.

Gina believed, however, that people might have mis-construed her as being drunk because, she alleged, Tony used to drop Rohypnol, or roofies (aka "the date-rape drug"), into her Cokes.

"One morning I woke up," Gina recalled, "and I'm sleeping with Amber and she's one of these people who sleeps like a gymnastics person. So, I woke up in Amber's bed and she had her foot up my nose and I'm like, 'How the hell did this happen?'" At first she blamed it on stress.

It wasn't until years later when Regina Shore asked Gina, "Did you know that he was drugging you?"

"No!" Gina exclaimed. "You're kidding!"

"Oh, yeah," Regina affirmed, "he laughs about it and about how gullible and stupid you were."

"Well, maybe if he was spreading rumors that I was intoxicated and drunk all the time," Gina pondered, "maybe that was the cover-up."

Gina was frightened by what her ex-husband Shore was capable of doing. "It was scary. I had no idea how long he may have been doing that. How many years? I have no idea what he did to me or may have done elsewhere while I was knocked out."

CHAPTER 36

Saturday, October 25, 2003, 12:43 A.M.,
Houston Police Department,
Interrogation Room #6,
1200 Travis Street,
Houston, Texas.

The following text is the transcript from the actual interrogation of and confession on tape by Anthony Allen Shore in regard to the murder of Diana Rebollar:

TS: *Tony Shore (TS): The Diana Rebollar case, Rebollar, however you say it.*

John Swaim (JS): Rebollar.

TS: *Rebollar. At that point in time I was living in The Heights on East 18th Street, corner house at East 18th Street and Beverly behind the elementary school with my, she wasn't a wife, but a live-in. Girlfriend. She had two sons and I had two daughters when we were living there.*

> *Her car had broke down. I didn't have transportation*

at that time. She had an old Dodge van. I have no idea
what year it was. Sports van.

JS: What'd it look like?

TS: It was beige with white trim down the center. And it
had one big door on the back and it—

JS: And whose was this?

TS: . . . Was an extended van. Yolanda Elizabeth
Martin. She was a live-in. Not married.

JS: Elizabeth Martin.

TS: Elizabeth Martin.

JS: This van was . . . ?

TS: This van belonged to her. It belonged to her dad. It belonged to somebody but we were using it. It didn't
have a transmission. I put the transmission in.

JS: It was a Dodge you said?

TS: It was a Dodge sports van. It was an older model.
It was an extended van. It had the long rear end.
      Anyway. She and I had been on the rocks, up and
down. It was a bad rollercoaster kind of relationship.
We had four kids living in the house and we had a
two bedroom house, not enough space, 'cause Lizz
had come out of a lesbian relationship to be in our relationship and she was going out, sometimes with her
gay friends and stuff and I was unhappy and things
weren't going well.
      And, uh, Diana Rebollar. That was a freaky pack
of specifics I don't understand exactly. Too young. Not
developed. That was an opportunity, a freaky thing
that I don't know why I did that. I remember seeing
this girl walking alone.

JS: Do you know what street you're on?

TS: I wanna say on Main Street. North Main somewhere

around 21st to 26th. I'm not really sure where in
there. I know there is a parking lot and I pulled in
and I talked to her and . . . there wasn't anybody
around and I don't know what the hell. I'm sitting
there going . . . the girl. I just picked her up, put her
in the van. Nobody saw shit. And I told her to be
quiet—

JS: Did you wrap anything around her or anything or
just took her into—

TS: I just threw her in initially and I told her to be quiet
and that it was kidnapping and that she wasn't
gonna get hurt, this and that. She made like she was
gonna not cooperate so I remember using duct tape to
bind her. Hands and feet.

Then we drove around. I don't know where we
ended up. I remember this was a big, big parking lot
and a building. Looks like it had been vacated. And,
uh, in the bay area where the trucks come back up
and stuff. And I was gonna molest her and she
fought like hell. Strangely, she fought like hell. Just
couldn't go on with anything.

JS: Hispanic girl?

TS: Yeah, Hispanic girl. And I knew it wasn't gonna
happen and she was so afraid, I'm sure, but she shit
herself on her underwear. Made a huge mess. And I
remember using her clothes and stuff to clean her off.

She fought and fought and I don't recall what type
of cord or strand, a piece of wire or something. And
the same thing, I knew I was fucked and I don't know
why the shit kept happening. I couldn't stop it. I could
say, "Yeah, there are voices in my head," but it's my
own sickness.

JS: You don't remember what, it was a cord or . . . ?

TS: *That I don't recall. It seems like there was a pencil that I used to twist.*

JS: *But you don't know what the cord looked like, what color it was?*

TS: *No, that I don't recall.*

JS: *Okay.*

TS: *But, uh, then I tried to have sex with her but it wasn't happening, wasn't happening. She just fought so bad, and she's so small, and I just said, "God, you sick fuck. What the hell is wrong with you? Why have you lost your fucking mind?" And I just wanted, I just wanted it to end. I just couldn't, every time I'd tell myself, I'd just kept saying, "Oh, this has gotta stop. I'm a sick, sick puppy."*

There wasn't anybody around. I could've taken time, I could've done this or I could've done that and I had this sick, sick [thought] going through my head but I just wanted it to be over. I just wanted to get away from there.

I knew I couldn't just let her go because I knew that, well obviously, she's gonna go tell and then my life would be all fucked up. Just selfish, self-centered, fucked-up thinking, I know.

So, I did the ligature and she was [messy] because of shitting herself. I cleaned up the mess. I used her clothes. I don't remember. I think I left her t-shirt on. She was wearing a black t-shirt as I recall. I used the rest of it to clean her up.

She bought a bag of sugar and she cleaned it and I took that and cleaned that up and there was shit in her hair and I cleaned that up as best I could.

JS: *So, you took the shit and threw it away?*

TS: *Yeah, I just took all the shit, what was left in the van,*

*and I took it to a car wash and I tried to scrub the
fuck out of it.*

JS: *What'd you do with the shit in—*

TS: *Uh, I drove around with it the day before I got rid of
it. And, once again, I threw it in a trash bag and
I threw it in a Dumpster somewhere.*

JS: *So you remember having a black t-shirt on her and
you left that on her and then you took her pants?*

TS: *Pants and underwear and shit. I had to clean up the
shit that was everywhere. And it seems like I stopped
at a resell shop somewhere and bought myself a t-shirt
and used my t-shirt to clean her up good. I ended up
going to a car wash to try to clean up the mess. It was
a big mess.*

JS: *How much was that mess?*

TS: *I didn't want anybody to know that there was shit in
the van or the smell and everything.*

JS: *Okay. Alright. It's now about twelve minutes to one.
12:48 A.M.*

CHAPTER 37

August 1994,
700 block of East Eighteenth Street,
Houston, Texas.

Less than one week after Tony Shore murdered nine-year-old Diana Rebollar, he officially broke up with his girlfriend, Lizz Martin, who angrily left him, and then moved in his new girlfriend, eighteen-year-old Amy Lynch. The slim, attractive Lynch was a senior at Pearland High School, located in the soon-to-be sprawling suburb located more than twenty miles from The Heights. *(Full disclosure—the author graduated from Pearland High School ten years before Lynch, but has no knowledge of or relationship of any kind with her.)*

Shore met Amy while he was still dating Lizz Martin. Their meeting was rather inauspicious, as Shore happened to be doing some telephone repair work at Amy's father's house. He spotted a photograph of the young Amy on a mantel in the Lynch household. He asked Amy's father about the girl in the photograph and learned her name and that she loved to sing. When Shore heard that, he perked up. He informed Mr. Lynch that he was a "piano man" and that he and Amy should come out to see him play sometime. Mr. Lynch felt comfortable with Shore and agreed that he would take his daughter out to the watering hole where Shore would be performing.

Amy and her father went to see Shore play and were duly impressed. They hooked up after the gig and promised to keep in touch.

According to Gina Worley Shore, Amy was a "nice kid" who began to see Tony Shore for vocal lessons. Soon thereafter, Shore and Amy began to see each other romantically. Amy's parents were less than thrilled, mainly because of the age disparity. Shore was fourteen years older than his newest conquest.

Tony Shore moved Amy Lynch out of her mother's home and into his house on East Eighteenth Street in The Heights within just a few months of meeting her. The couple shared their place with Shore's daughters, Amber and Tiffany. Amy's parents became completely disenchanted with their daughter and refused to speak with her, but Amy continued to attend classes at Pearland High School so she could graduate.

Shore and Amy became quite the musical team. Together, as piano man and chanteuse, they headlined several gigs at nightclubs, restaurants, private parties, and weddings. The couple truly made beautiful music together while on stage. Shore even approached the guys in St. Vitus Dance to see if Amy could join the band as one of their lead singers, to which they agreed. Tony Shore believed his chances for stardom had increased dramatically with Amy Lynch in his life.

Amy loved living with Shore. She respected his musical ability and creativity. She loved the fact that he created his own drum kit from scratch. She used to watch as he would stretch the skins over the drums and tie them down with a specific knot. She watched as he tied the skin tighter using a "stick-type thing, a little dowel rod," which usually measured three to four inches. He told her it made "a good grip for a handle." It was one of the many things he could do that thrilled the impressionable young girl.

Gina Worley Shore was shocked when Amy called her up and asked her advice about Shore. "Bless her little heart. I used to call her 'my little sunflower' because she is so open. She would call and ask me, 'Was it like this for you?'"

Amy gushed about Shore to anyone who would listen. "He's creative. He's smart. He's talented. He's brilliant and he's charming." She felt lucky to be with such a wonderful man.

After a while, Amy's luck began to change. As Shore wowed her with his creativity and alleged brilliance, he also began to manipulate and control the young lady. It started simply enough. Shore informed his rather thin girlfriend that she was "larduous," a nonexistent word he used to describe her weight and physical appearance. Her older beau believed that Amy was just a little too feminine for his tastes. He encouraged her to lose weight so she would lose her "curves." He wanted his eighteen-year-old girlfriend to look even younger.

Amy, who wanted to please her man, did as she was told. She eventually slimmed down to ninety-eight pounds. Shore was thrilled, as he could now go out and buy her the type of clothes he wanted to see her in. Mainly, children's clothes. At her smallest, the adult Amy could fit into size-14 children's clothes. Shore loved to visit the junior kids section of the nearby resale stores and shop for his little girl. He also used to get a kick out of ordering Amy's clothes for her out of a Dillard's catalog. Amy even stated that "he's got a good eye for fashion."

Rob Shore noticed that his son had become a "control

freak." He and his wife, Rose, ran into Tony and Amy at the Montrose Art Festival in downtown Houston. Rob stated that his son's wife did everything Tony told her to do.

"How he made Amy dress when we ran into them," Rob Shore recalled. "And with the daughters, the same way. Rose noticed it and it just wasn't the way you'd expect someone to dress. It's like he wanted Amy to dress like a little girl and look like his daughters. It just struck me that he was—and the way that they acted was—just strange to me."

Shore had other demands of Amy as well. He preferred her hair to be very straight and long. Amy, of course, complied. Anything to make her man happy.

One thing that Shore did do that disturbed Amy was drugging his daughters. She found it "uncool" that he allegedly used to put Benadryl in their hot chocolates to make them go to sleep. Amy actually confronted him about this seemingly bizarre practice.

"That's how I've always done this," he calmly replied. "If they needed to go to bed and they weren't going to sleep, I'd just slip them a Benadryl and it would knock them out." He smiled as if it were no big deal. "Besides," he added, "I'm the dad and they do what I tell them to do."

Amy rarely confronted Shore on any issues. Her reason for not doing so was simple in a very stereotypical 1950s way. "He's the man," she reasoned. "He's in charge. He knows best and he directs me toward the best choices." She added that in addition to her appearance, he also helped her with what music to sing and how to present herself when on stage. "He was my piano man," she dreamily remembered.

The following year, on January 11, 1995, both Tiffany and Amber Shore went to visit the school nurse at Love

Elementary School. The sisters were nervous as they sat down with the nurse and began to tell her of the molestations perpetrated on them by their own father. The nurse immediately reported Tony Shore to the Child Protective Services agency. When a CPS representative came to the family's house, they could not do anything to Shore, as his daughters failed to confirm their accusations. The sisters actually denied having ever told the nurse such a thing. As a result, CPS's figurative hands were bound and they could do nothing. Tony Shore was allowed to keep living with his daughters.

CHAPTER 38

Saturday, October 25, 2003, 12:51 A.M.,
Houston Police Department,
Interrogation Room #6,
1200 Travis Street,
Houston, Texas.

The following text is the transcript from the actual interrogation of and confession on tape by Anthony Allen Shore in regard to the murder of Dana Sanchez:

Tony Shore (TS): Last and final case. Dana Sanchez.

John Swaim (JS): Right.

TS: I got that name from the newspaper. She told me her name was Ruby. I don't know where Ruby came from. And she told me when her birthday was. I was driving—

JS: Do you know when her birthday was?

TS: I don't remember now.

JS: Or what she told you?

TS: *But, it also never came out in the papers, um, it's verifiable but I'm telling you—*

JS: *Okay. I believe you.*

TS: *I was driving, at that time I was driving a Ford Econoline van, old piece of shit, beat up, green—*

JS: *'78?*

TS: *How in the world you get '78 from?*

JS: *Nah, whatever.*

TS: *That I don't know. All I know is that it was an older model van about an '88. It was green, not Army green but like a dark metallic green. It was beat up.*

JS: *You traded it in?*

TS: *Yeah, I traded it in. I think I traded it in for the uh, Dodge custom conversion van that I ended up buying.*

JS: *Do you know where you traded it in?*

TS: *Yes, the Auto Sales on Shepherd somewhere between 11th and 15th. Somewhere on—*

JS: *Okay.*

TS: *Anyway. One of the things you can put in your report, I had done the interior with Berber carpet which is uncommon.*

JS: *Alright.*

TS: *I was driving around and I saw this girl, I'm gonna say she was wearing white coveralls and a striped shirt underneath and she was mad. She had this look that she was angry and upset and she was at a payphone.*

JS: *Where was this at?*

TS: *Corner of Cavalcade and Airline.*

JS: *Okay.*

TS: *And she, I guess, had called somebody from the pay-phone. She started storming off and I was making the "Say, hey . . ." She said, "Man, I'm going to see my boyfriend" somewhere. Forget where she told me.*

JS: *No problem.*

TS: *And we went driving and we had [a] conversation and I had this sick fantasy going through my mind like there could be something, relationship there, or some type of thing between us. I was flirting with her heavily. At the time I had really long hair. I thought I looked good or maybe I just looked like a freak, I don't know. But, she was real friendly, you know. Talking about, I think she said she was a runaway. Don't know what happened.*

JS: *She's a Hispanic girl, also?*

TS: *Yeah. She is Hispanic. But she wasn't Hispanic in the sense, she spoke good English. And we drove, if I remember correctly, 45 North. I have no idea where she wanted to go. I don't remember where she wanted to go. 34th sticks in my mind, I don't recall. And she told me her name was Ruby. Why she told me that, I don't know, but, I remember she told me her birth-day and we drove somewhere off of 45.*

She never even questioned why I was taking so long getting where I was going. She was just happy to have conversation and everything. So, I thought, "What the hell. I'll go for it." I pulled into this park-ing lot. I started flirting with her and pettin' on her. She was jokingly, "No, no, no, I gotta boyfriend" this and that.

So, I grabbed her, pulled her into the back of the van, and she cried. She bit me hard. Drew blood, I forget. My chest, hold on a sec.

JS: Mmm, hmm.

TS: So, I restrained her, tied her hands with, I wanna say duct tape. I can't remember but I think duct tape. I remember that I taped her.

JS: Alright.

TS: And she was fighting so hard. And I was there and getting sick about this whole thing.

Oh, I'm with the psychopathology [and its] craziness is . . . and I just knew that this was fucked and I didn't want it to happen and once again I knew that I couldn't stop. I knew there was nothing I could do to get out of this. And I used a ligature.

JS: In what way?

TS: I wanna say it was a yellow twisted nylon rope, but I don't remember. I think that's right. Like boat rope. Ski rope. Nylon.

JS: What color?

TS: Yellow, I wanna say.

JS: Okay.

TS: And, uh, there wasn't gonna be any sex with her. I had these sick, sick notions.

JS: Did you use any kind of tool to cut on there, Tony?

TS: Same, same thing. I don't recall, I just remember the yellow rope. I'm not even positive about that. Just the whole thing, I was getting sicker in my brain. I just couldn't, at this point I was almost in like a state of shock or dream state. I just, I wanted the shit to stop. I didn't want to keep not knowing what was going on. I just knew that I couldn't get caught but I wanted it to stop. And, I uh, couldn't get aroused, I remember that I was so sick in my brain and I knew, in my mind I knew that something had changed in

my head. *This wasn't at all what I bargained for.
So I drove and drove and drove and drove.*

JS: *With her in it?*

TS: *With her in the van in the back. I don't remember for
sure.*

JS: *Mmm, hmm.*

TS: *And I found this area way out in, got some streets in
'em—*

JS: *You remember what area?*

TS: *I don't. Off the north freeway somewhere. It was way
out, way out.*

JS: *Alright.*

TS: *And during that time I was thinking, "God, this is
so fucked." And I remember seeing it in the paper for
some type of thing she made or something . . . and
I was just, I thought I was in a different county.
I just knew I was way the hell out, so . . .*

JS: *Mmm, hmm.*

TS: *. . . I pulled her out into a field and [took off] like a
bat out of hell. I was scared to death.*

JS: *How far out in the field? Did you drive out in the
field or not?*

TS: *No, I just pulled up to the side. This was like an area
that was so overgrown with trees and—*

JS: *Trees were removed? The streets were cut or something?*

TS: *Yeah, they look like they were putting in a subdivision
or something. It was remote enough. I just, as fast
as I could, probably a hundred feet, maybe, off the
road. I jumped in the van, sped away scared to death
and anytime I think I had taken every identifiable*

thing I could think of: clothing, jewelry, all of that. I wanted to sit it all up and I didn't know what to do with it. I didn't throw it in a Dumpster this time.

I drove around somewhere away, way away from where she was at but still way north and I don't even know where I was at. I was in a shock state. My brain wasn't the same. It's just everything is something or nothing. I was scared and I knew this was fucked.

And I remember seeing another area similar where the streets cut in and the big utility easements cut out and it was overgrown and stuff.

JS: *Was it on the same side of the freeway or on the other side of the freeway?*

TS: *It was on the other side of the freeway but I don't remember for sure. This time I drove down an off-road and I threw all the shit out and I drove back.*

JS: *What kind of . . . clothes?*

TS: *Clothes and duct tape and—*

JS: *Whatever she had?*

TS: *Whatever she had.*

JS: *So, she was like completely naked?*

TS: *As I recall. I can't remember because my brain wasn't straight that day.*

JS: *Okay.*

TS: *And the jewelry I didn't throw in the same area. I threw that out on the freeway behind my back.*

JS: *And that was that one? Do you know how her body got found?*

TS: *Yes, I do. An anonymous phone call.*

JS: *And who made that phone call?*

TS: *I did.*

JS: *And what did you say and who did you call?*

TS: *I was out in the area of T.S.U. (Texas Southern University), Third Ward. I was a telephone main installer and repairman. So I used an effects box and tapped into one of those college campus lines and I couldn't be traced.*

JS: *Right.*

TS: *I don't remember what I said.*

JS: *Who did you call?*

TS: *I talked to Crime Stoppers, it wasn't Crime Stoppers. Crime Stoppers wouldn't give me the time of day. I want to say it was "Tips." The 222-TIPS, "Please use this line," something. Whatever it is you call and—*

JS: *They wouldn't take your call?*

TS: *At first Crime Stoppers didn't, they didn't, they thought I was full of shit and didn't listen. That's two calls that I made. The second one was to TIPS and I changed my voice and I remember telling them where to find her and I remember telling them her name and I remember telling them her birthday.*

JS: *You remember who you were talking to? A male or female?*

TS: *Honest to God, I don't recall. I want to say female but I don't recall.*

JS: *You told them what? I'm sorry I interrupted you.*

TS: *I told them where they could find her and at that time I had a better recollection of approximately where it was and I told them her name was Ruby and I told them what her birthday was so they could identify her. There was a part of me that just wanted to be caught and stopped.*

CHAPTER 39

Thursday, February 15, 1996,
Harris County, Texas.

Upon researching Tony Shore's background and court records, police discovered that he had been arrested a little more than six months after he allegedly killed Dana Sanchez. Shore apparently did not receive enough of a Valentine's Day gift from Amy Lynch, so he decided he would head out and look for some companionship. What he found was an attractive young female who offered her body for cash. Shore willingly accepted and looked forward to experiencing some new ass.

Instead, Shore had his own ass handed to him. He did not solicit sex from a prostitute, but rather from Alicia Ross (pseudonym), a Houston undercover police officer. She cuffed her john and dragged him downtown, where he spent an uncomfortable night in a holding cell. Shore made bail the following morning.

On March 26, 1996, Shore's lawyer, Bill Gifford, struck a sweet deal for his client. No jail time and only three months of unsupervised probation that would end on

June 25, 1996. Shore also was required to pay $122 for court costs.

Nothing ever came up about Dana Sanchez or the other girls, but Shore kept his cool and got off with an extremely light sentence.

CHAPTER 40

Christmas 1996

In 1996, Tony Shore lost control of the girls. "My kids were growing up fast," he recalled. "Too fast." Shore claimed his daughters were tired of being treated like little girls. "They demanded cable TV, wanted a new stereo, and had become tired of the little-girl furniture I made them. They wanted all new stuff and more respect." Tony had provided the girls with a nanny, but they asked him to get rid of her. They told their father they wanted a "more mature environment." Shore also realized that the girls knew how much he spent on the nanny and that that money would be better spent on their material needs.

Shore also claimed that his daughters "spent time listening to inappropriate music and watching inappropriate videos."

In his words, the girls had become "out of control."

Shore seemed to be following the pattern established by his father. He worked at least sixty to seventy hours a week with Southwestern Bell, taught piano

Maria del Carmen Estrada, 21, hoped to make something of herself in America. *(Felipe Estrada Santana)*

Estrada's partially naked body was found dumped behind a Houston Dairy Queen. *(Houston Police Department)*

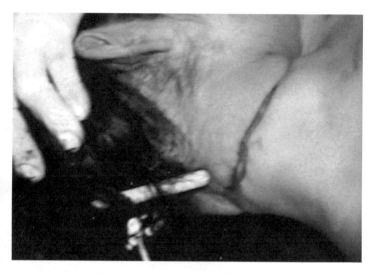

Estrada's neck with ligature used to strangle her.
(Harris County Medical Examiner)

Wooden dowel and rope knots used to kill Estrada.

Diana Rebollar, 9, was well-loved by her neighbors in The Heights. *(Virginia Piedra)*

Rebollar walked two blocks down Main Street to buy sugar. She never made it home. *(Houston Police Department)*

Cemetery and abandoned building where Rebollar's body was dumped.

Rebollar wore a Halloween T-shirt with a black cat and pumpkin on the night of her murder.

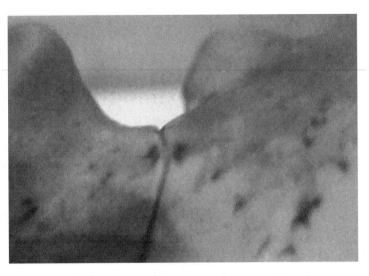

Rebollar's neck with ligature used to strangle her.
(Harris County Medical Examiner)

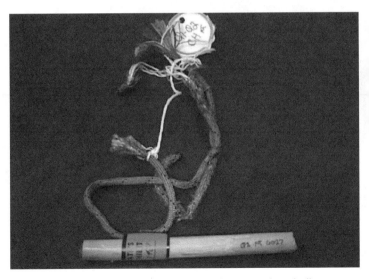

Wooden dowel and nylon rope used to strangle Rebollar.

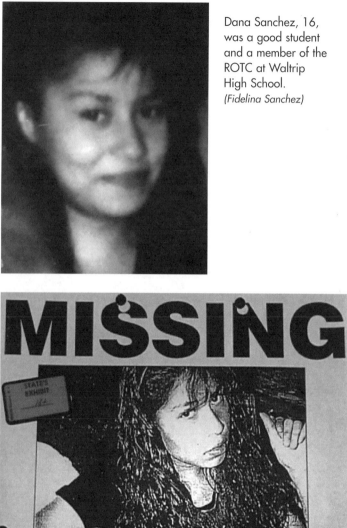

Dana Sanchez, 16, was a good student and a member of the ROTC at Waltrip High School. *(Fidelina Sanchez)*

Missing persons poster for Sanchez. *(Houston Police Department)*

Sanchez's severely decomposed body lay outside in the Texas heat for eight days. *(Houston Police Department)*

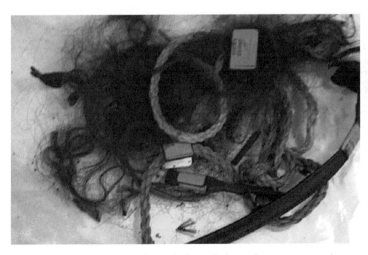

Nylon cord, toothbrush, and plastic belt used to restrain and then strangle Sanchez.

Anthony Allen Shore and Gina Worley Shore on their wedding day. *(Gina Worley Shore)*

Anthony and his mother, Deanna Shore, before his wedding day. *(Gina Worley Shore)*

Robert Shore, Anthony's father, was not around to raise his son.

Anthony, Gina, and their two daughters, Amber and Tiffany.
(Gina Worley Shore)

Anthony Shore was accused of molesting his two daughters.
(Gina Worley Shore)

Shore was a musical savant who gave piano and guitar lessons.
(Gina Worley Shore)

Shore played keyboards in the band St. Vitus Dance, an eleven-piece alternative rock cover band. *(Gina Worley Shore)*

Shore was arrested eight years after he murdered Dana Sanchez. *(Houston Police Department)*

Detective Bob King never gave up trying to find the murderer of Diana Rebollar.

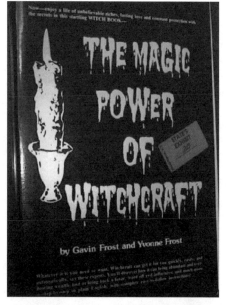

Shore carried a book on witchcraft with him.

Shore later confessed to the murder of 15-year-old Laurie Tremblay. *(Yearbook photo)*

Tremblay's body was tossed behind the Dumpster of a Mexican restaurant. *(Houston Police Department)*

Impression caused by ligature clearly seen around Tremblay's neck. *(Harris County Medical Examiner)*

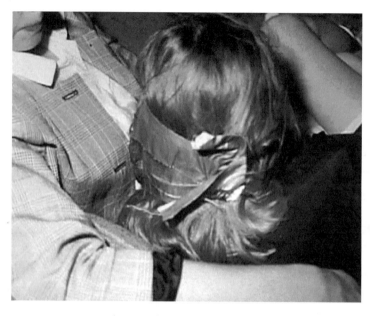

Rape victim Selma Janske, with duct tape around her head, being consoled by her mother. *(Houston Police Department)*

Shore kept boxes of pornography in this storage facility.

Gina Worley Shore, Tony's first wife and mother of his two children, had no idea her husband was a serial killer.

Harris County Assistant District Attorney Kelly Siegler worked in conjunction with the Houston Police Department to bring Shore to justice.

Shore informed his attorneys that he wanted the death penalty. His wish was granted. *(Gina Worley Shore)*

Shore checking out some young girls. *(Gina Worley Shore)*

lessons, and played nighttime gigs, and he claimed he spoiled his family.

"I had the foolish notion," he surmised, "that spending money to spoil my kids and Amy with material items and activities was somehow making up for not being there in person."

CHAPTER 41

Thursday, May 1, 1997,
700 block of East Eighteenth Street,
Houston, Texas.

After nearly three years of living together, Tony Shore made Amy Lynch an honest woman. They were financially stable as his job paid nearly $80,000 a year, and, to that end, they had a nice home, two cars, a nanny, who doubled as a housekeeper, and a yardman. He described their lives together as "the all-American dream." As far as he was concerned, "our life was one big vacation from the reality of the responsibilities of daily life." Eventually Shore and Amy got married and were eager to continue their fun times together.

Shore made sure that he and Amy enjoyed their honeymoon. He sent Amber and Tiffany to live with their grandmother, Dea, in Sacramento. Allegedly, Dea balked at first, but her son threatened her with never letting her see her granddaughters again so Dea relented and took the girls into her home.

Fairly soon thereafter, Dea was not able to care for both girls and was forced to send Tiffany to stay with

Shore's sister, Gina, up in Oregon. Gina gladly took her niece in and made her feel welcome and loved.

Gina immediately noticed that Tiffany did not seem like the upbeat, exuberant niece she used to know. According to an Out Patient Department Progress Record filed with the Sacramento Child Protection Center, and dated August 25, 1995, Tiffany would "sleep in her clothes, wear multiple layers of clothes, won't bathe regularly, has sexually advanced speech; speaks violently."

It was also disclosed in the same report that Tiffany confided in her aunt that her father had been raping her. When Gina told Dea of the molestation, she also informed her mother that Shore had also raped her and Laurel when they were young girls.

Tiffany later told her grandmother that Shore had "penile penetration" with her.

According to the report, Tony Shore was at home with the girls because Amy had to spend the night in the hospital. Tiffany claimed that he "crawled naked into bed with her" and raped her. She managed somehow to kick him off her and ran into the bathroom, where she locked herself away from him.

Tiffany stated that this was the only time that her father ever raped her; however, he had been exposing his genitals to her and Amber for years. Tiffany told her grandmother that she tried to slit her wrists and kill herself after her father attacked her. Tiffany also unsuccessfully attempted suicide by overdosing with a handful of pills taken from the medicine cabinet.

Tiffany reported that her father had even crawled into bed with one of her little girlfriends who had spent the night.

Tiffany spoke violently of what she wanted to do to her father. The eleven-year-old told her aunt that she "wanted to kill him" for what he did to her and Amber.

It was understandable, especially when she reported the violence perpetrated on her by her father. According to Tiffany, her father "beat her, threw her against a wall, pulled her by the hair, and kicked her." She added that he "tied her in sheets" and that "he would place a pillow on her face if she cried and threaten to kill her."

Once Tiffany opened up to Gina, Amber disclosed to her grandmother what her father had done to her. Amber said that her father had been peeping on her in the nude since she was less than six years old. She claimed that he would pull his penis out of his pants and stare at her or Tiffany until one of them stirred and then would hurriedly leave their room, and that her dad used to "come to her bed and fondle her buttocks with his hands, feeling her anus and fondling her breasts."

Amber also said that her father "hit her all over her body," and added that "she sleeps on her stomach on her pillow to make it harder for him to get at her." Amber, like Tiffany, also claimed that Tony "pulled her hair, placed a pillow on her face, and threatened to kill her."

Tony Shore's ex-wife, Gina, was skeptical initially. "As much as he and Amber never got along, she always wanted to do something to spite him. There's some part of me that says if that was going on, it seemed like she'd be blabbing it to everybody.

"The way that they were raised, that if the doctor touches you like this, it's okay; but if it's like this, then it's wrong. We'd give them the speech over and over about people touching you and even if it's one of your parents, it's still wrong," Gina insisted. "I had that discussion with them from a real young age and so it wasn't as though they were presented with a situation with which they had no coaching. They had been told, even if it's a grown-up you know, it's wrong, even if it's me, it's wrong. Even if it's your dad, it's wrong." Gina never heard a peep from the girls about their father molesting either one of them.

Gina believed the girls needed to come back to Texas and stay with her until they straightened up their acts. "They went to California and then they started doing bad in school; they hung out with the wrong crowd; they had pentagrams and pentacles on everything. I was thinking about having [them] home-schooled, and they were going, 'No, no, no, we don't want to do that. You know what, Mom? You're really too far away to make us come back,'" the girls defiantly challenged her.

"I can make you come back," their mother retorted.

"It just seems like an unusual set of circumstances for them to be strutting around. And, according to Amber, Tony's favorite thing to say to her, 'I'm gonna put you in military school.'"

But Gina had her doubts as to whether her second ex-husband actually molested her daughters. She believed it had more to do with Tiffany. "She wanted to stay in California. It's beautiful there. And she was always doted upon by Tony's mom." Gina also believed that Shore's interest in his new wife, Amy, took away from the attention he paid Tiffany. Gina further suggested Tiffany was embarrassed because her father was married to someone so close to her in age.

"The school nurse used to make fun of her," Gina said of Tiffany, "because Amy would walk in and say, 'Yes, I'm their mother,'" which Tiffany emphatically denied.

Interestingly, today Gina believes that her ex-husband did indeed molest their two daughters. "Obviously, if he hadn't had that charge against him, he wouldn't be where he is today, so everything happens for a reason."

She doesn't, however, believe the sexual assaults could have begun when Amber was six years old. "I don't know how he could have done that. It wasn't like they didn't go and have physical examinations.

"And Amber didn't have a good sense of personal hygiene," Gina continued. "I think I would have noticed any irritation down there. And of course in Houston it's hot, so you want to pay attention to little girls in case they get rashes. They get yeast infections. I used to tell her, 'You better clean it or it'll fall off.' So, I really think I would have noticed.

"Up until he left the house, and up until that summer, I still saw the girls naked all the time, bathing, dressing, all that. And they never had any redness, rashes, irritation, inflammation, any of that. My mom was a stickler for nighttime baths and she never saw any of that. If a kid itches, they're gonna tell you, 'Hey, it itches' or 'It burns.' And they never had anything. Anything."

Gina also had her doubts as to the veracity of Dea Shore in regard to the girls' molestations. "Tony's mom was all this, that, and the other thing, talking and telling my mom. Whenever the evidence came back regarding their gynecological exam, nothing."

In conclusion, Gina could only surmise one thing in regard to Tony Shore possibly raping his own flesh and blood. "I had been greatly uninformed as far as that goes."

Rob Shore, likewise, was clueless as to what his son had allegedly done to his granddaughters. "I had no idea," he remembered. "I had so little of a relationship with them."

* * *

Friday, October 31, 1997,
Harris County Courthouse,
1201 Franklin Street,
Houston, Texas.

Regina Shore, Tony's sister, made sure that charges were officially filed against her brother for the alleged molestation of his two daughters, Amber and Tiffany Shore.

CHAPTER 42

Friday, January 23, 1998,
Harris County Courthouse,
Courtroom #337,
1201 Franklin Street,
Houston, Texas.

Tony Shore appeared in court for two charges of indecency with a child. Shore's case would be heard that day by a visiting judge from Dallas, Judge Jon Hughes, who was filling in for Judge James L. "Jim" Barr, who was suspended from the bench. Judge Barr had been accused of making sexually inappropriate comments to female prosecutors after referring to them as the "all-babe court." Judge Barr also made another comment to a female district attorney (DA) that raised several eyebrows: "I could just reach over and slap the crap out of you." Judge Barr even got into a shoving match with a deputy who refused to release a rape suspect who had been acquitted before being processed. Judge Barr was later disciplined and removed as the sitting judge.

But Judge Jon Hughes's temporary tenure in the

courthouse started out with a bang. During one of his earliest courtroom appearances, the visiting judge got into a verbal disagreement with an attorney, Joseph Rumbaut, which nearly escalated into fisticuffs. Apparently, each man called the other a liar.

Tony Shore was walking into a very strange courtroom.

Shore took his seat behind the defense table next to his court-appointed attorney, Bill Gifford. Seated nearby at the prosecution's table was Assistant District Attorney (ADA) Michelle Stansbury. The defense attorney and prosecutor had spent the previous two months going over Shore's case. Gifford earned his paycheck as he hammered out a sweetheart deal with the prosecutor.

Stansbury, on behalf of the Harris County District Attorney's Office, agreed to reduce the charges against Shore from two counts of sexual molestation of a minor to two counts of indecency with a child. Even such a reduced sentence at the time could net a defendant five years to life in prison. Somehow, the district attorney's office decided it would be acceptable for Tony Shore not to have to serve any time behind bars.

In lieu of prison time Shore would be placed on probation for eight years and forced to pay a $500 fine and $126.50 for court costs. He also received a payment plan, wherein he would only have to pay $10 a month.

As a further condition of Shore's probation, he would be required to register as a sex offender with authorities every ninety days and to report to his parole officer, Chester "Chet" Machen, every fifteen days. Shore would be assigned 240 hours of community service and not be allowed to leave Harris County without Machen's approval. He could not drink alcohol or take any illicit drugs, would be required to have drug and alcohol counseling, and would be subject to the occasional, random urinalysis.

Shore would also have to attend a sex offender therapy program. He further could not be in public where children gathered and could not live with a child.

The final requirement for Shore was that he had to provide a DNA sample for the court to keep on file.

If Shore managed to slide through the next eight years unscathed, he would receive deferred adjudication and the court would expunge the charges from his record.

A usual requirement in a case involving sexual misconduct with children is to forbid them from being within one hundred yards of a school. Strangely, Judge Hughes allowed Shore to return to his residence on East Eighteenth Street, directly across the street from Field Elementary School and its playground full of young kids.

The waiver was penciled in by the judge himself. The agreement actually stated that Shore was not allowed to "reside, go in, on, or within 100 yards of premises where children commonly gather, including a school, day-care facility, playground, public or private youth center, public swimming pool, or video arcade facility." Next to that declaration, written in the judge's hand, was "except for your residence" at East Eighteenth Street.

When it came out, nearly six years later, that Shore was a suspected serial killer who stalked, raped, and strangled little girls, the critics came after Judge Hughes.

"There is no justification for it," stated Andy Kahan, director of the Crime Victims Assistance program, out of the City of Houston Mayor's Office. "Unless he was taking care of invalid relatives, there is no reason why he should have been allowed to stay in that house."

Kim Valentine, administrative coordinator for the

Harris County Community Supervision and Corrections Department, clarified that it was the judge who made the decisions on any extra conditions or waivers when it came to parole. "The judge is really the only one that can answer that question."

When Judge Hughes was asked about it in 2003, he feigned ignorance. "I don't recall that case." He then added that such a decision to waive the one-hundred-yard rule would be given only in the rarest of circumstances. "Generally speaking, the only time I would allow them to stay in their home is if it was their homestead," which was the case.

Further, while it is normal for probationary requirements to forbid the defendant from seeing his or her victim or victims, Judge Hughes inexplicably allowed Shore to have contact with Amber and Tiffany.

Denise Oncken, chief of the Harris County District Attorney's Office Child Abuse Division, told *Houston Press* reporter Sarah Fenske that such a light sentence wasn't normal, "but it's not outside the norm either."

When Dea Shore found out about the plea bargain, she was shocked. She claimed to have not been consulted by the district attorney's office. "They just don't care. They told me they didn't want the girls to feel guilt. I said, 'Why should they? They are children. They don't feel guilty.'"

Dea added that the girls feared for their lives. They were having bad dreams that their father would hunt them down at night and kill them. "I was furious. I'm still furious," the girls' grandmother declared.

* * *

Everyone and their mother knew Tony Shore got an incredible deal. Everyone, that is, except for Tony Shore.

When word of his probation got around to Southwestern Bell, he was unceremoniously fired. Within weeks of his sentence he had Bill Gifford file a motion to withdraw his plea agreement. He claimed that he had no idea that the requirements for a sex offender would be so stringent and that he had only heard the terms of the plea offer fifteen minutes before his hearing. He believed that was not a sufficient amount of time to digest the information and make a rational, sound decision.

When Regina Shore heard about the new motion, she wrote out and signed an affidavit that stated she believed her brother had molested more girls than just her nieces. She wrote about how he used to grope the little neighbor girls when they were kids. "I think there were a lot more girls he molested," Regina wrote. "A lot more."

A judge denied Shore's motion to throw out his plea bargain.

Gina Worley Shore, Tony's ex-wife, talked about the molestation charges. "If you go back through all of the news accounts of this," Gina surmised, "he was really the one who tripped off all of this Predator Watch stuff. They did find him right across the street from a school. They just kind of glossed over it. They found him living like that and, really, all he got was a slap on the wrist. That was when they kicked off all this news mania about Predator Watch and they said, 'Is there a sex offender close to your home?'"

Despite the seemingly light sentence, Tony and Amy

Shore lost the services of their nanny/housekeeper and
their yardman, suffering what Tony suggested was the ultimate indignity. "Suddenly we were faced with doing
dishes, laundry, yard work, house cleaning, and this,
combined with an inordinate amount of stress and
mental strain from losing the kids and doubts in me
about the offense, took its toll."

CHAPTER 43

One of the major requirements of Tony Shore's probation was to attend a sexual offender therapy program. Shore started off with a licensed sex offender treatment provider by the name of Dr. Barbara Levinson. This particular union only lasted two months, until he was reassigned to a new program through an organization called Crimson & Associates. Shore would deal mainly with Dr. Sharon Burns.

One of his big assignments in the treatment program was to keep a journal of his thoughts in regard to his offense and to other pertinent issues in his life. His notebook contained several insightful passages.

Tony Shore wrote about God.

In an essay entitled "Forgiveness Self," he declared that he harbored "a lot of mixed emotions [regarding] . . . forgiveness" and wanted to know "how can I ever truly forgive myself for what I did?" Shore believed God sent him guardian angels and that he was protected. "I've confessed my sins and know I'm forgiven and will never go back."

Shore always seemed to write exactly what he believed

his counselors wanted to read. "I'm only a man. I have, however, forgiven myself on some level," he detailed. Nowhere did he mention regret for having done what he did to his daughters.

Shore believed he was a prime candidate for rehabilitation "but until I am able to reconcile with my daughters . . . it will be impossible for me to find complete forgiveness for myself."

Eventually Shore's essay displayed a sense of remorse. "I have faith and believe God will see us through and bring us together someday," he wrote in reference to Amber and Tiffany. "Someday I will have the opportunity to apologize and let them know this was totally my fault and nothing they did could have caused any of this."

In his essay entitled "Drugs & Alcohol," he wrote that he did not abuse alcohol or drugs. "I just never developed a taste for alcohol and don't care for the woozy feeling it provides. I don't like drugs and usually feign away from even prescribed drugs. I generally won't even take Tylenol or aspirin."

His one weakness was cocaine, which he claimed he used periodically in high school and college because it enhanced creative and artistic thought.

"In retrospect, it definitely clouded my judgment and, ironic, I feel it was a contributing factor when I offended Tiffany." Shore could not quite place all of the blame on himself. "I left California when I was nineteen and had only used three or four times since then about every three to five years whenever a certain friend would come to visit when passing through Texas. He just happened to be visiting that week."

Shore contended that if it weren't for the cocaine, he would not have laid a finger on Tiffany. "I never would have imagined it possible for me to have done this horrible offense in the first place and know in my heart if my judgment wasn't clouded at the time I believe I would have acted differently."

Apparently, sex offender therapy class taught Shore one thing. Tell them what they want to hear.

"I can honestly say," he contended, "I would rather die than harm my kids." As a result, he swore off cocaine "because of the potential for disaster, harmful pain and suffering, loss of reason, and clouded judgment that comes with it."

Tony Shore wrote about restrictions.

In an essay entitled "When I Offended Travel Health Recreation," he wrote, "When I offended, my ability to travel and recreate were affected enormously." He went on to list several places he could no longer visit due to travel restrictions. He missed out on San Antonio and the Riverwalk, Austin's Hill Country, and camping at Ink Lake. He wouldn't be able to hit the beaches of Galveston or go offshore fishing. No more camping or sailing for Shore either.

He lamented the fact that the restrictions basically ruined his shot for musical stardom. "I used to play piano for country music artist Brian Black on tour and contracted to play piano for several visiting artists at the Woodlands Pavilion."

The reason his music career stalled was because "I am not allowed to attend events where children congregate." He also could not play anywhere that served alcohol.

Shore again redirected the results of his incestuous molestation back on himself. "My restrictions on travel and recreation have all but brought my performing music to a complete and permanent halt." He felt he was no longer the same man without his music. "I lost a major part of who I was when I offended."

He described the pain derived from no longer being able to play music for others. He used to enjoy playing for crowds. "I loved touring and loved the limited fame and attention," he reminisced. Music was his escape and now he no longer had that outlet.

Shore's pain became even more dramatic.

"I really don't know exactly how I survived it," he recalled, referring to not being able to make a living from his music, "or why I didn't give up all hope."

Shore concluded the essay with "a large part of who I was for over thirty years is lost, gone forever, and there is a huge empty void in my soul. I know I'll never be the same as a result of what I did."

Tony Shore also wrote about self-esteem.

In his essay entitled "Self Esteem, Hopes, Religion Spiritualism," he wrote, "When I offended, my self-esteem took a dive, my hopes and dreams were shattered, and my religious beliefs and spirituality were jeopardized and became suspect."

He wrote of how he always thought highly of himself.

"I was . . . living the All-American dream," Shore believed. Never shy about his abilities, he conveyed that he was "confident, talented and self-assured." People turned to him in their time of need. He was the answer man. "I was the solid Rock of Gibraltar."

Shore wrote that he was amazed at what he did to his daughters. "I hated myself for what I had done and was loathe [sic] to find words or acceptance." He added in a melodramatic flourish, "Our lives were all destroyed and the future was devoid of any hope. Literally, everything was lost."

Shore wrote that he believed his nefarious actions had severe religious implications. "I was spiritually empty [and] felt that even going to hell was too good for the likes of me."

Allegedly, he found salvation with the help of friends and therapy. "I really decided to come to grips with the harsh reality of what I had done and the weight of the harm and hurt I caused."

Shore believed God would take care of him and his daughters. "I . . . do have faith in myself, my daughters, and God's will to bring us together to find healing."

Tony Shore wrote about why he would be a good candidate and a bad candidate for sex offender therapy treatment.

The good reasons he listed were because he was a sex offender and he wanted "to learn and understand empathy." He wanted to be able to forgive himself and he wanted to work on his anger. "I'm angry at myself," he wrote. "I'm angry at the system and hope to learn to redirect that anger into positive and constructive behavior and hope to be a better person."

His bad reasons were "because I am educated and intelligent and think I already know everything I need to know." He described himself as "hard-headed and resistant to other people's ideas." He also declared that he was a bad candidate due to the financial stress such treatment would toll. He was also a bad candidate because he "is a good person and [doesn't] need someone else to tell me right from wrong." He also declared that he did not like confrontation and was resistant to change.

Interestingly, Shore wrote down "because I already know that I will never offend again" and then scribbled the passage out.

He was also asked to write more about his restrictions. He stated that "no contact with children" would not be a problem because "children irritate me." In regard to his social life, he stated that he was "not very social" but that he did "occasionally enjoy the company of other adult friends and intellectual conversation." He also stated that he would continue to perform music at private parties and restaurants. He would not play weddings and funerals, because he hated them.

Shore also wrote about not being able to go to bars. "I don't and never did enjoy bars, clubs, big festive events where people get drunk and stupid." On the other hand, he declared, "I don't impose my values on others."

Tony Shore wrote down his thoughts as to relationships. "I would just as soon be alone than to be with someone too independent."

He also wrote about any additional hobbies he may have had. "I don't have any outside of the preoccupation of fashion [worn by] young women in music." He was determined that his daughters would become "famous rich successful rock stars on MTV to succeed in the music industry where I failed."

Tony Shore wrote about his mother.

In an essay entitled "What I Would Lose If I Decided to Forgive My Mother," he spoke of the resentment he had toward his mother. "It is extremely difficult to not be consumed with hatred when I am reminded daily of the loss and pain she imposed on me as a result of her greed and obsession for money."

Shore described his hatred for his mother as an "incurable cancer" that had caused him "irreparable damage." He claimed that he had forgiven her, but "it is a very difficult task because hating her and choosing to lie blame there has been like an addiction for me."

Shore claimed that if he forgave his mother, he would "lose the comfort of depression and feeling sorry for myself."

In the end, however, it did not appear as if he would ever forgive his mother. "It is difficult to let go of a bad habit," he wrote of his hatred for his mother. "But I'm willing to try." He described his mother as evil and he had a unique way of dealing with her. "I will try for now to just write her off as a non-person. Dead to this world and try to cope by not wasting any more time thinking of her."

Not exactly the most forgiving soul on the planet.

Tony Shore wrote about how he messed up his life.

He described himself as "a primadonna [*sic*] know-it-all who offends people." He also wrote that he was stubborn and set in his ways, extremely critical of himself, and a poor listener. He also stated that he was irresponsible and would often make excuses for his shortcomings. He quoted the axiom: "Argue for your limitations and they are yours forever."

He added that he wanted to appear better than everyone else and that his situation in life was different and more important than everyone else's.

* * *

Tony Shore wrote about his daughters.

"I spoiled my girls," he admitted. He had a nanny do their chores for them and he gave them both $50-a-week allowance for shopping. "I allowed them to wear makeup, dye their hair, play in a band, dress and act much older than they were."

Shore thought very high of his daughters. "They were talented, beautiful, and physically well-developed," and he liked to show them off.

He allowed the girls to wear "promiscuous" clothes as an act of defiance. He believed the girls' schools were too strict with their required dress codes. "I let them because I wanted to encourage their artistic freedom of expression."

Shore loved to go out in public and put his three "young women"—Amy, Amber, and Tiffany—on display. "It stoked my ego to be seen with such beautiful young women in public. I had a huge ego."

His interest sounded a bit unfatherly. "I spent a great deal of time watching them perform. I ritually enjoyed looking at them." His interest seemed to go beyond that of the loving father role. "Internally I knew there were times I looked at them more as young women than my little girls." His interest increased as the girls grew older. "I spent an inordinate amount of time worrying about how boys/men might try to take advantage of my young beauties."

Shore even described the lustful feelings in his heart that he held for his girls. "There were times that I would imagine their young well-developed bodies and feel ashamed of myself at the thought, but I nevertheless allowed myself to look at their muscular bodies and firm full breasts."

He added in his treatment notebook that "I was guilty of dissecting and disrobing [them] with my eyes." His descriptions of his lustful feelings became more graphic: "I imagined what they looked like under their clothes. I would watch them in their short skirts or dancing around in braless tops." He knew what he was thinking was wrong, but he could not stop. "I would fantasize about what these young rock stars look like naked. They were still my little girls."

Shore succinctly described his behavior in regard to his daughters as "predatory."

He used to call his daughters "my little babes" and tell them that they were "too cool for school." He claimed he said these things to them so it "might inflate their inner egos."

Tony Shore wrote specifically about what he did to his youngest daughter, Tiffany.

In an essay entitled "Despair—Tiffany," he stated, "Despair with Tiffany was huge from the start. I was in despair before, during, and after the offense."

He blamed his actions on outside stimuli. "My judgment was impaired by cocaine and I made several bad decisions, one after the next, which intensified the feelings of despair and hopelessness."

He described how he felt as he molested his youngest daughter. "I remember feeling afraid and confused, but when I heard noises outside the restroom and realized the risk of my indiscretion being discovered, I immediately came to my senses."

He described the fear he felt. "Confusion, shame,

helplessness, all increased dramatically. Panic about being caught. Panic how Tiff would react. Shame at my actions, scared of consequences not only for myself but for my family, our future. Scared of what possible trauma I could have caused my daughter."

Shore chastised himself for his behavior. "I broke the promise to myself that I would never touch my daughters that way. My despair was huge."

At least he admitted his selfishness. "I believe my despair at the time was mostly for myself." He also acknowledged that his daughter's despair had to have been worse than his own. He wrote of how he violated her while she was "sick and confused. Rather than giving her care, comfort, and safety when she turned to me for help, she was betrayed."

In another essay Shore wrote that Tiffany and her friends stole some alcohol and got plastered. "My daughter was a complete mess. I was angry. I wanted to discipline them and most specifically her for allowing this to happen."

In yet another essay he claimed there was a party going on in his house, he was high on cocaine, and the girls were drunk. He also wrote that Tiffany was "vomiting all over herself." He claimed he was afraid the girls' parents would find out that their daughters had been drinking and "I would be shunned, embarrassed, and surely in trouble for not being more aware of what was going on and preventing this from happening."

Instead of being a mature adult and taking responsibility for his poor chaperoning skills, he said, "I panicked. My decision was to cover up. Do damage control and hide from the reality. I told everyone to go to bed and sleep it off.

"I carried Tiffany to the bathroom," he continued, "as

she could not walk and put her in the shower." Shore washed the vomit off his daughter in the shower.

He wrote that he was aroused by his daughter. "There she was," referring to Tiffany, "wet and totally incapacitated. She didn't look like my little girl any more [*sic*]. It was at this moment I experienced some level of arousal, her body was that of a woman, very developed and muscular."

Shore described how he was supposedly overcome by an intense sensation. "Somehow though, for a split second, suspended in time, I lost control and my mind gave way to fear." He seemed to blame his behavior on extenuating circumstances. "I was scared, confused, high, and she was wet and vulnerable." Apparently, the combination was too much for him to withstand. "I could not have been in my right mind, for in that moment I was overcome by some sick desire to touch her vagina by hand."

Tony Shore wrote specifically about what he did to his oldest daughter, Amber. "I was in a dream state, half awake, half asleep, snuggling with Amber on the couch when I caught myself touching her breast through her clothes. She was asleep and I stopped the moment I became conscious." Shore never could accept full responsibility for his actions. He continued, "I was sick and embarrassed. That was the moment I realized I was preoccupied sexually with touching Amber. Prior to that, my fantasy was more just disrobing with my eyes."

Unfortunately, his preoccupation flourished. "After the incident with Amber I think the fantasy grew and I would wonder how supple her breasts might feel."

* * *

Tony Shore wrote down what he considered to be triggers that aroused him when it came to his daughters:

- Long clean brushed and flowing hair
- Athletic/shapely long bare legs
- Short skirts/shorts/braless tops/swimwear
- Bare breasts
- Beautiful dark eyes and nice smile
- Form-fitting clothes like a tee or tank top
- Crop tops with nicely shaped firm flat tummy showing
- Flirting is a turn-on, complimenting me
- When women would play with my hair (used to be long)
- Kissing and touching me in an inviting way
- Provocative or suggestive dancing

"These were all triggers in both cases which I feel led to preoccupation with each of my daughters."

Tony Shore wrote about the denial he went through after he molested his daughters. He justified his actions by convincing himself that what he did was an accident, or that the girls didn't know what happened to them, or by buying them expensive musical equipment, or that since no vaginal penetration was involved, his behavior was acceptable.

He added that he obviously lost the girls' trust and that "their stress was beyond words and they lost their ability to focus their attention." He added, "I'm certain they were consumed with anger, rage, terror and confusion and in the end they lost contact not only with Dad, but with everyone whoever mattered."

Tony Shore wrote about the consequences of his actions and how they impacted his own personal relationships. "As for my immediate family, my dad, mom, aunts, uncles, sisters, without exception, they abandoned me." Tony Shore claimed that everyone abandoned him. "They hate me. I have lost all contact with any/all of my relatives. As far as my family is concerned, I'm deceased and do not exist anymore."

CHAPTER 44

Tony Shore's probation turned out to be a joke. Not once, but twice, he submitted a urine sample laced with cocaine. Instead of facing serious time behind bars, Shore did not receive any punishment. He truly seemed to be charmed.

Shore made sure that Amy was by his side every time he had to make a courthouse appearance. He wanted to create a familylike atmosphere with Amy playing the supportive wife role. She was with him at each hearing.

Amy talked about Shore's bizarre behavior during this time. She stated that he often told her he was "going trespassing." According to Amy, that was "a sport for him to go and see if he could go in some place where he wasn't supposed to be and then leave again without getting caught. Without anyone knowing that he had been there."

She also talked about how Shore would dress up in disguise, usually in a long black wig, so he could mingle about in crowds where there would be children.

A friend of Shore's named Mort also mentioned that Tony used to wear disguises whenever they would hit the bars. Mort claimed that he and Shore worked together and hung out and got wasted over a period of two years.

"He was a good friend to me," Mort recalled. "Tony was very strange, not unlike myself or any of the freaks I run with.

"He always told me, 'You think you know me, but you don't know me.' I assumed that what he was saying was a roundabout way of saying he was into some homosexual stuff, so I never made too much of it. I guess I was asleep."

Mort had some words for his friend. "He was always kind and giving, but everyone has a dark side. His was just darker than others."

Amy also talked about a dark side to her husband that others did not see. She recalled one time when he came home very late and his shirt was covered in blood. He told her that he had helped a little girl in a white dress who was bloodied in a car accident. Shore claimed he knew CPR and was ready to help if necessary. Amy doubted the sincerity of that explanation.

CHAPTER 45

Fall 1998,
700 block of East Eighteenth Street,
Houston, Texas.

Amy Shore entered her home to see her husband frantically pacing the hallway. "What's wrong?" she asked.

Tony Shore stopped, looked up at her, and continued to pace.

"Tony, what is wrong?" she asked again.

"I'm gonna make you famous," he said to her.

Amy thought that maybe he was talking about her musical career. He had always told her he would make her a star one day. She felt in her skin, however, that he was not talking about pop stardom.

"Tony, what are you talking about?"

Shore continued to pace. Finally he stopped and looked up at her again. "One of my conditions for probation," he stated, "is to give a DNA sample. Why should I have to give my DNA for something I didn't do?"

Amy was amazed at her husband's demeanor. He had always looked so calm to her. Always in control. Always in charge. Now he was bouncing around like a jackrabbit on cocaine. She was worried for him, but also nervous because of the way he was acting.

"You know I didn't do this, right?" he asked her.

Amy nodded her head.

"I don't want to do this. I just don't," he declared. Shore turned around in a flash toward Amy. "I'm gonna run! I'm gonna run!"

Shore began pacing again as he told Amy what they were going to do. "First I'm gonna get a boat and you're coming with me. You're my guardian angel." He loved to call her that. He was her protector and she was his guardian angel. He also used to say that he was her "Rock of Gibraltar."

"We'll take a boat and head out into the Gulf and make our way out to the Atlantic. We'll get away from American soil and that way we can't be extradited back to the States."

Amy stared at him in amazement.

He turned around and looked at her again. "I'm gonna make you famous."

Tony Shore waited until the last possible day before he finally complied and supplied a DNA sample.

CHAPTER 46

Saturday, January 16, 1999,
700 block of East Eighteenth Street,
Houston, Texas.

Despite his strange behavior and the child molestation charges brought against him by his own two daughters, Amy stayed married to Tony Shore. She even stuck with him when he began to intimidate her physically.

Shore attempted to get Amy to join him in some riskier sexual encounters. He wanted Amy to let him choke her while they had sex. "If you're asphyxiated, then you will get off better and you'll cum," he told her, expecting her to get excited by the prospect. Amy smacked him on the shoulder and told him, "Get out of here, Tony. I'm not doing that."

The next morning Amy woke up groggy and incoherent. As she stumbled out of bed, she had difficulty righting herself just to walk to the bathroom. While Amy shuffled forward, she felt a severe pain in her neck. At first, she assumed she must have slept wrong and gotten a crick in her neck. She then felt the pain in her chest and then a pain in her throat. She thought it was rather odd coming so soon after her husband said he wanted to choke her during sex.

Despite all the warning signs, Amy stayed with Tony Shore.

That is, until one night in winter 1999. Shore and Amy were in their home making love when things got out of control. According to Amy, Tony Shore drugged her drink and she became woozy and passed out. She awoke to her husband's hands wrapped around her throat. Shore squeezed her throat as hard as he could, so hard that Amy could not physically defend herself. She started to fall unconscious as he kept choking her.

Miraculously, Tony Shore stopped just short of killing her. Amy, however, believed he had every intention of doing so. She blamed his cessation of choking her on her acting skills as she played possum and faked falling unconscious.

As Amy lay there in a semiconscious state, Shore decided to have his way with her. He rolled his wife over onto her stomach, pulled off her panties, and took her from behind. Amy continued to play possum during the rape. He started to pound away at her and make bizarre grunting noises. Suddenly he stopped, ejaculated inside her, and dismounted. He then grabbed Amy and tossed her on her back. He began to pound on her chest with his fists. He leaned over her face, grasped her nose and pinched the nostrils shut, and placed his mouth over hers. He began a rhythmic breathing pattern while alternately applying pressure to Amy's chest. He was trying to resuscitate her.

The force of her husband's breath into Amy's mouth caused her more pain. She began to cough so violently that he pushed himself off her. Amy sat up and kept hacking until her air passage seemed clear. She looked at Shore, but did not say a word.

Amy could not believe what her own husband had just done to her. But she dared not utter a word of discontent, for she feared for her life. Instead, she lay awake in bed next to the man she agreed to stay with until "death do us part."

Amy Lynch was determined that she would not be that person.

The following morning Amy bolted from her home and sought comfort from a friend, telling her what Shore had done to her the night before. Two days later, Monday, January 19, 1999, she found herself on the steps of the Harris County Courthouse, ready to file for divorce. But there was one problem: Monday was a federal holiday due to the observation of Martin Luther King Day. Amy was ready to cry. It was almost as if Tony Shore had some irreproachable control over every aspect of her life.

But Amy pulled herself together, realized the foolishness of her thinking, and returned to her friend's residence for the night.

The following morning, Tuesday, January 20, Amy returned to the courthouse, where she successfully filed a petition for divorce from her husband, Anthony Allen Shore.

Shore blamed the dissolution of his marriage to Amy, not on the accusation of and sentence for molesting his own two daughters, but rather on Amy's supposed materialistic needs.

"When I could no longer support (and spoil her) in the fashion she was accustomed to, she left me," Shore said of his second wife.

CHAPTER 47

January 1999,
700 block of East Eighteenth Street,
Houston, Texas.

Tony Shore's downward spiral continued unabated.
He spent Christmas alone, he had not heard from either
of his daughters, and his divorce from Amy was pending.

Then he met Pauline Cody. Pauline was a not-so-fresh-
faced gal from the school of hard knocks. Despite hard-
ships and setbacks, she had a strong work ethic and was
doing everything she could to get her life back on track.

One of the avenues Pauline undertook to better care
for herself was spending a year-and-a-half in a drug rehabilitation center known as the Door to Recovery. They
helped her kick her addictions to marijuana and alcohol. They also moved her from Austin to Houston, supposedly to separate her from any bad elements.

After Pauline successfully completed her drug treatment, she moved into her aunt and uncle's home. They
lived in The Heights.

Pauline was lucky enough to land some work at the

nearby C & D Hardware, located down the street from her aunt and uncle's. She worked the cash register and also helped customers find items they couldn't locate on their own. It was an honest job with a decent paycheck that kept her close to home. She also scored a second job working for Buchanan's Nursery, across the street from the hardware store. She eventually did so well for herself that she was able to lease one quadrant of a four-plex in the same neighborhood, only a few streets from her jobs.

Pauline felt very confident that things were only going to get better for her.

One day, while working at C & D Hardware, a gentle-man with short dark hair and a dark goatee walked through the store's front door and asked Pauline if they had a specific piece of hardware. She had never heard of what the man was looking for and told him so. The man smiled and said he would find it himself. Pauline thought he was cute and that he seemed very courteous, despite the fact that she could not answer his question.

After a few minutes, the man returned with the mys-tery item in hand. He had a big smile on his face. Pauline returned the smile when she saw that he found what he needed. He gave her the item and some cash, and then said, "Would you like to go out with me tonight?"

Pauline was embarrassed. But pleasantly so. She had been flying low on the dating scene ever since she had been admitted to rehab. The fact that a fairly attractive, congenial man expressed interest in her warmed her soul. She smiled and agreed to go out with him. She told him where she lived and he told her what time he would pick her up.

Tony Shore arrived at Pauline's apartment right on

time and whisked her away to a nice Mexican restaurant called Spanish Flowers. The two dined and conversed easily together. After they finished their meal, he drove her to a coffeehouse called Café Artist, where they both nursed hot cups of joe.

Pauline asked Shore up to her apartment and he eagerly accepted. The couple spent the rest of the night talking about each other and writing poetry. He told her about being on probation, but Pauline did not seem to mind. Of course he lied to her and told her his own mother had put his daughters up to it. Pauline believed Shore and actually felt sorry for him. They spent the rest of the night enjoying each other's company. He was a complete gentleman and eventually left her and went home.

Pauline was instantly enamored with Tony Shore. Even though he was nearly fourteen years older, she believed he understood her and she felt he was a great listener. She also found him very attractive and was especially enthralled with his creative side. "He swept me off my feet," she recalled.

Pauline added that "he was very charming. There was a lot about him that seemed attractive. He was really smart. He was very articulate and musically inclined and just opened my world to a lot of new things."

Shore spent the next several days courting Pauline. They ate out frequently at several nice restaurants. They went to the movies together. Shore wowed her with his musical prowess on the piano, guitar, and drums. Pauline told Shore of her tainted past. He informed her that he was separated and would soon be divorced.

Within a couple weeks, Pauline had moved all of her possessions out of the fourplex and into Shore's home on East Eighteenth Street. "It just kind of happened," Pauline recalled. "We didn't really discuss moving in."

After she moved in, Tony decided it was the appropriate time for them to engage in intimacy. The first night they went to bed, Shore got in his preferred doggystyle position. As he thrust into his new girlfriend's willing orifice, he reached down with his hand and gripped it around her throat. Pauline was oblivious at first, but as he continued to put the G.I. Joe kung fu grip on her, she began to get light-headed.

"I realized, after some time, that this was really not something I was interested in doing," Pauline recalled. She asked him to stop and he complied. She then told him to never do that to her again.

"Tony, why would you want to do that?" she wondered.

"Some people get off on it." He smiled. "I don't know. I just thought it might enhance your pleasure. I'm sorry."

He never tried to choke Pauline again.

She did notice, however, that he seemed to choke on his responsibilities. In the beginning of their relationship, Pauline saw him write and mail child support checks to his mother in Sacramento. Apparently, this task did not last very long and Shore quit sending in payments. "I just didn't see him do it anymore," Pauline recollected. "It kind of fell off."

Pauline also began to notice Tony's fluctuating work situation. One week he worked for one towing-truck company and made good money. A month or so later, he was no longer working there. This transcience became a pattern. He told her that these moves from company to company resulted in better pay.

Shore also became more reclusive as time went on. About the only person he invited over to the house was his neighbor Rick Huey. The other visitor to the house was Shore's probation officer, Chet Machen, and Shore wasn't ever happy to see him. Almost every time Machen paid Shore a visit, Tony would instruct Pauline not to make a sound while the probation officer knocked on the door. He hated dealing with Machen. Shore even knew where all the squeaky sections of the hardwood floors were and pointed them out to Pauline so she wouldn't step on them and make noise.

Pauline recalled that Shore did a lot of unusual things in the house. When she first moved in, he had been painting the inside in exchange for rent payments. He put up brown paper on all the windows to keep the paint off the glass. It took him nearly two months to complete the job; however, he did not take down the paper.

Around the same time Shore suffered a major blow when he received a letter with official divorce documents from Amy. Things once again began to plummet downhill for him.

One of the reasons postulated by Gina Worley Shore as to why Tony lost his house was that he spent too much money on cocaine, despite a ban on all illicit drugs as part of his probation. Indeed, Shore's drug usage was probably the main reason why he used to hide out from Chet Machen, according to Pauline.

Just as he had done with Amy, Shore frequently snorted coke in front of Pauline. Though she spent time in rehab, cocaine was never her drug of choice. She claimed that she had only partaken in the substance one time prior to meeting Shore. Pauline admitted that there was cocaine in the house "from one to three times a week."

Pauline added that Tony Shore was very cognizant of his required in-office probationary meetings with Chet

Machen. Whenever he had a scheduled appointment, he made sure he did not snort coke for three days prior to the meeting. He told Pauline that "he would clean his system out" in case he was required to submit a urine sample for drug testing.

Shore got good at fixing his drug tests. One time, according to Pauline, he even put some pickled onion juice in a jar and gave it to Machen instead of his potentially drug-laced urine.

On August 29, 2000, Shore's deception caught up with him. He told Pauline that he had to appear in court because he was ten hours shy of completing his mandatory community service and was probably going to get nailed for it. The reality was quite different. Shore had finally gotten snagged for cocaine usage. A routine drug test turned up traces of cocaine in his urine.

Shore spent the next twenty days behind bars. While he sat in jail, he made friends with another convicted sex offender. Allegedly, he and the other man concocted a grandiose scheme to steal a large sailboat and travel around the world stopping in various ports of call, where they would abduct and rape little girls and then sail away.

When Tony Shore got out of jail near the end of September, he told Pauline that "time was running out" for him. She had no idea what he was talking about. He kept telling her that something big was going to happen and that his time was limited.

"He was always so trustworthy," she declared in a near state of shock. "You just believed everything he said."

Eventually, Shore and Pauline had to move out of their home because the landlord decided to sell it to someone else. The couple packed up and moved into a townhome on the 6100 block of Marinette Drive. Ironically, it was directly across the street from where America's most prolific serial killer, Coral Eugene Watts, stabbed and killed Elizabeth Montgomery on September 12, 1981, and a mere two blocks away from where Watts also killed Suzi Wolf later that same night. (See *Evil Eyes* by Corey Mitchell, Kensington/Pinnacle, 2006.)

Shore broke even more conditions of his probation after they moved into the townhome. Though his other major condition (aside from illegal drug usage) was no pornography, Shore had plenty of it. Pauline expressed concern for her boyfriend because she knew he could get busted, but he simply blew her off.

Shore was also not supposed to have any contact with minors. He, of course, ignored that condition as well. According to Pauline, they would go out to Dave & Buster's, a restaurant with pool tables and video games that was frequented by teenagers, preteens, and adolescents. He also took Pauline to the Renaissance Festival two or three times in one year, which was teeming with teenage girls. Further, he was not supposed to leave Harris County, but the Renaissance Festival was actually held in nearby Plantersville, outside Harris County.

Shore also took Pauline to the Art Car Ball, a parade with lots of children present.

Each time he went to one of these events, he never did seek approval from Chet Machen. Shore just did not care which rules applied specifically to him.

Eventually, he and Pauline could no longer afford payments on the townhome, so they packed up their belongings and moved into the InTown Suites at the 30000 block of Highway 6th South, on the west side of Houston. InTown Suites is a pay-as-you-go hotel/apartment complex with basic amenities, such as a refrigerator, stove, and microwave, where residents can pay on a week-to-week basis.

But probation be damned. Tony and Pauline's stay at InTown Suites consisted of lots of cocaine and tequila. The blow snowed and the liquor flowed.

Pauline recalled a few unusual instances with Shore at InTown Suites. One time, when the couple stayed home to watch a movie, Shore paid careful attention to the scene in which a man strangled a female victim. Shore looked at Pauline and said, "That's not how a strangulation victim would look. Her eyes should be more red, almost bloodshot. And they should be bulging out."

Pauline raised an eyebrow as she listened to what her boyfriend just described. She did not pursue the issue any further.

Another time Shore had a friend, Chris Stone, over for some coke and tequila. It was their usual recipe for fun. But at this particular shindig, Pauline did not have such a good time. Usually, when she partook in cocaine, she tended to bounce off the walls. Sleep was usually out of the question. This time, however, she felt sleepy and lethargic. She was barely able to hold her head up.

Pauline stumbled over to the refrigerator to find some cool water to help clear her head. When she opened the refrigerator door, she was perplexed by something inside. She grabbed what, at first glance, looked like a glass of water. As she tilted the cup toward her mouth, she caught a glimpse of what was inside. The drink looked like it had powdered soap particles in it that were dissolving. Pauline stopped short of taking a swig of the polluted water.

She then noticed a cellophane wrapper from a pack

of cigarettes inside the refrigerator. She picked up the wrapper and saw a fairly large quantity of white powder in the wrapper. She assumed it was the same substance that had clouded up her potential drink.

"What is this?" Pauline called out to Shore.

Her boyfriend laughed as he saw what she was asking about. He said it belonged to Chris and that he was going to help him use it on "a woman they all knew" so "he [Tony] can take advantage of her." While Pauline did not like the fact that Shore possibly was going to drug a woman, she was too tired to do anything about it, and soon passed out.

Later that night Pauline was surprised when she woke up naked. She was even more surprised to see Shore on top of her, choking her with his hands. She already had told him she was not into the choking-during-sex thing, but he obviously had not listened. Pauline became frightened when Shore ignored her pleas to stop and kept on going. She tried desperately to fend him off by pushing him, but he would not budge. She began to struggle and roll around, and, somehow, she managed to disengage from him.

"What the hell are you doing?" Pauline screamed. She began to sob hysterically. "Are you trying to kill me?"

"No," Shore declared. "I'm so sorry. I didn't mean it. Really, I didn't mean it. I promise it will never happen again." It was the same promise he had made to her the first time he tried it a few years earlier.

Shore's attack scared the hell out of Pauline. She ran off and went to stay with her sister, Charlotte, in Texas City. When she told her sister what Shore had done, Charlotte demanded that she leave him immediately. Pauline agreed and, soon thereafter, told her boyfriend she was leaving. He did not put up much of a fight and even packed her bags for her.

It was time for Tony Shore to move on to the next woman in his life.

He needed someone to take care of, and he knew it would not take long to find that certain someone.

CHAPTER 48

300 block of Freeport Street,
Houston, Texas.

Lynda White was feeling slightly dejected. The fifty-year-old single mother of three had not been on a date in seven years. She had actually been engaged to the last man she dated, but she had broken it off after five years because she was not ready for marriage.

Lynda had high standards for the men she wanted to date. Her fiancé had been a very successful man who used to spoil her with lots of attention and trips to Hawaii. She had not found a man equivalent to him in the intervening seven years and seemed resigned to her fate of singledom.

Lynda's cousin, however, believed Lynda was a vibrant, beautiful, fun lady who could use some good male company. So, she took matters into her own hands. She signed her cousin up with an Internet dating service. When she told Lynda about it, her cousin *acted* upset, but admitted that she was pleased and even somewhat excited about the prospect of meeting a nice, entertaining man.

The man she got was named Tony Shore.

Lynda liked Shore's biographical data as listed on the

dating Web site. He described himself as "bohemian, funny" and said he had a love for music. She believed the two had a lot in common and decided to give him a shot. They e-mailed each other several times, until Lynda finally decided to give him her telephone number. They spoke on the phone several times and got to know one another a little better until, finally, Lynda decided it was time for the couple to take the next step. She was always big into family. For her first date with Shore, she put him to the test. He was to meet her at her mother's house for a get-together with her mother, Lynda's three children—twenty-one-year-old Josh and her twenty-year-old twins, Jason and Kristin—and her five-month-old grandson. She figured if he could feel comfortable around her family, he might be all right.

Shore was much better than all right. He appeared to be in his element. He charmed the entire family with his sense of humor and his piano playing. He led the family in sing-alongs and chatted amiably with the kids. He spent lots of time with Lynda's son Josh, talking about their mutual love for true-crime books and true-crime television shows. Josh was in a heavy rock band and enjoyed hearing Tony regale the group with stories of St. Vitus Dance. Lynda beamed as she saw him interact with Josh. *This might be the one,* she thought on that first date, which lasted only one hour.

One date turned into several. Lynda had no qualms about the fact Shore drove a tow truck for a living. She was used to men who had made more of themselves, but she just could not resist Shore's charms. She found him to be "funny, engaging, and charismatic." He was also romantic, cordial, and made her feel as if she were the only woman on the entire planet.

Although Lynda felt good about her relationship with Tony Shore, she felt he was rushing things along too quickly. Within just a few months he began to hint constantly about moving in with her, into her comfortable one-story home, located near, ironically, North Shore High School. Lynda kept begging off because she was not quite ready to make that commitment.

One reason she was not quick to agree to cohabitation was that she came across a sheet of paper that mentioned some type of treatment program. She was not sure what it was exactly, but when she asked Shore about the program, he seemed embarrassed and began to tell her about his sexual assault charges.

Lynda sat horrified as he told her what had happened.

Of course he left out one key element to the charges: the truth.

He told Lynda that the charges were bogus and that he had been falsely accused of raping his daughters. He told her he had been framed by his mother. He also claimed his mother tried to extort money from him and that his mother's behavior stemmed from years of abuse she inflicted on him.

Somehow, Shore convinced Lynda that he was innocent. He even got her to feel sorry for him for being wrongfully accused.

After Shore spun his lies, he gave Lynda an ultimatum: if she did not let him move in with her, he would end their relationship. Lynda agreed and Tony Shore moved his belongings into her home.

The new living arrangements worked out well for the couple. Lynda enjoyed Shore's company and he treated her kids wonderfully. She described him to her friends as "fun" and said that he had "no temper" and did not even use curse words.

Lynda noticed that Shore took a special liking to her oldest son, Josh. They had music and true crime in common. They also both had drug histories. Lynda stated that her son got hooked on drugs in a bad way, but with Shore's help, he was able to kick the habit.

After Josh cleaned up, he spent even more time with Shore. He was truly grateful for his mom's boyfriend's help. According to Lynda, one time the two men were sitting on the couch talking about true-crime books and serial killers. Josh professed his interest in the case of Ted Bundy, the charismatic, handsome, intelligent serial killer who went on a cross-country killing spree during the late 1970s.

Shore wasn't impressed with Bundy. He believed Bundy was sloppy and should not have been caught.

"I know how to commit the perfect crime," he told Josh. "And I can tell you how to get away with it and never get caught."

Josh laughed and punched Shore in the shoulder as if to say, *Yeah, right, Tony. Whatever.*

Shore just smiled at the young man.

Not long after Shore moved in with Lynda, her daughter, Kristin, and her six-month-old grandson moved in with the couple. One of Shore's probation conditions was that he was not allowed to live with children. He conveniently failed to inform Lynda of this fact.

Shore was also not allowed to consume alcohol, but he did. He was also not allowed to live in a home that had a computer, and, of course, Lynda owned one.

One time Lynda came home from work earlier than usual. She usually got home after Shore did. On this particular occasion she walked in on Shore while he was on the computer surfing the Internet, and he seemed startled when she walked into the room. She glanced at the monitor and noticed he was looking at a Web site for missing persons. She found it rather unusual and asked him why he was looking at the site.

"I'm looking for my daughter," he replied.

"Your daughter? What do you mean?" Lynda replied.

"My daughter Amber. I'm looking for her. I think I found her," he said, and pointed at a photo of a young woman. He did not explain himself any further.

Lynda had never seen a photo of either one of his daughters, so she had no idea if the photo was really one of Amber or not. She also failed to ask him why his daughter would be listed as a missing person.

Shore was not allowed to look at or possess any type of pornography. Once again, in Lynda's home, he blatantly violated his probationary condition. This time it was with a giant box of porn that he kept in Lynda's garage. He had all sorts of pornographic magazines, from *Barely Legal, Chic,* and *Hustler* to *Cheri, International,* and *Live XXX.* He had converted Lynda's garage into his own personal jack shack. Of course he was able to keep it away from Lynda, who had no idea what was up.

The relationship between Shore and Lynda continued to blossom—as he kept his secrets from her. Lynda, however, became very disturbed one night while she and Shore were making love. He had mounted Lynda doggy-style, when suddenly he grabbed her by the throat with his hand. Caught up in the moment, Lynda did not break her rhythm and simply swatted his hand away. Instead of backing off, however, he instinctively reached back up with his hand and encircled it around her throat. He began to squeeze extremely hard.

"What the hell are you doing?" Lynda demanded as she dismounted her lover and knocked his hand away again.

Shore started to laugh as he looked at Lynda. Fully naked, he said to her, "It's just a predatory thing. Don't worry. I would never hurt you."

Lynda nervously laughed it off.

After the rather unusual sexual encounter with her lover, Lynda began to see other strange quirks in his behavior. He seemed to have a fixation on penis size. According to Lynda, he seemed overly concerned with having a small penis. She stated that it wasn't just an occasional mention or bemoaning, but rather, he brought it up "often." She stated that he seemed obsessed with his less-than-generous endowment.

Lynda also recalled an unusual incident when she called a plumber over to fix the pipes in the kitchen sink. When she came home, she found Shore curled up in the fetal position in her bedroom closet. He told her he had a terrible headache and needed to block out all the light.

Eventually Lynda started to get fed up with him. She soon learned that he was "immature" and also very "arrogant." She also called him "antagonistic" and stated that he liked to pick fights with her over trivial details. Shore would argue with Lynda over everything they discussed. Sometimes the couple's fights were so bad Lynda would storm out of the house and spend the night at a nearby hotel on I-10. She did this on at least three separate occasions.

Shore got to stay in her house.

With her kids.

With her grandson.

Alone.

When Shore and Lynda fought and she took off, he was just as relentless at getting her back home. He would call her on her cell phone. If she did not answer, Shore would hang up and dial again. He would do this for hours until she picked up.

One time, during one of their fights, Lynda recalled a very unusual situation. She and Shore argued and she stormed off, got into her car, and drove to a nearby 7-Eleven convenience store to put gas in her car so she could make it to the hotel. As she stepped out of her vehicle, the entire world started to spin. She stumbled out of the car and could barely shut her car door. A young man in the parking lot saw Lynda and cautiously approached her.

"Ma'am, are you okay?" he asked her.

When she didn't respond, the man gently grasped her by the arm and asked her again. This time she mumbled something incoherently. The man then asked her where she was staying and Lynda managed to blurt out the name of the hotel where she usually hid away from Shore.

The young man placed Lynda back into her car on the passenger side, took her keys, and jumped into the driver's side. He fired up the car and took off. Luckily for Lynda, the young man was an upstanding citizen and drove her to the hotel. He even checked her in, paid for her room, took her and her baggage to the room, and left her car keys on a table.

She never learned the young man's name.

The following morning she woke up to the sound of her hotel door slightly creaking as it was being opened. As the sun pierced through the crack, she saw a figure enter her room, but was hazy as to who it was. As the figure entered the room, it blocked the light. Lynda was slowly able to make out the face that belonged to the figure. It was Shore.

Lynda had no idea how Tony Shore knew to come to get her, because she had no recollection whatsoever of having spoken to him. She definitely did not remember asking him to come and retrieve her. Shore packed her up and took her home, where she immediately fell back asleep. Lynda slept almost another twenty-four hours before she was able to regain her senses.

CHAPTER 49

Friday, October 24, 2003,
Houston Police Department Headquarters,
Homicide Division—Sixth Floor,
1200 Travis Street,
Houston, Texas.

After receiving the call from Katherine Long indicating that she had received a positive match on the DNA underneath the fingernail clippings of Carmen Estrada, Detective Bob King began to research Tony Shore.

"Found out he had been a telephone repairman. Started looking into his work history. Looked at his residences. Started looking at his vehicles. The state came up with a list of them. One was registered to a shop or a garage and we went and talked to that guy."

When Captain Richard Holland determined it was time to go after Shore, he had King contact ADA Kelly Siegler to assist with a warrant to search Lynda White's house.

In the warrant King declared that Shore was a "possible serial killer" and that "there exists the distinct possibility that the defendant has kept as 'trophies' something from each of his victims, as in perhaps, items of clothing or similar items from the crimes he has committed. Your affiant believes that the defendant may still have in his possession such items from the victims."

The legal wheels had been properly set into motion. Now they needed to find Shore, arrest him, and search his residence.

"It got to the point where Captain Holland said, 'This guy's too big a threat to the public. We can't let him just stay out there. We need to go ahead and get him in,'" King recalled. "I got with Kelly Siegler and drew up a probable cause arrest warrant. He's not actually charged. It's also called a pocket warrant. You lay out your probable cause for arresting him.

"She and I went to the judge in the court where he was on deferred adjudication, so he signed off on that warrant and the search warrant for Lynda White's house. I called back over to Lieutenant Neely, who had headed up the task force since March, and he had Hal Kennedy sitting up on a wrecker storage lot where Shore worked."

Friday, October 24, 2003,
Champion Collision Center,
8747 Daffodil Street,
Houston, Texas.

Houston Police Department patrol officer Robert Farmer had only been on his shift for two hours when he received a call to arrest a man suspected of murder. The suspect was dressed in a black T-shirt with a Mini Cooper logo that said "Let's Motor" on it, tucked into a pair of faded light blue jeans, and he wore a medallion around his neck. He was standing outside Champion Collision Center, at the corner of Daffodil Street and Crossview Drive, smoking a cigarette.

Officer Farmer spotted the man, pulled his squad car within twenty feet of him and stepped out of his vehicle. He approached the man in black and said, "You're under arrest."

The man looked up at the officer, did not say a word, and then continued to smoke his cigarette.

"Put your hands behind your back, sir," the officer told the suspect. The man complied without saying a word.

Officer Farmer reached in to cuff the suspect's wrists together when he noticed that the suspect still had the burning cigarette in his hand. "Sir, please drop that cigarette," he ordered the suspect.

The man defiantly held on to the cigarette.

Officer Farmer reached for his flashlight and "cracked him on the knuckles" so he would finally drop it. "After that," Farmer later recalled, "there was no further resistance."

Much later, Tony Shore's father was stunned by the news.

"I was very surprised. Got a couple of calls from Lynda White. He brought Lynda over once. She seemed really nice. Really nice. She was really torn up about this," Rob Shore sympathized. "It was kind of a sad situation. Tony was calling her a lot and she didn't know what to do. My take on it was 'Don't stay in contact with him.'"

Tony's first wife, Gina, was just as taken aback.

"It just blew me away. Especially since the way I first heard about it was from Amber on the answering machine. I said, 'Yeah, that's so funny. Ha! Ha!'" She thought it was a vicious prank, even for her daughter.

Eventually Gina went home and turned on the television.

"I heard it on the news and I screamed," she recalled. "I was astounded. It was such a shock. And then the phone starts ringing. Media. Everybody thinks you know something, but you don't. I said, 'I don't know anything. I'm just as surprised as anyone else.' Shit, the wife [Lynda White—girlfriend, actually] he was living with had no clue. Nobody had a clue."

Gina was just as confused as the media was about what Shore had been charged with. She would ask reporters why they thought he did it and they would say they didn't know either.

"I think in the very, very beginning of everything, I wondered, 'Is it something I did? Is it my fault?'" Gina expressed a sense of guilt, a trait often seen with surviving family members of suicide victims. She finally came to the conclusion that it was all Shore's choice and that it had nothing to do with her or anything she did.

"You have to accept responsibility for your own deeds," Gina concluded. "When you're a little bitty kid and people dominate your life, then you can blame somebody. But once you're an adult, and you go out and make these decisions, you really can't blame [someone else], unless you have 'Stockholm syndrome,'" Gina said, referring to the condition wherein a captive individual eventually acquiesces to the seemingly untenable demands of their captor, such as in the Patty Hearst kidnapping by the Symbionese Liberation Army. "Or you're an Iraqi prisoner or something. That might tend to warp ya.

"But he didn't have such a terribly awful childhood." As far as the alleged abuse Tony Shore supposedly received at his father's hand, Gina stated, "I don't even remember him talking about his father being violent like that. His mom, on the other hand, she has the raging Italian temper!" But Gina believed Dea reserved her punishments for Shore's sister. "I think she used more physicality with Regina. I remember the family talked about a couple of physical contacts when Regina was a teenager. But, I never heard anything about Tony except that he was a free spirit up there, that he was in a band, Foxfire, and that he wasn't going to school."

According to Gina Worley Shore, "Dea had one rule: 'Do not go into my closet.' It's like everything that's holy to her she kept in her closet. She worked like sixteen hours a day as a waitress at Denny's."

Gina recalled when Tony got in trouble with his mother. "She left Tony to take care of Regina and Laurel. I think it was his fifteenth birthday [and] he had a really wild party, and there were people in her closet making out. That was it. She threw him out."

When asked what was so important in Dea Shore's closet, Gina Worley Shore stated, "She was a costumer. She did alterations and costumes and she did portfolios on the side with models, so most of it was clothes that she had sewn and costumes and the boas and things like that." Understandably, Dea Shore did not want her hard work to be soiled or tainted in any way. "She'd go in there and smell the smoke in the fabric, which would ruin them. She told Tony, 'That's the one thing I asked you not to do. I can't handle it, Tony. I have to work. If you can't give me that one courtesy, then you have to move your stuff out.'"

Gina added, "Dea was working sixteen to eighteen hours a day. One day she got a box of chocolate-covered cherries from someone. It was the one treasure that she was looking forward to after working so hard. Waitresses work very hard. She was coming home looking forward to eating this box of chocolate-covered cherries, but someone had eaten the whole box. Man, she was so mad. She wanted to know who it was. Each person blamed the other. Even to this day I've asked about that and I still

don't know who ate the chocolate-covered cherries." She
does have her suspicions, though. "I think it's probably
Laurel." She laughed.

Gina also wondered if an automobile accident might
have triggered something in her ex-husband.

"He and a friend were driving down some dark country road, and he went to pass someone, but the car
wouldn't let them pass, nor would it let them back in the
lane and they had a head-on collision with a truck," Gina
recalled. "His friend got a cut across the forehead. Tony
shattered all of his fingers. Shattered his jaw. The ignition went up through his spinal cord. I think he was in
the hospital for almost a year. He has little dots where
the pins were."

According to Gina, the doctors told Shore that he
would never play piano again. "But he got one of those
handballs and he worked through it himself. He didn't
have enough money to pay the hospital bills. Rob, the
trombone player (from Foxfire), played a platinum
trombone. Tony sold it so he could pay his bills. Needless to say, that didn't go over too good with Rob."

Gina continued saying that Shore "couldn't even pay
the anesthesiologist when he had his pins taken out, so
he had them taken out without any anesthetic."

Gina later saw a picture of the car. "I'm surprised he
even survived. The front of the car was all the way in the
backseat. It looked like a little car."

CHAPTER 50

Lynda White's Residence,
300 block of Freeport Street,
Houston, Texas.

Lynda White sat in her living room holding her grandson, enjoying some alone time with her little bundle of joy. She was a bit concerned, however, because she had not heard from Tony Shore and was beginning to wonder when he would show up.

Her silent reverie was loudly interrupted with a loud bang on her front door. She jumped at the noise and then realized there were people standing outside. She walked briskly to the front door and opened it up. Standing in front of her was Detective Bob King. She smiled until she looked over his shoulder and saw what appeared to be the entire Houston Police Department on her front doorstep.

"While they were talking to him, I was out with D. D. Shirley at Lynda White's house," King recalled. "Knocked on the door. She answers the door. Broke the news to her. There were seventeen of us. Different uniforms. Plainclothes guys. So we're out there while most of the interrogation is going on."

Lynda was scared to death. She had no idea what was going on. She did watch the officers, in addition to searching her entire house and garage, confiscate her personal computer.

After the arrest the news media would not leave Lynda White alone. She said that they literally camped out on her doorstep.

Lynda was also distraught when she lost several of what she thought were close friends because of the ordeal.

"They shunned me."

CHAPTER 51

Bob King felt a sense of relief. Nearly ten years of holding on to the Diana Rebollar case file, and staring at the photograph of her face every day as he sat down to work, took its toll on him. With Tony Shore's confession in hand, however, he finally began to relax—just a bit.

King worked in a cubicle alongside Boyd Smith, the sixty-one-year-old veteran homicide investigator who had been involved in the Tony Shore case with the Laurie Tremblay murder. Of course, neither King nor Smith knew Shore was involved in their respective cases until Shore opened up the floodgates. Both officers seemed incredibly relieved to have possibly closed the long-dormant murders.

Detective King returned to his cubicle after a late lunch. He stopped cold in his tracks, however, when he saw several of his fellow officers standing over something near his desk. He noticed two paramedics dressed in white and brandishing a banged-up stretcher. King briskly moved toward the commotion.

"What the hell is going on?" he asked one of the other officers standing nearby.

"Smith," the officer replied.

"What about him?" King shot back.

"He's got a fucking hole in his head." The officer shook his own head as he responded.

"What?" King asked incredulously.

King brushed past the other detectives until he could see for himself. There he was. Boyd Smith's near-dead body lay crumpled on the floor near King's desk, blood splattered everywhere. Smith's head appeared to still be gushing blood. Somehow, miraculously, Smith was still breathing. The paramedics worked furiously to keep him alive and get him transported to Ben Taub Hospital, which was only six miles away.

There was confusion in the department as to whether the wound was self-inflicted or if Smith had been attacked by another officer and shot in the head. Either way, the paramedics hustled his body onto the gurney and hoisted him out of the Homicide Division. They slowly descended in the elevator to the lobby, headed out the doors, and inserted him into a waiting ambulance, which rushed him to the hospital.

It would be several hours before Bob King and the rest of the Houston Police Department Homicide Division detectives heard the status of their fallen comrade. As they waited on edge, the story began to clear itself up. Apparently, Smith had not been attacked, but had instead taken his own service gun, a .45-caliber Colt Model 1911 and placed it to his head and pulled the trigger. It appeared to be a suicide attempt.

* * *

Approximately three hours later the worst possible news was delivered. Boyd Smith did not survive. He died of a self-inflicted gunshot to the head. Official cause of death was ruled a suicide.

Needless to say, the detectives were devastated. Smith was considered to be one of the most well-liked and fun-loving officers in the whole of the Houston Police Department.

Acting police chief Joe Breshears, who was giving a press conference on the closing of the HPD toxicology lab, stated that Smith was "a man dedicated to his city. It's a tremendous loss to the police department. He was a good man. He was a great man. He will be missed."

The sentiment was echoed repeatedly, to the man, about their esteemed colleague. Retired Homicide detective Bobby Adams declared that Smith was "a star for the Homicide Division." Adams also noted that "when he and his partner were on a scene, you knew it was going to be done right. And I never recall him ever being asked to do something that he didn't do absolutely correctly, and with a good attitude."

Adams was shocked that his friend may have committed suicide. "He always had a smile on his face," the retired detective fondly recalled. Adams had even spoken with Smith one week earlier at a retirement party for another detective. "He was smiling. He looked good. He looked happy."

Several of the officers commented on his work on several high-profile cases. He worked on the case of Coral Eugene Watts, the country's most prolific serial killer, who was almost set free to roam the streets of Texas due to a legal technicality that would allow him to be released despite killing at least twelve women. He also was one of the detectives who questioned Andrea Yates, the Clear Lake housewife who killed her five children by drowning them, one by one, in her bathtub. In addition, Smith had worked on the possible serial killing case of Henry Lee Lucas and Ottis Toole.

Smith was noted for his tenacity. He had a reputation as a strong man who never gave up on a case. One such instance was the rape and murder of Mary Ann Castille, a twenty-year-old girl murdered back in 1982. Smith worked the case the entire time, all the way through 1999 when a DNA hit came back and led the way to Castille's killer, Michael Brashar. The Castille case had been featured on the highly respected crime-fighting television program *America's Most Wanted.* Indeed, the capture of Brashar was referred to by producers of that show as "one of the most stunning moments in the history" of the program. John Walsh, show creator and TV host, chipped in that Smith was "a dear friend of *America's Most Wanted,* and one of the most dedicated cops I've ever known."

One of the program's producers, Cindy Anderson, was shocked by the news of Smith's suicide. She had spoken with him on Tuesday, one day before his death, about the fact that *America's Most Wanted* was airing an updated episode of the Castille case on the upcoming Saturday. She stated that Smith sounded "ebullient and excited." She also stated that he was in "very happy spirits yesterday, very happy. This is something this guy had worked so hard on." Anderson seemed shocked at the news. "He was excited, he was feeling good. Then we got [to] talking about Michael Brashar's trial. He said, 'Maybe now, someday, I can retire.'"

Boyd Smith's retirement was not that far off. Four years to be exact. Smith had mentioned that one of his kids was about to start college, so he wanted to continue working. That was another big reason why so many of his coworkers were stunned by his death.

Furthermore, Smith was ecstatic about finding the killer in another long-term case he had been involved in—Laurie Tremblay's murder. Smith had recently been taken off duty after having undergone minor surgery. Despite not having yet been cleared to return to work, Smith came in every day during the week to help out on the Tony Shore case.

"That's the kind of policeman Boyd was," declared Harris County district attorney Chuck Rosenthal. "That's the kind of man he was."

Warren Diepraam, an ADA under Rosenthal, agreed. "He was a good guy who always made the extra effort to help out."

The mood around the department had changed by Thursday. In addition to the depressing air in the room, there was also an issue of consternation. Apparently, some people in the department did not believe that Smith had killed himself. Instead, they believed he may have been the unfortunate recipient of a weapons malfunction. Indeed, only a few days prior to Smith's death, another detective's Glock was set off when the officer placed the holstered gun on a hook on a bathroom door in the men's restroom.

Allegedly, officers had had problems with the model gun Smith carried. The Colt models are cocked and ready to go so the officers can have a fast reaction time, if necessary. They use a thumb release that locks the trigger; however, the thumb release is not always reliable. The releases occasionally deploy accidentally and cause a misfire. Over the years various accidents had occurred in HPD, including one officer who shot himself in the foot and another who shot his horse.

In addition, one of the local television news stations

reported that Smith had been in an argument with another detective right before he was shot. All of the other officers in the department categorically denied the station's claims.

On Friday, October 31, the Harris County Medical Examiner's Office officially declared that Larry Boyd Smith had committed suicide via a gunshot to the head. Police department chaplain Edwin Davis expressed concern that some of Smith's fellow detectives were not going to buy the determination. "There's going to be an overwhelming number of people very shocked and in disbelief about it. I think you're going to have some who are not going to believe the ruling."

Davis spoke the following day at Smith's funeral. He spoke of how the death had been hard on Smith's coworkers. "I'd say the mood is somber. Everybody is just stunned. We're just trying to make some sense of it. To have something like this tragedy occur at the workplace, it's just been very devastating."

As some of Smith's friends and coworkers went over the details of his life, they started to see a pattern of loss. He and his wife were divorced just two years earlier. Soon thereafter, his mother passed away. In addition, all four of his adult children had flown the coop and set off on their own. And, like a bad country song, his dog died two weeks earlier.

"Might not sound like a big deal," stated one of Smith's coworkers, "but when he got home at night, that was his only companion."

At Smith's funeral the next day, there were people from all stripes of life in attendance: coworkers, friends, family, families of crime victims, defense lawyers, prosecutors, judges, and even the waitresses from his favorite restaurant.

HPD Homicide captain Richard Holland likened

Smith to Lieutenant Columbo, the seemingly bumbling
'70s television detective played by actor Peter Falk, who
always got his man through sheer persistence and tenacity. Holland said Smith was better than Columbo, who
always had one last surprise question for a suspect.

Retired HPD police officer Jim Boy summed up his
friend nicely: "Every investigation that man did was for
the family, it was for justice, it was honorable the way he
did business. He was a good man and a good detective."

Two-and-a-half months after Boyd Smith's ruled suicide, his toxicological reports came back with a record
of a drug in his system known as Citalopram, more commonly known as Celexa, which is used in the treatment
of depression.

In addition to Smith's suicide during the month of
October, Harris County ADA Kelly Siegler informed the
media that the district attorney's office would pursue the
death penalty for Tony Shore.

CHAPTER 52

Friday, November 14, 2003.

Tony Shore wrote a note "To Whom This May Concern" asking whoever found the note to "notify my wife: Lynda White that Tony would no longer be a burden to her." He bequeathed all of his belongings to his stepson Josh.

The note appeared to be a suicide note. Shore added, "Hope to see you all again on the other side."

He ended with a dramatic flourish: "I'm not afraid to die! Only afraid to live. Dieing [*sic*] is easy."

He signed off with his name and also as "Lynda's Tony."

Tony Shore then proceeded to swallow twenty-five sleeping pills, the specific type of which no one was sure. Shore was rushed to a hospital to be treated for the overdose.

He did not die.

CHAPTER 53

Friday, February 6, 2004,
300 block of Freeport Street,
Houston, Texas.

Nearly four months later, Lynda White opened up a letter addressed from the Harris County Jail. Obviously, it was from Tony Shore. She had no idea what to expect.

She was immediately taken aback by the large all-caps exclamation "I LOVE YOU LYNDA!" that adorned the top of the long letter. Before she could even begin to read the tome, she noticed notes running up and down the sides of the page that were vertical and sideways. The largest said, "YOU ARE BEAUTIFUL! YOU ARE MY WIFE! WE WILL BE TOGETHER AGAIN . . . SOON! I LOVE YOU!"

Lynda was now sufficiently mortified.

She began to read Shore's letter.

After starting off proclaiming his love to her yet again, Shore commanded his "wife" that she "must destroy this 1st page after you read it." His words sounded like the ramblings of a paranoid schizophrenic who was planning a serious, all-out, balls-to-the-wall, bloodletting jailbreak.

"When I go, it will be do or die . . . a one shot deal," he declared. "In the event I cannot snatch you within the first twenty-four hours, then I will of course bide time to insure your safety and well being."

Tony Shore, ever the gallant white knight.

He warned Lynda that as soon as he escaped, she would be put under surveillance. But he was determined to see his damsel in distress.

"Once we are together again," Shore assured, "and I have you in my custody, my love, I can promise your safety and guarantee your safe return at your discretion."

Again, to insure her safety, he commanded she burn the letter. The second page had another side-page message, which read, "Burn this Lynda . . . Read it . . . Memorize it if you want BUT DO <u>BURN</u> IT!"

Shore indicated that he might be able to escape as early as that April.

He wanted her to be ready at a moment's notice and to even pack her bags. "There will be no time for any last minute arrangement. So any evidence must be destroyed in advance to insure you will be completely free from suspicion or harm."

He ordered her to "think ahead" and to "be ready at all times." He instructed her that the best way to be prepared would be to already have any necessary medications on her person, expenses, arrangements for food, shelter, transportation, and identification.

Shore also promised Lynda "love and ecstasy, adoration and devotion beyond your wildest dreams," and that he would satisfy her "every fantasy."

In case there was any doubt about his sincerity, Shore closed with "I'm going to make it happen or die trying. There is a way, though it will by no means be easy or safe for me to get out. I will make this happen. I promise!"

Apparently, the offer was not quite good enough for

Lynda to accept. Instead, she picked up the phone and contacted Detective Bob King.

Later that evening, Tony Shore's jail cell was searched extensively for any tools, notes, or plans for an escape. A thorough search turned up nothing. He was kept under closer scrutiny from that point on.

CHAPTER 54

Saturday, March 6, 2004,
Houston Police Department,
Digital Forensic Lab,
Houston, Texas.

Nearly half a year after Tony Shore's arrest and the subsequent confiscation of his personal home computer, Officer J. T. Smith, of the Houston Police Department Digital Forensic Lab, got his hands on it. The twenty-seven-year veteran Smith's job was to scan suspects' computers to see if the police could locate any evidence to use in the case against them. Smith used a program known as In Case, which helped detect every bit of computer usage by a suspect, including files that might have been deleted by the user. Smith, who had been in the Digital Forensic Division for three years, had received all of the necessary training and certifications to conduct a thorough investigation.

What he found was quite compelling—hundreds of snapshots of Web sites that Shore had visited on Lynda White's computer. A large portion was dedicated to straight sex between a man and a woman. Some of those sites included Lickable Teens, Pregnant Perversion, and Sexy School Girl. Interestingly, Shore visited as many gay male porn sites as he did heterosexual porn sites. Some of these he visited were Hot Male Butt Sex, Well Hung Studs, and Asian Twinks. There were also a few random lesbian-oriented sites, bondage sites, Asian female sites, and legal teen female sites. Shore's sexual interest ran the gamut from bondage and discipline to golden showers to fisting and everything else under the sun.

Shore also visited several child porn sites—almost as many as he had of the straight sex sites and gay male sex sites. The vast majority of the teen and preteen porn sites he visited focused on boys. The sites were extreme in nature and contained full-frontal nudity, graphic sex between minors, and graphic sex between minors and adults. Some of the sites he visited were Boys Factory, Nudeboys World, and Lolita Slumber Party.

Officer Smith found something else of importance on the computer used by Tony Shore. He was able to access Shore's search moves on the missing persons' Web site that he had been surfing when Lynda White walked in on him. Smith confirmed that Shore surfed the site and that he looked up the names of Dana Sanchez, Maria del Carmen Estrada, and Diana Rebollar.

Perhaps even more disturbing was that he also looked up two more names: Collette Williams and Gloria Gonzales.

CHAPTER 55

Harris County assistant district attorney Kelly Siegler was coming off a hot streak. Her recent prosecution of Susan Wright, the former stripper who stabbed her husband 193 times and then pitifully buried his body in their backyard, had garnered her national media attention. The attractive attorney drew the majority of the attention when she faithfully re-created the Wright murder scene by actually bringing the Wrights' bed into the courtroom, straddling her co-counsel, ADA Paul Doyle, and acting as if she were stabbing the tied-down man nearly two hundred times. It did not hurt her case that the district attorney also had a nice figure. Siegler's performance was bandied about on every twenty-four-hour cable news show and "yellivision" screamfest.

Siegler was born and raised in Blessing, Texas, located in Matagorda County, less than one hundred miles southwest of Houston. Blessing, a town of only nine hundred residents, was originally going to be called "Thank God"; however, the United States Post Office shot that name down.

According to Siegler, Blessing has "one blinking light,

not even a red light. You have to go to the Post Office
to get your mail. No Dairy Queen. People say, 'What's
your address?' It's on the first street off the highway.
'Yeah, well what's your house number?' I go, 'No, no. We
don't go by house addresses.'

"UPS used to stop by my daddy's barbershop and ask,
'Where does so and so live?' It used to be, until a few
years ago, that he would dial four numbers and call
someone and tell him to come pick up his package.
That's where your mail was that didn't make it to the
Post Office."

Siegler graduated from Tidehaven High School,
which was the consolidated high school for all the small
towns in that area. The tiny AA school was located in the
middle of a cotton field.

Like many Texas youth during that time period,
Siegler was actively involved in sports and played volley-
ball and basketball.

"It was a great way to grow up. I wish more kids would
grow up that way."

Siegler also excelled academically. "I was valedictorian. I was a geek."

Siegler's family tended to be at the center of Blessing's
comings and goings. Specifically, her father's business,
Billy's Barber Shop, which she described as "half barbershop and half liquor store. Funny story. TABC [Texas Alcohol and Beverage Commission] requires that there is
a wall separating the two businesses. And Daddy was like,
'Wait a minute. There's an air-conditioning window unit
that cools both places. I can't put a wall up. So Daddy
put chicken wire up so the air could still go across it, but
he wasn't violating the TABC rule."

Billy's Barber Shop became a veritable library of
knowledge for Siegler on how to read people, how to

understand basic human interaction, and—best of all—how to spin a good yarn. "You live in a little town. You have to get along with everybody or you're gonna have problems. And I think we're friendlier than people who grew up in the city because you know everybody, everybody knows you. There are no secrets. You do something stupid on Friday night, your mom and dad know the next day."

The cast of characters that traipsed in and out of her daddy's barbershop had a great impact on Siegler's personality. "You know, when you're little, growing up, you just think everybody's like that. Everybody's just kind of funny or whatever. Now, when I go home and I'm sitting there drinking beer at Daddy's barbershop and everybody's coming by and they say, 'Hey, Kelly's home. Let's go visit.' We sit out there listening to country music, of course, drinking beer, and I just go, 'Man!' You know, you go home and see it, it looks a little different than growing up.

"It was always wonderful. They were all friendly and happy. Easygoing. A lot more easygoing than we are."

After she graduated valedictorian at Tidehaven, Siegler applied for admission to the University of Texas (UT) and was readily accepted.

"Looking back, that wasn't a good idea," she wistfully recalled. "Culture shock.

"I wanted to get out. I wanted to be different 'cause very few went to college, but if they did, they went to Blinn [Junior College] or maybe they went to A and M [Texas A&M University], but I wanted to go to UT, so I went to UT."

But Siegler was none too thrilled with UT. "I hated it and got out in three years." She did not quit; she earned her degree and graduated in three years.

While she was there, she had intentions of majoring in international business. "I was gonna go off and be a lawyer and travel the whole world. It was another bad idea, but I was gonna get out of that damn school in three years and I wasn't gonna change my major. Learn about tariffs and quotas and all that miserably boring stuff."

Siegler did decide, however, to go to law school. She attended South Texas College of Law, in Houston. "I could have gone to a couple of law schools," Siegler recalled, "but I picked South Texas because I could live with my aunt and I didn't want it to be three more years of misery like UT was."

Siegler moved in with her father's sister and focused on her classes during the first year. Her second year, she landed a job at a civil law firm. She stated that South Texas was a clearly divided school between the students who went to school on "daddy's dime" and those who had to work to pay their way through school. Siegler fell into the latter category.

"South Texas, back then, was more of a 'you could go to school around the job if you needed to make the money to be able to go to school' school." So, to make the money, she worked at a civil firm. "It was horribly boring. And that's when I realized even more, international business and this civil law stuff was just bullshit. I didn't know how I was going to do this the rest of my life."

Siegler realized she needed something more. "Around the middle of my second year, a friend of mine, who interned here [at the Harris County District Attorney's Office], needed to make more money and said, 'Kelly, I'm gonna quit my job. Why don't you go interview for a job as an intern at the DA's office in the Family Criminal Law Division, Domestic Violence.' So I came over as an intern [during her third year in law school], got the job, and never left."

Siegler was not thrilled with law school; however, she did fall in love with her criminal law courses while at South Texas.

"They were my favorite classes, which I thought probably everybody thought. It wasn't like I was thinking going in I was going to be a prosecutor, I was going to be a criminal lawyer. I was going to be the international business lawyer."

Her experience at the civil law firm convinced her that she needed to try something different. "The civil firm I worked at, they were very nice, but I'd sit there and try not to fall asleep all day when there were chores and assignments. I just couldn't wait to get out."

Once Siegler landed the intern position at the Harris County District Attorney's Office, she knew she had struck personal nirvana. "The days just fly by, even now, almost twenty years now. Every single day just flies by. You're doing something different and fun. Talking to people every day, all day.

"You research, get what you need. But you're talking to people all day. Defendants, lawyers, witnesses, cops. It's pretty much you just bullshit all day long," she added with a laugh.

Siegler's first responsibility as an intern was to interview abused spouses or battered girlfriends and convince them not to drop charges. "And I was in charge of protective orders, which are like restraining orders for domestic violence cases."

Siegler spent one year as an intern. She then interviewed for a precommit job. She passed the State of Texas Bar Exam and became an assistant district attorney the day after she received her results.

"You start out in Misdemeanor when you're new here. And then you progress up in Misdemeanor court, starting with possession of marijuana cases, DWI, 'no test' cases, to the more serious misdemeanors. Then you go up to Felony court for a little while doing the less serious felonies. Then you're a Misdemeanor supervisor. A Misdemeanor chief supervisor, supervising the brand-new people. Then you go back up to Felony and progress up until you make chief of a Felony court. The longer you're here, the more serious cases you handle, and the more people you supervise," Siegler explained.

"When you make Felony II, there are three people to a court. When you make Felony II, you start handling murder cases. Of course there are always the bar murders and the gang murders and the murders with problems. And rape cases. So, I think when I made Felony II, I was already handling murders and aggravated robberies and aggravated sexual assault cases, and that was probably in 1989."

Kelly Siegler enthusiastically recalled her first murder case. "Guy's name was Terry Gilpin. He murdered a man because they had a sexual relationship and the man was gonna disclose that they had the sexual relationship and he didn't want people to think he was gay. So, he just beat him to death. Blood spatter case. My first dealings with blood spatter. And the cool thing was that they found a roll of film stuck under the bushes in the backyard of the dead man's house. We developed that film and it's all the pictures of them having sex where my defendant has a kind of dog collar around his neck and a leash and all that kind of stuff. So, you really don't forget those pictures. And the defendant was a beautiful man, a gorgeous guy."

Siegler added that the district attorney's office also sought the death penalty against Gilpin's son, Terry Gilpin Jr., in 2004.

Siegler was modest when it came to her record as a successful prosecutor. Her 95 percent success rate had been bandied about in the newspapers around the time of the Susan Wright case.

"You know, I don't know where that number came from, the ninety-five percent," Siegler said. "But think about this—by the time you get to Felony, you're supposed to win all of them. So, ninety-five percent really ain't that great. Everybody should have that in Felony. Jeez!"

Eventually Siegler made her way up the DA food chain until she hit her ultimate goal—Serious Offenders. She preferred to work the cold cases, ones that had gone unsolved for a number of years. By the time Tony Shore's death penalty was to be tried, Kelly Siegler had worked almost fourteen cold cases, with four of those being death penalty cases.

"I guess cold cases are just different and more challenging because they're old and they got old because people before then wouldn't take the charges, wouldn't file the charges. Or, there wasn't enough to file the charges. To sit down with these officers, which I did, you go through all those boxes. But you sit down with an offense report and you read it, and the whole time you're reading it, you're thinking, 'Okay now, would this be better today? How can we tweak that or make another run at this witness or what played out with that?'

"And a lot of the cold cases, believe it or not, in the real world, have nothing to do with DNA. It's just other things that all the sudden make it better," Siegler surmised. "Here's the question with a cold case. It's not always that they're a whole lot better, but it's that you read it and you know in your heart that he did it. And what are you gonna do? Let him get a way with it or give it a shot?

"You have to ask yourself, 'Is it good enough to prosecute, because you've got one shot, or are you getting too cocky?' Making sure you've got the best information before going forward. But that's the best job."

Kelly Siegler transitioned to cold cases in 2001. She had been a Felony chief for seven years.

"My mom passed away and an opening came up in Special Crimes in the Major Offender Division, which is the division that works more closely with the police officers on more difficult cases. If a murder happens in Harris County, and it's a regular ol' murder and they know who did it right away, they just file the charges through our intake division. If it's one that's more complicated, more problems, it takes longer to file the charges. . . . They get advice from Special Crimes in Major Offenders. So I went there in '99, started doing that work and that's the greatest job in the world."

She has become best-known for the Susan Wright murder case. Even then, she begs off excessive platitudes for her work. "That was a slam-dunk case. That was just more about the sentence."

Kelly Siegler practically wore both cop and lawyer hats on the Tony Shore case. Her involvement began with an e-mail from Captain Richard Holland. "It said, 'Kelly, we have a team together of HPD guys, county guys, and cold case guys, Roger [Wedgeworth] and Harry [Fikaris], and we want you to be our go-to prosecutor. Would you be willing to do that?' So, I'm like, 'Heck, yeah, but let me go and make sure it's okay with my boss, Chuck Rosenthal.' Chuck says, 'Sure, y'all can have Kelly.' So I go over there and meet with the task force.

"At that time, understand, this case was not the whale it turned out to be," Siegler clarified. (A whale in legal parlance usually refers to a bloated case that is easy to prosecute.) "This case was Bob King working on it for ten years, who finally got all these players involved, and, at times, there were many other suspects. They went through a lot of aggravation on this case."

Siegler continued, "It was all this, 'We ain't got shit, but we think it's Anthony Shore. Come over and let's strategize and come up with a plan.' So I went over there with fifteen of the best cops you'll ever meet. You talk about the A Team; man, it was great. Hal Kennedy, Todd Miller, Allen Brown, Swaim. Swaim is unbelievable."

Siegler continued, "We had this group meeting and we have a plan. I remember the Friday the plan started. I typed the first warrant when we got the CODIS hit that led to one case. We knew it led to the one and he was gonna be put through the rest, but he didn't know, Anthony Shore didn't know, no one knew how many we thought he was good for."

Siegler typed up the warrant herself, then waited. "So we're all sitting around all day and waiting to hear and wondering, 'Is he gonna talk, is he gonna talk, is he gonna talk?' It's going on five o'clock, eight o'clock, nine o'clock. All the guys are talking to him. It was just a very strange day. Now people say, 'Goddamn, Anthony Shore. Who couldn't try that?'" Siegler, however, understood how much work went on behind the scenes.

Terese Buess would be Siegler's co-counsel and second chair on the case. Siegler was pleased, because she knew the prosecutor was a stickler for details.

"Terese got involved in the case after it became a whale because it landed in her court. We have a rule around here that death penalty cases require two prosecutors," Siegler acknowledged. "So, it lands in her court and she becomes the second chair. In the beginning it was all about strategy and planning and luck with those guys and that's why, I think, I was good friends with them before, through other cases, but I would do anything for those guys and they would for me, because we all know each other so well and about getting the job done.

"But it all turned out the way it turned out because Richard Holland and John Swaim and Bob King and Todd [Miller] and Allen [Brown] said, 'We're gonna figure this out.'"

Siegler also spoke about luck. "Another kind of corny thing that I believe is that when you work on a case and you have the courage to file it or work it up, you wouldn't believe what ends up happening. They say in Major Offenders, 'Goddamn Kelly's luck' and the cops say the 'black-witch touch' or the 'voodoo touch,' or whatever you want to call it, but, I swear, if you file 'em, all the sudden these wonderful things happen that make it better every time. Some new witness will pop up or DNA or some little thing will come along. I swear. I swear it happens."

It happened in the Shore case, according to Siegler, during the John Swaim interrogation. "When he [Shore] tells [Miller], 'Get me some cigarettes and send Swaim back in here.' And John Swaim went back in, I think it was one in the morning, and he just started talking."

As far as Siegler's actions on the day of Shore's arrest, she was a very busy woman. She sent Hal Kennedy out to a Public Storage facility, where Shore kept even more porno magazines. She then got together with Bob King around 11:00 A.M. to discuss the search warrant, since he was the affiant, or the person who makes an affidavit.

"We did something kind of cool on that," Siegler recalled. "We did an Exhibit A, which was a picture of the ligature. And then Exhibit B was the picture of another ligature, to help the judge see that this was kind of odd and coincidental, to get him to sign the warrant. I thought that was kind of neat.

"After that, it was just a question of 'can we keep all this stuff straight' because it was just coming in like an avalanche. Evidence. The case just kept getting more beautiful and more beautiful. Once the good luck happened, it just kept on happening. It never stopped."

Kelly Siegler and Terese Buess gave themselves two months to prepare for Tony Shore's death penalty case. "Anthony Shore was really four death penalty cases, because every one of those was a capital. People say it was a whale, and it was a whale, but there was a lot of shit we had to keep straight and also think about not turning off the jury with overkill."

Siegler and Buess worked well together. "It was a very, very good team," Siegler recalled. "Terese is very organized and methodical. A lot of times on death penalty cases you're not so sure your partner is doing their part thoroughly enough. Not a problem with this case. She's anal, just like I'm anal. But the only thing she said she really wanted to do was Selma Janske, the rape victim."

As far as how the two women coordinated their preparation, Siegler said, "Whenever she got ready with her final plan and I got ready with my final plan, we ran it by each other. We talk vaguely about who's gonna go first or second, how much time we're each going to talk and the points we want to touch on, but we don't ever do like a dry run in front of each other."

Siegler explained how she has a unique reverse psychological method of picking a jury. "We didn't want the jury to have any idea at what they were looking at, because we didn't want them to come in with high expectations of the evidence. This is typically how I do cold cases because you *want* a jury sitting there saying, 'That poor girl ain't got shit.' Then, when they hear the evidence, they're pleasantly surprised.

"Even in the opening statement, don't let on to how much evidence you have and show your hand too early."

Part V

THE STATE OF TEXAS
v.
ANTHONY ALLEN SHORE

The ego is willing but the machine cannot go on.
                                        —Will Durant

CHAPTER 56

Monday, October 18, 2004,
Harris County Courthouse,
1201 Franklin Street,
Courtroom #337,
Houston, Texas.

Kelly Siegler and Terese Buess were ready to do battle. After all the preliminaries were dealt with, voir dire, indictments, and more paper shuffling, there was nothing left to do but face the jury and lay out the evidence.

Assistant District Attorney Siegler was given the floor for opening arguments. The seasoned trial lawyer gave out the background on Maria del Carmen Estrada; how she came to the United States from Mexico as an illegal immigrant to make a better life for herself; how she worked extremely hard to achieve that goal; how she met her untimely demise at the hands of Anthony Allen Shore.

Siegler talked about Shore's weapon of choice, a tourniquet. She spoke of the intimacy of killing someone with a tourniquet.

Siegler let the jury know that there was plenty of evidence recovered at the murder scene to implicate and convict Tony Shore. She also spoke of the problems with the Houston Police Department Crime Lab and how officers used Orchid Cellmark for DNA testing and got a match on Shore.

Siegler concluded by saying that the jury would hear the actual confession to the murder from Tony Shore's own mouth, on tape.

Next up was defense lawyer Gerald Bourque. He opened up with an interesting salvo.

"The evidence in this case is going to show you that I am thankful that the Houston Police Department arrested him. The evidence is going to show that I am thankful he is off the streets. 'The evidence in this case is going to show you that I cannot live in the free society that you live in and my lawyers live in. The evidence in this case is going to show you that I'm guilty.'"

Siegler objected, "Judge, he's arguing as if he's testifying as if he's the defendant."

"Rephrase your argument," ordered Judge Caprice Cosper.

"The evidence in this case," Bourque started over, "is going to show that Carmen is how I knew her. The evidence in this case is going to show that Carmen Estrada got into my car. . . ."

Siegler interjected, "Judge, I object to him arguing as if he were the defendant, as if the defendant was going to testify."

"Mr. Bourque, phrase in terms of third person, please?" Judge Cosper asked.

"Yes, Your Honor," Bourque sheepishly agreed.

Bourque went on to paint the picture that Tony Shore and Carmen Estrada had a thing and that he did not kidnap her and that her murder should not count as a capital crime. The defense strategy was simply to prevent their client from getting the needle.

"The evidence in this case is going to show that Anthony Allen Shore has done some monstrous, maniacal things in his lifetime. The evidence is going to show you those things, but oddly enough the evidence is going to also show you in some twist he's not maniacal and he's not a monster.

"The evidence is going to show that he's not stupid. The evidence is going to show that he's not insane. The evidence is going to show you he's not crazy. The evidence is going to show you how he's not much different than we are in just a bizarre way."

Bourque concluded his opening by saying, "If they don't prove capital murder, you cannot convict of capital murder."

CHAPTER 57

Wednesday, October 20, 2004,
Harris County District Court,
201 Franklin Street,
Courtroom #337,
Houston, Texas.

All in all, the state called nineteen witnesses during the trial phase, including Maria del Carmen Estrada's father, boyfriend, and friend. They also called in Tony Shore's second wife, Amy Lynch Shore, as well as Detectives John Swaim and Bob King.

Kelly Siegler felt great about her next witness.

"The state calls Katherine Long."

"Come on up, Ms. Long," ordered Judge Cosper. "She has been sworn. You may proceed." The judge nodded toward Siegler.

Siegler smiled at her witness. "Could you introduce yourself to the jury?"

"My name is Katherine Long," the distinguished-looking woman said as she smoothed out her skirt.

"Who do you work for?"

"I work for Orchid Cellmark, a laboratory in Dallas,

a private forensic laboratory. We used to be known as Genescreen."

"How long have you worked for Orchid Cellmark?" inquired the prosecutor.

"A little over four years now."

"And what exactly do you do for Orchid Cellmark?"

"I'm a forensic DNA analyst. Anytime there's been any type of criminal activity that involves a transfer of physical evidence, be it blood, seminal fluid, it's my job to identify the blood or seminal fluid." No one on the jury batted an eye in this day and age of excessive legal-procedural television programming. "And from there, we can include or exclude someone who may have contributed to that fluid through the use of DNA testing."

"Have you been qualified before in courtrooms in Texas to testify in this area?" Siegler queried.

"Yes, I have."

"Few or many questions?"

"On many questions."

"How about in other states?"

"Yes, in other states."

"Can you give the jury the benefit of your educational training and background that led to having this job?"

"I have a Bachelor's of Science degree in medical technology from the University of Texas at El Paso. I've also received graduate credit hours from the medical school in Dallas, the University of Texas at Arlington, and also the University of Virginia," said Long, laying out her lengthy scholastic résumé.

Prosecutor Siegler looked up and turned her head toward the jury. She then asked, "In regard to this particular case involving a complainant named Maria del Carmen Estrada, did you receive some evidence to do some testing on, last year, from HPD?"

"Yes, I did," Long responded.

"And before we get into the nitty-gritty of DNA, Ms. Long, can you tell the jury how easy or hard it is to understand all that you're fixing to be talking about?" A couple jurors, whose heads were down, popped their faces up.

"It's really not that difficult." Some of the jurors looked relieved at her response. "Basically, what we're doing is obtaining a genetic profile of individuals, and we can then compare these profiles to other profiles." Long had a PowerPoint presentation on hand to assist her with the narrative of her testimony.

"And can you and I agree that during your testimony today, we'll try to keep this as simple and as short as possible so it's understandable to the jury?" Siegler understood what a jury wanted.

"Yes, we will try to keep it as simple as we can," Long agreed. Again some of the jurors smiled.

It was of the utmost importance to Siegler to keep the jurors focused on this key testimony. She felt it best to walk them through the process beginning with the basics.

"What is DNA?" she asked.

"DNA is basically your bloodprint. It makes you what you are. It makes your eyes brown. It makes your hair red. It's basically just codes for everything that you are," Long began to explain. The jurors seemed alert.

The prosecutor and her witness then proceeded to detail the benefit of DNA in a criminal trial. "It's somewhat stable," Long detailed. "It's consistent. It's the same throughout your body. So your fingernails will have the same type DNA as your blood cells." The allusion to Maria del Carmen Estrada's fingernails was apparent.

"Every person is different," Long continued. "Ninety-nine-point-nine percent of your DNA between all of us is the same. It's that point-one percent that we're looking at that makes us different. Except for identical twins, they have the same DNA.

"The testing that we're using today," Long expanded, while still captivating the jury, "we can actually say this one individual contributed to this body fluid or skin cells because we get such high discrimination."

"Tell us about the different sources of testing for DNA," requested Siegler.

"As you can see from the slides"—Long pointed to the overhead screen showing her PowerPoint presentation—"blood, sperm cells, tissues, bone marrow, hair. We can get DNA from almost anything."

"When you get evidence submitted to you at Orchid Cellmark," Siegler began, "explain to us the process by which you receive it, take care of it, transfer it, and test it."

"The minute it hits the door, it's assigned a case number. It's assigned an item number. This is so that we can keep track of the evidence because, heaven forbid, we should misplace something.

"We keep a chain of custody," Long continued. "The package is in a sealed condition the entire time that it's at Orchid Cellmark."

"When you're dealing with evidence from old cases, like we have in this case," Siegler asked, "what sort of factors influence the ability for you to get any kind of results because of the packaging that was done in the old days?"

"Sometimes things are placed in plastic bags that could be detrimental to DNA, because if there's any kind of moisture present, mold and mildew can build up and that actually degrades the DNA.

"Some of the boxes were not stored in ideal conditions," Long continued. "They were exposed to heat, water. So some of the packaging is detrimental to us."

"So, as in the case when HPD sent you some evidence back in October of last year, within a couple of days you told them that you could get DNA off of the evidence submitted?" Siegler wanted to know.

"Correct," answered Long.

"What determines a match?"

"Actually, a match can happen at just one location on your DNA. What we're testing is thirteen locations. And if all those thirteen locations are identical to the evidentiary sample, then that's considered a match."

"Explain the steps you went through in analyzing the evidence in this case."

"First we extract the DNA out of the cells that it's in. From there, we then identify the portions of the DNA that we want to test. We then make copies, which is called amplification. The actual copies are labeled with fluorescent tags and those are detected with an instrument.

"We then do some tests," Long continued. "Our software actually identifies what part of the DNA that we've actually gotten. And from there, we can perform statistical analysis using different software programs."

Siegler could see that the jury was starting to get restless. She decided to get to the meat of the discussion. "And in this report we're fixing to show, you prepared on Maria Estrada, do the back pages show the loci, or location, of the DNA?"

"Yes, it will actually show the number of repeats each sample had."

"And is what's scanned in here on the following pages your actual final report on the evidence you tested on Maria Estrada?"

"Yes, it is."

Siegler and Long went over a copy of Long's report for the Estrada case. The prosecutor asked the scientist to look at page 4 of her report. "What are you looking for as far as being able to tell if you have a match?"

"We're looking at the numbers and comparing the numbers to each other. And if the number of repeats match, that gives us an indication that we may have identical samples or identical DNA."

"Specifically, what items did you test in the Maria Estrada case?" Siegler inquired as the collective jury panel leaned forward.

"I tested the samples that were submitted to me, specifically, a wooden rod, a rope, an empty swab box and swab sticks, Maria Estrada's left-hand fingernails, Maria Estrada's right-hand fingernails, a stain card from Maria Estrada, which is basically blood that's been put on the cloth, one plastic tube that was labeled 'Oral Swab,' one plastic—it was a DNA oral swab, P-1 female, one plastic tube DNA oral swab Q-2, which was male, and buccal swabs, Anthony Allen Shore."

"When you received that evidence, were you able to tell that the evidence had already been dealt with and tested by the Houston Police Department Crime Lab?"

"Yes, it was," Long confirmed.

"Has it been your experience that when HPD's crime lab did their DNA testing, they were not in the habit of saving and leaving enough samples for future testing?"

"That's correct."

"Just like what happened in this case?"

"Yes."

"So, were you able to duplicate or replicate the findings that HPD had already done in the items that we're talking about right now?" Siegler asked.

"No. I was not able to, because there was not enough DNA left."

"So, you focused for the first time on what?"

"I tried to focus on the stuff that I felt they hadn't tested. In this particular case it would be the fingernails from Maria Estrada."

"Before we get into the fingernails, did you focus on

the wooden rod and the rope, the ligature, the two parts of the ligature?" Siegler quizzed Long.

"Yes, I did," Long responded.

"And what were the results?"

"They were insufficient. There wasn't enough DNA to provide a profile."

"Nothing came off the ligature?"

"Correct."

Siegler then asked Long to talk about Maria Estrada's fingernails.

"We actually had the physical fingernails that were cut from Maria Estrada's body," Long responded.

Siegler showed the small packets of Maria Estrada's fingernail end clippings that were used by Orchid Cellmark. "You didn't need to scrape anything off. You just used the fingernail itself?"

"That's correct."

"Tell the jury how you do that. What do you do with it?"

"Typically, what I do," Long continued as she held the jury's rapt attention, "is basically rinse off the fingernails. Any DNA that may have been picked up by those fingernails is separated from the fingernails themselves. I then remove the fingernails from the solution and perform DNA [test] on what came off the fingernails."

"In order to compare the unknown fingernail evidence, you have to compare it to the knowns?" the prosecutor asked.

"Correct."

"And in this case the knowns were what and what?" Siegler queried.

"The known initially was the known stain card from Maria Estrada."

"And how about from the defendant?"

"From the defendant we actually had what's called

buccal swabs, which is basically just a swabbing of the inside of your cheek."

"Have you done much testing with fingernails and fingernail clippings?"

"I've done quite a bit," responded Long. "That's one of the better evidentiary items that tends to hold up over the course of time . . . because they tend to be better preserved. They don't get wet. It's just a nice little place for DNA to hide."

"Why?" pondered Siegler.

"It's protected. You've got a hard surface and it's just one of those things when a female is attacked, typically a female will scratch her attacker."

"In this case"—Siegler was lining up her witness for the key information—"when you tested the fingernails, left and right hand of Maria Estrada, what were the results?"

Long sat slightly more erect and stated, "There was a foreign DNA profile, foreign to Maria Estrada under her fingernails."

"Which hand?"

"The left hand."

"What were your results? What is your opinion as to who that foreign contributor, under her left hand fingernail, belonged to?"

Long did not hesitate: "Anthony Allen Shore contributed the male DNA that was found under the fingernails of Maria Estrada."

Shore did not flinch. He never looked up at Long. He also ignored the jury.

Siegler perked up and continued her line of questioning. "What number base do you use and how do you go about making sure your statistical analysis is correct?"

"The statistical analysis is checked by another analyst and everything in the file is reviewed by the supervisor."

"And where is the database originating from?"

"It originates from the—it was provided to us by the FBI," Long asserted.

"Based on your statistical analysis and the results that you got on the left hand fingernails, Ms. Long," Siegler ramped it up, "tell us the statistical probability involved in this case."

"This particular genetic profile, we would expect to see it once in 4.72 trillion times in the black population. We would expect to see it only once in 3.53 trillion times in the Caucasian population and one in 57.1 trillion times in the Hispanic population."

"Now, in everyday normal language, restate what this says to the jury with these numbers," Siegler directed Long.

"This is just how many times we would expect if we had 3.53 trillion people. We would expect to see this particular profile only once."

"How many people exist on the face of the earth today?"

"There are approximately 6 billion people."

"So, is another way of saying this, you would have to go through 3.53 trillion people to come up with someone with the same DNA as Anthony Allen Shore?"

"That would be the expected frequency of this particular profile," Long concurred.

Kelly Siegler turned toward the jury, then looked back at Katherine Long. She smiled. "Pass the witness."

The state rested on the third day of testimony.

The defense, hamstrung by their client's need to control everything, did not call a single witness.

CHAPTER 58

Thursday, October 21, 2004,
Harris County Courthouse,
1201 Franklin Street,
Courtroom #337,
Houston, Texas.

Terese Buess and Kelly Siegler were set to make their closing arguments. Terese Buess took the floor. "Sometimes the wheels of justice grind very slowly," she opened, looking at the jury. "Ask Maria del Carmen Estrada's father who's waited twelve long years wanting to know who kidnapped, sexually assaulted, raped, and murdered his daughter.

"Ask Mr. Torres, who had a four-and-a-half-month relationship with her, who had discussed marriage."

Buess continued down the list of people touched by Estrada's death, including the police officers and detectives who worked her case. She explained that they were all ready for justice to finally be served.

The assistant district attorney went on to explain why the prosecution had successfully proven, beyond a reasonable doubt, that Tony Shore had committed capital murder.

"The evidence is clear," Buess reminded the jury. "It's astoundingly loud and clear for all of you. And Kelly and I are both going to be asking you to return the proper verdict in this case, of guilty of capital murder."

Buess's closing argument was short and sweet.

Gerald Bourque stood on behalf of Tony Shore.

"I'm sick and tired of trying to make something out of something it's not. This is clearly, clearly, clearly a murder case. And if he spends the rest of his life in prison," the attorney turned and looked at Tony Shore, then back to the jurors, "I have no problem with that."

Bourque then proceeded to separate "capital" from "murder" for the jury. "So, let's talk about what we have. We have a murder, a despicable, disgusting, tragic— I don't have a sufficient number of adjectives to describe this death, the homicide, this murder, this intentionally taking of a twenty-one-year-old young lady's life. I don't have words to describe it. All we have is the word 'murder.' It is not a *capital* murder."

Bourque's argument was based on the defense's belief that Shore knew Estrada, that he had a relationship with her, and that she willingly had sex with him. He had an interesting way of analogizing his argument.

"There is no evidence that the deadly weapon, the ligature, was used to force compliance. There is what?" Bourque asked rhetorically. "Speculation and conjecture. Well, if you put it around a horse's neck and you drag them to the barn over here, he'll follow you. And if you tell him to get down on his knees, he'll get down on his knees. Okay?"

The imagery of ropes and forced compliance was probably not the most well-timed.

The self-described "little bald-headed, big-eared, short

guy" Bourque concluded, "I understand what really happened in this case. He intended to kill her. He killed her. It's disgusting. It's depraved. It's maniacal, but it ain't capital murder."

The state, as is the norm in Texas, was allowed the final closing argument. Buess reiterated the evidence against Shore and that his case was indeed capital murder.

Siegler was also allowed to proffer a closing argument. She stood up and looked over to the jury. "One question that Terese and I know you've all asked yourselves is how could a defendant so smart, so intelligent, so brilliant, how could he confess?

"And let there be no doubt in this courtroom that this man's intelligence level, his IQ, is higher than everyone else's in this room. He's that smart." The jury shifted at this statement. Tony Shore did not even bother to look up.

"So why would someone so smart confess?" Siegler wondered. "Because as high as his IQ level is, his desire for control is even higher. Rape is never about sex. Rape is always about power and control. That's why he gave a completely voluntary, Mirandized—six different times—confession. Because to him it's all about control."

Siegler pointed out how Shore needed to be in control in the police interrogation room and how he casually referred to Sergeant Swaim as "John" and Officer Miller as "Todd." She mentioned how he was completely able to mask his deception.

"It's human nature," Siegler continued, "to want to figure out how he could turn out this way? What happened in his childhood? What happened to him to allow him to turn out to be the kind of man that he is today?"

Siegler again faced the jury and stated, "Well, you know what? In this case Tony Shore is in a world all by himself because even among the people, the criminals—

the sick, depraved criminals that you can't figure out—you can line up shrinks from now to doomsday to talk to him and evaluate him and test him and ask him questions and you would never understand what kind of man he is."

Siegler turned toward Shore. "It was never sex that he wanted from Carmen. It was always control." The prosecutor turned her back away from Shore. "Why do you think he used the tourniquet, not a gun, not a knife? That's too easy. That's too clean. That's too simple and that's too fast."

Siegler stood in front of the jury box and began making twisting motions with her hands. "See, with a tourniquet, he can torture her. He can terrorize her. He can look into the fear and the terror in her eyes and he can take his sweet, sweet, sick, sick time doing it."

Siegler directly addressed the jury. "Can you imagine what she was thinking and feeling in the last moments she was alive as he twisted and untwisted and tightened and untightened, as he decided when he was going to let her breathe, when he was going to let her loose, and when he was going to let her stop breathing?"

The assistant district attorney brought up the knot on the ligature. "So why is the knot in the back?" she wondered. "Because he's raping her from the rear, then she's more than just a thing there in front of him and he can control as he looks down upon her and he twists and he tightens as it turns him on."

The entire gallery seemed uncomfortable at the imagery.

Siegler talked about how Shore carried around a ligature and wooden dowel for strangling purposes and how he must have imagined the day he would murder.

She also lobbed verbal fireballs at Bourque's argument that Shore and Estrada had engaged in consensual sex. "Use your common sense and know that what we're talking about here is a sexual assault case. Why would her panties be rolled around her ankles the way they were? Why would her panty hose be ripped and rolled around her ankles the way they were? When you have consensual sex, do you cut your bra in two? Of course not. Use your common sense."

Siegler then switched gears to commend all of the officers who worked on the case. "In a day where all we ever get is criticism, have you appreciated the fact that not only did they recover all the evidence and interview to the point he gave a statement, they also managed to find out exactly what kind of cord was used, number-four Venetian blind?

"The complete detail and thoroughness of the job that they did is to be commended. And mostly be commended for the fact that they never gave up."

Siegler then reverted back to the defendant, Tony Shore. "He tells you in the tape he has a sick consumption. He says, his words, not mine, 'I don't know what to call it.' Well, maybe Anthony Shore doesn't know what to call it, but you do. Depraved, sick, maniacal, monstrous."

Siegler asked the jurors to put themselves in Estrada's position. "What do you think about when you know you're about to die? When a man you don't even know is fixing to kill you for a reason you have no idea that you can understand. Can you imagine the terror that she went through?

"Can you imagine what she thought in those last minutes as she begged for her life? Can you imagine what it feels like to die and to leave this world looking into the eyes of that?" Siegler practically spat as she pointed toward Shore. "And that"—she thrust her index finger at Shore again—"is a capital murderer. It is time today to find him guilty."

Judge Cosper informed the jurors that the argument portion of the trial was complete and they were to deliberate Anthony Allen Shore's fate. She then released the two alternate jurors and sent the remaining twelve on their way.

The jury deliberated after lunch and into the early evening. By 5:00 P.M., they had not come to a decision.

Thursday, October 21, 2004, 8:45 P.M.,
Harris County Courthouse,
1201 Franklin Street,
Courtroom #337,
Houston, Texas.

The jury had reached its decision in the morning. They were called into the courtroom by Judge Cosper. The tension was not that thick; everyone was tired and not expecting any surprises.

"Has the jury reached its verdict?" Judge Cosper asked.

"We have, Your Honor," jury foreperson Larry Pechacek answered.

"If you would please hand the form to the bailiff."

Pechacek handed the verdict over to the bailiff, who, in turn, passed it on to the judge.

Judge Cosper looked at the paper with the verdict on it.

"This is *State of Texas* versus *Anthony Allen Shore.*

"We, the jury, find the defendant, Anthony Allen Shore, guilty of capital murder, as charged in the indictment."

Tony Shore simply kept his head down the entire time. He showed no emotion whatsoever.

There was not a lot of commotion in the gallery. Mainly, the spectators were relieved that nothing unusual occurred.

"Ladies and gentlemen of the jury, this concludes the guilt/innocence phase of the trial," Judge Cosper noted. "We will be moving into the punishment phase of the trial. We are going to begin tomorrow morning at nine-thirty."

CHAPTER 59

Friday, October 22, 2004,
Harris County Courthouse,
1201 Franklin Street,
Courtroom #337,
Houston, Texas.

The jury of twelve Houston citizens had no idea what they were in for next. They rightfully assumed that this was a one-off murder case. Little did they know what type of nightmare they were about to enter.

Kelly Siegler was going to make sure they knew.

"Evil lives among us," the prosecutor informed the jury, "and sometimes evil comes in the form of someone who looks completely normal, who we live with and talk to and work with, and never have any idea what they're really like."

Siegler told the jury that they were about to see and hear some of the most shocking evidence and testimony over the next few days.

"I expect there won't be a whole lot of cross-examination." Siegler nodded toward the defense table. "I would like to compliment these guys. They're some of the best lawyers that Terese and I know, but their hands are going to be tied by the evidence because there's not a whole lot of questions they can ask."

Siegler mentioned the names of Tony Shore's other victims to the jury for the first time. Only now did they know they had just convicted a pedophile, incestuous rapist, and serial killer.

After laying out her game plan, Siegler closed with, "You're going to believe when we're all done, that if Anthony Shore doesn't belong on death row, they might as well tear down the walls."

Next up was Siegler's counterpart, defense attorney Alvin Nunnery. Siegler was right; Nunnery was hamstrung by his client.

"Ladies and gentlemen, this is going to be very short," declared the polite African American defense attorney. "The Bible says that if you confess your sins, God said I'm faithful and just to forgive you and cleanse you of all your unrighteousness."

Nunnery looked directly at the jury. "Something unusual happened yesterday . . . when you returned your verdict of guilty in this case. Mr. Bourque and I may have been dissatisfied with the verdict." He turned to his client and gestured. "Anthony was quite satisfied." Nunnery looked back at Shore's peers. "Against our advice, against our better judgment, against forty years of experience, Anthony has asked on his behalf that we ask you to answer those questions in such a way that he's sentenced to death."

An audible gasp could be heard from the gallery.

Nunnery continued to address the jury. "I find that a very, very troubling thing, but it is his life. It is where he is and it is what he thinks should happen to him based upon how he lived his life.

"Ms. Siegler talks about control and she talks about

manipulation," Nunnery continued. "I disagree that this is the final instance of manipulation or control."

Nunnery attempted to paint a picture of a reformed Anthony Allen Shore. "From the time he got placed on probation . . . he accepted a different lifestyle. That is one where he accepted the Lord in his life, never with the courage to come forward, but with the realization that one day he was probably going to get caught."

In other words, jailhouse conversion minus the jail time.

"While he would ultimately be free from the pain of sin, that is, eternal damnation," Nunnery continued, "he has to pay the consequences of what he has done. And he believes . . . that [the] ultimate penalty is death by lethal injection."

Nunnery looked slightly exasperated as he addressed the jury one last time. "As difficult as that is for me to tell you, that is where he is. So throughout the course of this [penalty phase of the] trial, Mr. Bourque and I are going to sit silent because we, too, agree that maybe the victims in this case need this forum to have their say."

Indeed, Tony Shore's victims would have their say.

The prosecution made sure to bring forth many witnesses on behalf of the slain girls—from the detectives, such as Bob King and John Swaim, to the families and friends of the victims.

The prosecution also wanted the jury to hear from one of Tony Shore's surviving victims. Selma Janske, now twenty-five years old, was called to the stand. The attractive young woman seemed cowed by the experience of having to face the man who raped her eleven years earlier, in 1993. She would be questioned by Assistant District Attorney Terese Buess, who specifically requested to address Janske.

The young woman took the stand, was sworn in, and then ran through the usual battery of background questions. She was born in Houston, Texas. She attended Lamar High School. She graduated from Trinity University in San Antonio with a degree in biology and worked for a large medical organization in, ironically, genetic testing, including DNA.

Selma's family, including her mother, father, and older brother, accompanied her to the courthouse. Bob King described them as a "classy family." They were also devastated that their young daughter, once again, had to relive the nightmare that was Tony Shore.

"I want to go back in time," Buess began. "I want to go to October 19, 1993. I know you recall that date."

The lovely young woman quietly spoke up, replying, "Yes" as the jury focused on her.

"How old were you back then?"

"I was fourteen."

"Where were you going to school?"

"Lamar High School. I was a freshman."

"Tell us what kind of activities you were involved in at Lamar High School back then."

"Mostly, I played soccer," the young woman recalled. "I played soccer most of my life. And doing school and hanging out with my friends."

"Was your brother living with you at the time?"

"No, he had gone off to college that year."

"So, in your home, tell me who was living in your home on that day."

"My mom, my dad, and myself."

"Just the three of you?"

"Yes."

"Tell us how you got back and forth to school."

"I had a car pool with three or four of my friends. Our parents took turns driving us to and from school."

"What time did you normally get home from school with the car pool?"

"About three-thirty, or right around then."

"And how would you get into the house at that point?"

"I had a key. I'd just let myself in through the front door."

"And when you came home, would either your mom or dad be home at that time?"

"No, they worked."

"What time would they normally get home?"

"Somewhere in between five-thirty or six-thirty usually."

"And would they both come together or separately?"

"No, separate."

"When you would come home from school on a regular school day, what would you normally do once you got home?" the ADA asked.

"I would usually come in and get a snack, probably watch some TV, do some homework."

"TV first, then some homework?" Buess asked with a smile.

"Right."

"Typical freshman in high school," Buess stated as she smiled at the jury. They knowingly smiled back. Buess continued on with questions in regard to the Janske home. She then steered Janske back to the attack. "Okay, Selma. On October 19, 1993, did you come home from school on that day?"

"Yes," Janske replied calmly.

"It was a school day?"

"Yes."

"Got home at the regular time, about three-thirty, with a carpool?"

"Yes."

"How did you let yourself into the house?"

"I let myself in like normal."

"Do you recall what you had with you at the time?" Buess asked.

"I always had a backpack with me at school, and that's probably it," Janske answered.

"Tell me on that day what you were wearing."

"I had on jeans, I think, tennis shoes and just a T-shirt of some kind."

"Do you remember what color the T-shirt was?"

"I believe it was blue."

"Underneath your shirt, what did you have on?"

"A bra."

"Underneath your jeans, what did you have on?"

"Underwear."

"Let's talk about what you did when you came home. You said you came through the front door."

"Yes."

"And tell me what you were doing at that moment."

"I was checking the mail because the mail slot is in the front door and it goes on the floor. So, I would always walk in and just pick it up," the witness answered.

"What were you looking at?"

"There was a catalog in there. I had sat down on the couch and started flipping through it."

"What did you do next?"

"I started walking through the living room and I had walked through the dining room and was walking into the kitchen watching the clock."

"So, are you in the kitchen or almost there?"

"I'm walking through the doorway of the kitchen."

"And what happens next?" Buess queried as all the members of the jury sat at attention.

"I heard a noise behind me," Janske responded. "It

was a voice. I think he said, 'Hey,' and I turned around and saw a figure standing where the table usually sat."

"Let me stop you right there. Let me back you up a little bit. We're going to go slowly so we don't have to do it again. Okay?"

Apparently, a table had been moved from its normal location. "In its place, what was there?" Buess asked.

"There's a man standing there," Janske responded.

"When you looked at him, did you look at him in the face?"

"Yes," Janske replied, but she was unable to do so eleven years later.

"Could you see his face?"

"No."

"Why not?"

"His face was covered with a bandanna or something on his head."

"Could you see any part of his face?"

"I could see his forehead, maybe his eyes."

"What could you tell from seeing that much of him?"

"That he was white."

"When he spoke to you and he called your attention, do you recall the words he used?" Buess questioned.

"I can't remember if he said, 'Hey,' or if he just made a noise to get my attention."

"Aside from noticing the white forehead and the eyes, tell us what he was wearing."

"He was wearing large, baggy clothes. When I first looked at him, I thought he was a scarecrow-type-looking figure." The image seemed to cast a pall over the gallery.

"Was it a shirt or a jacket?" Buess asked. "What was it on top?"

"It was a shirt of some kind."

"How about the pants? Could you tell what kind they were?"

"Blue jeans, I believe."

"Did you look at his feet?"

"No."

"Tell the jury, when you hear that noise, when you hear him talking to you or saying something and you turned around and saw him, tell us what's going through your mind right then."

"I thought it was a joke," Janske responded while slowly shaking her head. "I thought someone was trying to scare me."

"What did you do?"

"I just stood there," Janske replied, and began to sob. "I didn't, I didn't know what to do."

Terry Janske (pseudonym), Selma's mother, began to cry as she watched her daughter struggle alone on the witness stand. Her husband comforted her stoically.

"Did you notice or learn anything about his hands?" Buess forged onward.

"He was wearing surgical gloves on his hand," Janske replied.

"How did you know that?"

"I just saw them as he was walking up to me." Shore ignored Janske on the witness stand. He also would not look at the jury. He kept his head down and focused on the sheet of paper in front of him.

"What did you think when you saw those gloves?"

"I wasn't thinking at that point."

"Tell us what happens next. What does he say to you?"

"He said he was just breaking into the house. He wanted to steal something. He was just breaking in to find money. He didn't know that I was going to be there and it was an accident."

"When he says that to you, what kind of voice is he using?"

"It was very calm, very soothing, almost."

"[Did he say], 'I'm just here to rob your house'?"

"Yes."

"'I'm not here for you'?"

"Right."

"Does that make you feel any better?"

"I believed him."

"So what happened next?"

"I was just standing right inside the kitchen. He came over, and he said he was going to put duct tape around my eyes so that I couldn't see him and couldn't identify him. And he kept saying over and over again, 'I'm just breaking into your house. It's an accident that I'm here when you're here.'

"And so I let him," Janske recalled in a soft voice. "And he wrapped my whole face around in duct tape, over my mouth, around the back of my head."

"What about your nose?" Buess wanted to know.

"Well, I could still breathe."

"So, your nose isn't covered?"

"Right."

"How about your eyes?"

"Yes."

"You say he went all the way around?"

"Yes."

"Back then, what kind of hair did you have?"

"Pretty much like I have today, long."

"What did he do with your hands?"

"He said that he was going to tie my hands behind my back so I couldn't come after him. And so he tied my hands real tight behind [my] back."

"What did he tie your hands back with?"

"Well, it was a wire of some kind. And later I found out that the alarm clock in my room wasn't working anymore, and he had cut the wire from that and split it down in two so it was long and thin," Janske answered.

"Just so we have a good picture of you at this point in time, your eyes are covered, your mouth is covered, you can breathe."

"Yes."

"Can you see anything at the time?"

"No."

"And are your hands behind you?"

"Yes."

"He left your feet alone?"

"Yes."

"What happened next?" Buess continued the tense questioning.

"He started walking me into my bedroom through the kitchen." The jury watched the witness with a collective intensity.

"How is he doing that?"

"He's leading me from behind with his hand on my—on my back."

"So, he just kind of guided you forward?"

"Yes."

"Because you can't see, right?"

"Right."

"Where did you go in the house?"

"We went through the kitchen and turned right into my bedroom."

"On the walk through the dining room, through the kitchen into your bedroom, is he silent or is he talking?"

"No. He was—he talked the whole time."

"What's he saying?"

"Just repeating over and over again that it was an accident that I was there when he was there."

"Did he tell you he wasn't going to hurt you?" Buess inquired.

"Yes."

"Did you believe that?"

"I had to," Janske stated emphatically.

"You said his voice was calm and soothing. Is it still the same way?"

"Yes."

"Tell us, Selma, when you realized that it really was about you."

"When we were walking back into the bedroom, he lifted up my shirt and just grazed my side. And that was the first realization that I had that it might not be just about the house; that it might be about me too."

"So, now you're in your bedroom. What happened next?"

"He sat me down on the bed."

"So are we at the foot of your bed?"

"Yes," Janske replied.

"You're sitting down at the foot of your bed?"

"Yes, with my knees over the end of the bed."

"What does he say?"

"I don't remember. He started taking off my pants," Janske spoke quietly.

"Did he tell you why he was taking your pants off?"

"He said he didn't want me to chase after him."

"Are you still thinking that maybe if you go along, it's going to be okay?"

"I don't remember. I didn't have a choice at that point."

"Did you let him take your pants off?"

"I think I struggled a little bit."

"Did your pants come off?" Buess asked.

"Yes."

"So, now at this point you've got your panties on?"

"Yes."

"Your blue T-shirt?"

"Yes."

"And your bra?"

"Yes."

"And you're sitting on the edge of your bed?"

"Yes."

"Okay. Tell us what happens next."

"He used a knife to cut off my panties."

"Selma, how did you know it was a knife?"

"Because he—I don't remember if he told me at that point, but at some point he told me that he had a knife that he would cut me with."

"So, when he cut off your panties, did you feel that knife on your body?"

"I don't remember if I felt it, but I knew that's how he did it."

"When he's cutting off your panties, did he say anything to you?"

"I don't believe so."

"At this point, with your panties off and your jeans off, are you still sitting upright in your bed?"

"I don't think so."

"Where are you now?" Buess queried.

"I'm laying on my back on the bed, but my legs are still hanging off of the bed."

"Off of the edge of the bed?"

"Yes."

"And you're laying back flat?"

"Yes."

"Where is he?"

"He was standing at my knees."

"Is he still talking to you?"

"I believe he was."

"Do you recall what he was saying at this point?" Buess questioned.

"He started talking, telling me to just relax, and he spread my legs open."

"How is he spreading your legs open?"

"Using his hands," Janske answered with a quaver in her voice.

"And you said you think you struggled at one point?"

"Yes."

"What do you recall doing?"

"Trying to close my legs and just screaming."

"At that point the tape that's around your mouth, is it still in place?"

"It's a lot looser by then because [of] the moisture from my breath and moving around."

"So, it's come a little bit loose?"

"Yes."

"In your screaming, can you hear yourself screaming?"

"Yes."

"Can he hear you screaming?" Buess posed.

"Yes."

"Tell the jury, please, as you're screaming, what changes with him?"

Janske looked directly at the jury. "As I was screaming, he got upset. He was telling me that I was being too loud, that I needed to be quiet. At that point he was threatening me with the knife, that he had a knife and he was going to cut me."

"And at that point you knew he had a knife, right?"

"Yes, because he had cut my panties with it."

"So, with that knife and the threat being made, did you believe that he was capable of doing that to you?"

"Yes."

"Of killing you?"

"Yes."

"You said you were screaming. When he told you to be quiet, did you stop or did you continue?"

"I think I did quiet down for a little bit."

"What happens next?"

"He was able to open up my knees."

"And what happened next, Selma?"

"That's when he raped me," Janske replied as the air went out of the room. The prosecutors looked fierce. The jury looked worn-out. Anthony Allen Shore looked neutral as he continued to stare down at the defense table.

"Did you ever hear him unzip his pants?" Buess asked the young lady.

"No."

"When you say 'raped,' tell us—I'm sorry to have to ask you this, but we've got to—the written record has to be clear. What part of him goes into you?"

Janske cast her eyes downward and quietly answered, "He put his penis into me, into my vagina."

"And again, just so the jury is clear, he's not on top of you, is he?"

"No, he's not."

"How is he at this point?"

"He's leaning over me. On me."

"So, he's standing in front of you?"

"Yes."

"And your legs are between his legs now?"

"Yes."

"Did he stay still or did he move? Just tell us what you recall."

"I think he stayed still."

"Selma, tell the jury, back then when you were fourteen years old on that date, had you even started your period yet?"

"No."

"Did you really know anything about sex?"

"No."

"Ever had anything enter your vagina before that you know of?"

"No. No."

"Tell the jury, when his penis went inside your vagina, what that felt like."

"It hurt."

"When that happened, what did you do?"

"I started screaming again."

"And what did he do?"

"He told me I was being too loud."

"Did he ever tell you—aside from the 'quit screaming' and 'quit being so loud,' did he tell you what to do?"

"No."

"Did he ever tell you to relax?"

"Yes, he did," Janske remembered.

"How many times did he tell you to do that?"

"I only remember once."

"Did he tell you what would happen if you didn't relax?"

"He told me if I relaxed, it wouldn't hurt."

"Did you believe that?" Buess asked.

"Well, not at that point. No."

"Tell us what you recall happening next."

"I want to say I started screaming again, and he told me I was being too loud. I remember, suddenly I wasn't able to breathe."

"You said the tape around your mouth is coming a little bit loose and you can hear yourself?"

"Yes."

"How about your eyes? Does that come off your eyes? Can you see at all?" Buess wondered.

"At some point I could see just a little sliver of light coming through," Janske responded.

"But you didn't see his face?"

"No."

"At any point up to this time, have you ever said, 'No. Stop'?"

"I don't know that I specifically said 'no.'"

"And while you're laying down on your bed, your arms are where?"

"They're still tied behind my back."

"So, you're laying on top of your arms?"

"Yes."

"You said you were screaming?"

"Yes."

"Are you crying?" the ADA questioned.

"Yes."

"When did you start crying?"

"It's hard to say exactly. I mean, probably when I started screaming."

"So, even before he had pulled your legs apart?"

Janske could not verbalize her answer at first. She slowly nodded her head up and down. "Yes," she finally said.

"You said you were still screaming and he was upset about it. And then you said it became hard to breathe."

"Yes."

"What was happening?"

"I realized that something was choking me."

"Could you see what was choking you, Selma?"

"No."

"Based on his position on you, do you have a good idea what was choking you?"

"Yes."

"What was choking you?"

"His hands."

"Tell us how far that went. That choking."

"I kind of came out of my stupor, I guess, and realized that I had to do something at that point," Janske recalled.

"Let me back you up just a moment." The jury actually seemed disappointed. They wanted to know what this brave young woman did to protect herself. Terese Buess, however, knew what she was doing. She wanted to lead Selma Janske to the reveal, with the most impact.

"You realized that you can't breathe. What's happening to you aside from the realization that you can't breathe?" The jury appeared as if it were not ready to breathe either. "Did you begin to black out?"

"No, I don't believe so."

"What are the thoughts going through your mind?"

"If I don't do something, I'm going to die."

"So what did you do?" The entire gallery was a cone of silence.

"I pulled my legs up to my chest and I pushed him off as hard as I could," Selma recalled.

"So, you kicked him?"

"Yes."

"What happened?"

"He didn't come back to me. I was really scared that . . ." Her voice trailed off at the memory.

"What did you hear, though, when you kicked?" Prosecutor Buess brought Janske back to her counterattack.

"I heard him knock into something."

"And you were scared that he was going to come back to you?"

"Yes."

"Because you knew he had the knife?"

"Yes."

"Did he come back to you right away?"

"No."

"What happened?"

"I don't think he came back to me at all after that. He started talking to me again."

"What's he talking about now?"

"Now he's talking about how he knows everything about me. He had been watching me. He knew I came home from school. That he knew I played soccer and where I played soccer at, and that . . ." Her voice trailed off again as several members of the jury glanced over at Shore.

"Specifically, what did he say about where you played soccer that he knew?" Buess asked Selma.

"He knew what field I practiced at."

"Did he name the school that you played at?"

"He named my high school that I went to and said he knew I went to school and it was Lamar and—"

"How did that make you feel?"

"Later it made me pretty scared."

"So, he's talking and you're still on your bed?"

"Yes."

"Laying flat on your back?"

"Yes."

"Where are your legs now?" Buess queried.

"I think at that point, once I kicked him off, I think I curled up into a ball on the bed."

"So, are you on your back or on your side?"

"On my side."

"And he's talking now?"

"Yes."

"Is his voice nice and calm, like it was in the beginning?"

"I believe so."

"Can you tell what he's doing?"

"I think I hear him putting on his pants or shuffling around."

"Now at this point, are you talking?"

"Well, he was making me promise—he was telling me the description that I needed to give to the police."

"What description was that, Selma?"

"That he was a short black man with a New York accent."

"Which was not what he was at all?"

"No."

"You knew he was white?" Buess asked.

"Yes."

"Did he have an accent?"

"No."

"And what did you tell him when he's asking you to do that?"

"I swore up and down that I would," Janske replied.

"What else?"

"He told me that if I told them, the police, the correct description of him, that he would come back for me and that he would come back and kill me."

"And did you believe that at the time?"

"Yes."

"Did he tell you he was leaving?"

"Yes, he did."

Selma Janske continued to testify that Tony Shore finally left her house. She rushed to pick up the phone and dialed 911.

"Someone had broken into the house and I needed the police," she told the jury.

Janske then testified that she called her mother at work. Neither one of these phone calls was a simple task, as she was still bound with duct tape. First she put the phone on the counter and dialed the numbers, then she laid her head on the receiver to speak. To call her mother, she testified, she had to "bunch my hands to the side, just to dial. And it really hurt because my hands were tied down so tight, but I just—I had to do it. And so I was able to bring it up to my head."

"What did you tell your mom?" Buess continued.

"I told her someone had broken into the house and hurt me."

"You didn't tell her that you had been raped?"

"No."

"What did she say?"

"She asked me if I had called the police. I told her I had and she said that she was coming."

"She was on her way home?"

"She left her office."

"And you're telling us with a pretty calm voice right now. What kind of voice did you use when you called your mom?"

"I think I was trying to be calm so I wouldn't totally scare her."

Selma Janske testified that a female police officer, Jeannine Maughmer, was the first person at the scene. Janske had to somehow manage to unlock the dead bolt on the front door to let the officer enter her home.

"When she came in, did you tell her everything that happened?" Buess asked.

"No," Janske admitted.

"Why not?"

"I was pretty scared."

"What were you scared of?"

"I didn't want to tell her his true description and I didn't want to tell her the false description. So, I told her I didn't know."

"Did you tell her what had happened to you yet?"

"Yes, I think it was pretty obvious."

"Who else came over to the house?"

"My next-door neighbor did. My mom's secretary had called my dad and my mom left the office and he, in turn, called my neighbor to check on me."

"And then your mom arrived?"

"Yes."

"When your mom arrived, did you talk with her?"

"Yes, I told her that he had threatened me if I gave the correct description and that I didn't want to tell them."

"What did she tell you to do?"

"She told me that I had to tell them the truth."

Selma Janske continued her testimony that she gave the appropriate description of her assailant. Her father then arrived at the house and her mother took her to Texas Children's Hospital, where doctors performed a rape examination on the young girl. She continued to testify that since she was unable to get a clear view of her attacker's face, the police could not do much to help her. The police, however, did keep in touch with her over the years.

Janske also testified that her attacker continued to harass her. A couple days after the attack, Selma answered the phone. "My mom was in the shower and my brother had come home from college for the weekend and he was asleep. I answered the phone. The voice on the other line just said, 'Do you know who this is?'"

"Did you recognize the voice?" Buess asked.

"Yes. The same man who broke into the house and raped me."

"When you heard that voice on the phone, what did you do, Selma?"

"I just dropped the phone."

"Were there other odd things that happened with the telephone?"

"Yes. One day, I think it was a couple of weeks after this incident happened, there was a message on the phone, and it was someone just heavily breathing into the phone sounding very sexually explicit and just around that time a lot of hang-ups, a lot of nobody being on the phone."

Selma Janske also testified that the attack forced her entire family to alter its routine. Her mother started coming home early from work. They installed an alarm, bolted the windows shut.

"How about school? How did you feel about going to your first soccer practice after that?" Buess asked.

"It was pretty scary, but I felt like I had to go back to some sort of normal life," Janske recalled.

"Did you go to counseling?"

"A little bit."

"Did you find that very helpful?"

"No."

"Was this something that you just put behind you and went on?"

"No, not at all," she stated as she emphatically shook her head.

"Selma, during the time that the sexual assault was happening, do you recall anything happening to your anus at all?"

"He touched my anus."

"You don't recall anything going inside your anus?"

"No."

"And you told the doctors that at Texas Children's?"

"Yes."

"Do you recall telling them that something wet was coming down?"

"Yes."

"Did you have any idea what that was at the time?"

"Not really."

"Did you know the basics of intercourse?"

"Yeah, from health class, but . . ."

"And at the time that this was happening to you, did you know whether or not the man ejaculated?"

"No."

"Selma, after the weird things started with the telephone, did you continue answering the telephone at your home?" Buess queried.

"No, I stopped for a couple of months. We finally got caller ID, which had just come out at that time." Selma paused for a moment, looked at the jury, then looked back at Buess and said, "I was terrified."

"You told us that your period hadn't started on that date that this happened. When did it start?"

"It started later that week."

"How did you feel about that?"

"Not very excited."

"When you were at the hospital and had a pelvic exam, were your feet up in the stirrups?"

"Yes."

"Had you ever gone through anything like that before? Had your genitals been examined in that kind of way?"

"No."

"Was there anything about what was done that hurt you at that time?"

"Yes."

"What hurt you?"

"The actual exam."

"The internal part of the exam?"

"Yes. Yes."

"Before you left, had they treated you for sexually transmitted diseases? Did they give you a pregnancy test?" Buess glanced at the jury after she asked the question.

"I believe so, yes." Janske seemed embarrassed as she answered.

"Do you know what kind of medications it was that you were supposed to take?"

"They gave me medicine in case I had gotten an STD, preventative type."

"And when you say 'STD,' to prevent you from developing any sexually transmitted disease?"

"Yes."

"Do you recall, later on, meeting with Officer Maughmer and giving her as much information as you could about what had happened? A statement? A formal statement?"

"Yes."

"Were there things that you recalled later on that you probably hadn't told the officer [when she] first arrived?"

"Yes."

"Selma, did you and I talk well prior to trial about a DNA match in this case?" Buess looked conciliatory as she asked Janske the question.

"Yes, we did," Janske calmly replied.

"And you knew who the DNA from your rape kit matched to?"

"Yes."

"Tell the jury how you felt about that at that time."

"Well, I had already known that he had confessed to raping me."

"How did you find out about that?"

"A police officer showed up at my door."

"Did they ask you if you had been raped?"

"They said that they had—my name had come up in an investigation that they were doing and that I needed to come downtown."

"Did you go downtown?"

"Yes."

"Was there anything for you to do there?" the prosecutor wondered.

"I gave another statement."

"How did you feel about coming here to testify today?"

"Pretty nervous."

"Are you glad to have it over with?"

"Very," she replied politely.

"Pass the witness, Your Honor," the assistant district attorney concluded her direct examination. The defense had no questions for Selma Janske.

"You may step down," Judge Cosper gently informed the young lady.

As she stepped away from the witness stand, it was evident that the entire audience in the gallery and the jury box had been moved by the young woman's plight. Bob King would later say that the jury was ready to give Anthony Allen Shore the death penalty based on Selma Janske's testimony alone, and she actually survived one of his attacks.

CHAPTER 60

Wednesday, October 27, 2004,
Harris County Courthouse,
1201 Franklin Street,
Courtroom #337,
Houston, Texas.

Prosecutor Kelly Siegler was eager to floor the jury. If Tony Shore wanted the death penalty, she was going to be sure he got his wish. She continued her portion of the penalty phase with testimony from two key individuals who had no involvement in the murders whatsoever—Tony Shore's own two daughters.

"Judge, the state calls Amber Shore McCabe," Siegler declared.

The young lady, now all of twenty, shuffled into the witness stand and was sworn in.

"Could you tell us all your name, please?" Siegler asked.

The witness leaned forward in her seat and spoke into the microphone. "Amber Fallon Shore."

"Amber, how old are you?"

"Twenty."

"Are you married?"

"Yes."

"And is your husband in court here with you today?"

"Yes."

"And also your mother-in-law?"

"Yes."

"How long have you been married?"

"Since January 24, 2004."

"Maybe the jury could tell when you walked up, but are you pregnant now?"

"Yes." She smiled as she answered.

"What's your sister's name?"

"Tiffany Shore."

"Can you tell the jury a little bit about Tiffany? What's she like?"

"She's really friendly, outgoing, a people-person type," Amber stated with a smile.

"Who's older? You or Tiffany?"

"Me."

"How much older are you than Tiffany?"

"A year-and-a-half."

"Have you ever testified in a courtroom before?"

"No."

"Are you nervous today?"

"Yes," she admitted as she shifted in the witness stand.

"Let's start off with some easy questions. What's your mom's name?"

"Gina Shore."

"And when you were little, did there come a time when your parents got divorced?"

"Yes."

"About how old were you when they divorced?"

"Nine or ten."

"When your parents got divorced, Amber, who got custody of you and your sister at first?"

"My mom."

"So how did you end up living with your dad after your mom got custody in the divorce?"

"My mom wanted to carry on with her new boyfriend, so she sent us to live with our dad."

"And how old were you when you went to live with your dad?"

"Nine or ten."

"What high school did you go to?"

"I didn't go to high school. It was, like, a home-school thing. And I didn't stick around long."

"How far did you get in school?"

"To the tenth grade."

"And why didn't you stick around, Amber?"

"I just didn't like it there."

"When is the last time that you saw your mom?"

"Last year in October."

"And are you planning on visiting with her while you're in town for this trip?"

"Yes."

"Tell the jury how you feel about being here to testify today."

"Not really good about it," Amber answered while purposely avoiding eye contact with her father. Tony Shore, however, looked directly at his oldest daughter.

"Amber, who is Tony Shore?"

"He is my biological father."

"And why did you say 'biological father'?"

"Meaning that he's not a stepdad or adopted or nothing. He's my blood-born father."

"When is the last time you saw your dad before today?"

"Thirteen."

"When you were thirteen?"

"Yeah."

"So, about seven years ago?" the prosecutor calculated.

"Yeah."

"Can you tell the jury a little bit about your mother? What sort of problems does your mom have? What kind of mom was she when you were little?"

"She was a good mother. She was more, like, a friend-type person; and as we started growing up, she was more of a friend."

"Amber, I want you to talk just a little while today, and we'll do this as fast as possible, like I told you. Did there come a time when you were little that your dad started doing things to you and touching you inappropriately sexually?" This time it was the jury members and the audience that shifted uncomfortably in their seats.

"Yes," Amber replied without showing any weakness.

"And that started when you were how old?"

"Like, kindergarten age."

"What house were you living in and who were you living with when it started?"

"Both my parents, and in an apartment."

"And then when you moved to the house on Eighteenth Street, did it continue?"

"Yeah."

"And who was the last lady your dad was living with, back when you were thirteen and it all ended?"

"Amy Lynch," Amber answered in reference to Shore's second wife.

"Tell the jury what your dad would do when you would be in your bedroom at night, when he would come to the doorway of your bedroom."

"He would stand unclothed and touch himself inappropriately."

"And would you and your sister be in your bedroom when that happened?"

"Yes."

"Did there come a time when he would come into your bedroom and touch you?"

"Yes."

"And this, the touching, started when you were how old, Amber?"

"Kindergarten age. Six." Some of the jury members actually flinched at the answer.

"And it continued until you were how old?"

"Thirteen."

"And your dad would touch you underneath your panties and your shirt?"

"Yes."

"And did he ever take your clothes off?"

"Just the underwear," Amber answered.

"And did he have clothes on when this would happen?"

"I don't know. My eyes were closed."

"How did he touch you?"

"With his hands."

"And when he would touch you with his hands, with his fingers, did he touch your breast area?"

"Yes."

"And did he touch your vagina?"

"The outside, yes."

"And how about your rear, your anus? Did he touch you there too?"

"Yes."

"When you were little, and he would touch you that way, did you say anything to him?" Siegler asked Tony Shore's oldest daughter.

"No, I was too scared to acknowledge that I was awake or even knew about it," Amber responded.

"Too scared to acknowledge what?"

"Too scared to acknowledge I was awake."

"Because you pretended what?"

"To be asleep."

"Why did you pretend to be asleep?"

"Because I was worried, if I woke up, he might do more or something."

"When you were little, did you tell any grown-ups about it, back when you were little?"

"Like kindergarten age?"

"Yes, ma'am."

"No, ma'am."

"Did you tell your sister?"

"No."

"Did there come a time when your school nurse kind of figured out or became aware of what was going on?"

"Yes."

"And how old were you when the school nurse kind of figured something out?"

"In the fourth grade."

"And after the school nurse figured something out, did CPS come to your house?"

"Yes."

"And is that the house on Eighteenth Street?"

"Yes."

"When CPS came, did they come and talk to you and your sister?" the ADA inquired.

"Yes."

"And did CPS talk to you in front of your father?"

"Yes."

"Did you tell them what was going on when they came to your house back then, Amber?"

"No."

"Tell the jury why not."

Amber focused her attention on the jury panel. "Because after they left, Dad told us that we would be taken away and probably put in separate homes with foster parents. And I wouldn't have my dog and it would be really sad and terrible how we felt about it, to be separated from our family."

"At that time, did he tell you anything about being sorry and that it wouldn't happen anymore?"

"Yes."

"What did he say?"

"He said he was really sorry. I don't know the words exactly, but, basically, he was very sorry and felt really awful about it and he would never do it again. And that's why he got me the dog. It was an apology. And that he promised he would never do it again."

"And after your dad made those promises to you, after the CPS people came to your house, did there come a night after that when you were in the bathroom when Lizz [Martin] found you?"

"Yes."

"What happened that night that made you go into the bathroom?" Siegler asked.

"I don't remember really," Amber responded.

"Do you remember Lizz finding you on the bathroom floor?"

"Yes."

"And the next morning, did you tell Lizz why you were on the bathroom floor and what was going on?"

"No."

"Why didn't you tell Lizz, Amber?"

"I didn't like to talk about things."

"Tell the jury why you didn't like to talk about things and why you didn't talk to grown-ups about any of all of this."

"I was accused of being autistic and I had an imagination and I just kind of brushed it off always, like, 'think before you speak' kind of stuff."

"What do you mean when you say you were accused of having an imagination?"

"Like, if I say I saw something or the cat looks sick or something like that, kind of just . . ."

"Blow you off?" Siegler interjected.

"Yeah," Amber responded.

"So why did you never tell a grown-up about what was going on with your dad?"

"Just not in the habit of it. Probably just didn't cross my mind."

"What sort of names and things did your dad call you growing up?"

"Shithead."

"Do you think you're smart, Amber?"

"Yeah."

"Who do you think is smarter, you or your sister?"

"Probably my sister."

"Did there come a time in 1997 when you and your sister went to California?"

"Yes."

"To see and stay with who?"

"My grandmother on my dad's side."

"And why did y'all go see your grandmother?"

"Because it was my dad and Amy's honeymoon and they wanted to be alone."

"And did there come a time while you were in California when you told somebody about what was going on back in Houston?"

"Yes."

"Who did you tell?"

"My sister."

"And eventually did your grandmother find out?"

"Yes."

"And also your aunt Gina, did she also find out?"

"Yes."

"And after y'all told your grandmother what was going on, did the police officers and the CPS people there in Sacramento come and talk to y'all?"

"Yes."

"And did they interview you on a videotape and take your statement and all that?"

"Yes."

"And is that what led to the charges being filed on your father down here in Harris County?"

"Yeah."

"But you were never called back to Houston to testify about all that back then, were you?"

"No."

"When all this happened, and [it] came out in California, were you also asked to go down to let a doctor look at you to do a sexual assault kit or rape assault kit or something like that?" Siegler gingerly asked the young lady.

"Yes," Amber answered.

"Did you agree at first to let the doctor examine you?"

"No."

"Why not?"

"I was uncomfortable about it."

"What do you mean you were uncomfortable?"

"Just emotionally, I was uncomfortable."

"When you went to California back in '97, and way back in those days, how did you dress usually?"

"I wore too much clothes."

"Tell the jury why you wore too much clothes," Siegler asked as she spun around and faced the jurors.

"To cover myself," Amber replied.

"And how good were you back then at taking care of your body and taking baths and all that?"

"Not very good."

"Why not?"

"Because I felt uncomfortable getting dressed," Amber answered.

"Even by yourself alone?"

"Yeah, I felt kind of paranoid or something."

"Did you sleep with your dog back then?"

"Yeah."

"Why?"

"Because I thought it would protect me."

"From who?"

"My dad," Amber admitted.

"When you went to California, had you noticed any changes in your sister sometime before you and her went to California?"

"Yes."

"About how long before then?"

"About a year, maybe two."

"And tell us the difference between the old Tiffany and the Tiffany you saw the year before you went to California," Siegler requested.

"The old Tiffany was really happy and outgoing," Amber remembered, "and she liked being around people. She liked lots of attention. She was a people kind of person. She liked to express her talents. She loved singing and dancing and playing her guitar. And she was really proud of her accomplishments at school, like being in Band Guard and such."

"And the new Tiffany? The different Tiffany?"

"Then she started getting less confident about herself. She started dressing more differently, like more bigger clothes. She wasn't interested in school as much. She was losing confidence in herself, in her talent. She didn't like to sing anymore. She criticized herself about her music and her other talents."

"Tell the jury why it is that you finally had the courage to tell what your dad had been doing to you."

"Because it really upset me that something like that would happen to my sister," Amber stated clearly, then looked at the jury with almost pleading eyes.

"How do you feel about your sister?"

"She's a really good person and I thought she didn't deserve that. She was doing better than I did. She probably had a better chance or whatever. I was Special Ed and destined to fail and wasn't as confident about myself as I was in her."

"When you were growing up in your dad's house, Amber, how would he react to y'all when y'all would cry?"

"He would act like it drove him crazy or something." Amber's voice became raised.

"What would he do and what would he say when you and your sister would cry when you were little?"

"He told us to shut up or he'd give us a real spanking and yell, 'Stop crying!' continuously."

"Tell the jury what you mean when you say 'give you a real spanking.'"

"He gave us a real spanking if we did something he didn't like," Amber recalled. "Like, when we were younger, we had lots of energy. We would go to bed at bedtime and then, like, wake up at two in the morning and run around the house. And he didn't like that too much. So, he figured if he yanked us by our hair and threw us over his knee and tanned our hide and spanked the bottom of our feet really hard, we would stay in bed and we wouldn't get back out because our feet would hurt. So, he would call that a 'real spanking.'"

"What would happen when your dad would leave the house as far as keeping y'all in the house? Tell us about that," Siegler queried.

"He was pretty particular about the locks on the doors and having our windows superglued shut, because he was paranoid of burglars, he would say. So, if he left for work and we weren't out of there to go to school in time, we were just kind of trapped in the house."

"How did he feel about y'all getting your hair cut?"

"He didn't like it."

"And tell us about the hot chocolate when you were little."

"He would put something in it, because it tasted funny and it made me feel drowsy."

"Did that happen very often?" the ADA inquired.

"A couple of times."

"I think the question that the jury would like to know from you today, Amber, is tell us how you are doing today."

"I'm doing really good. I'm really happy with my life right now," Amber professed with a somewhat hesitant smile.

"What are your plans for the future?"

"I'm currently enrolled in a school—like, a do-at-home-school kind of thing for dog training."

"I think we could all say that we wish you luck in that. Okay?"

"Okay," the young lady responded.

"Pass the witness." Siegler ended her direct examination of Tony Shore's oldest daughter.

"Any cross?" Judge Cosper asked.

"No questions, Your Honor," Alvin Nunnery answered, per his client's wishes.

Next up for the prosecution was Tony Shore's youngest daughter, Tiffany Shore. The young lady walked up to the witness stand, was sworn in, and sat down.

Kelly Siegler approached Tiffany with a smile. "Ma'am, could you tell us your name, please?"

"Tiffany Lauren Shore," she responded confidently.

"How old are you?"

"Nineteen."

Tiffany continued to testify that she lived out of state, had a good job, and was attending college.

"Tell us a little bit about your sister. What's she like? The jury just got to hear from her, but you describe her for us."

"She is different. She's had kind of a rocky past. She seems to be trying to make better of herself now. She just got married and she's pregnant, going to have a baby. So, it looks like she's trying to start a new life for herself."

"When y'all were growing up, was she diagnosed or called autistic?"

"Yes, she was."

"Do you know what autism is?"

"I have a general idea, just a learning disability."

"Do you think that Amber is autistic?"

"No, I do not."

"And why do you think people said she was?"

"I really don't know."

"How do you feel about her learning ability or disabilities or all that?"

"I feel that if she puts her mind to it, she can get something done, that she doesn't have a learning disability. She has problems focusing on things that's she's disinterested in, but I think that's common for anybody.

"I think the only thing that's a setback for her," Tiffany continued, "is that she spent her whole life being told she was autistic and that she wouldn't amount to anything and that she couldn't learn. So, that is disturbing on her part, I would think. But I would say, given the opportunity and the encouragement, that she would do fine."

"Besides being called autistic," Siegler asked the younger sister, "what else was she called when y'all were little?"

"Just, I don't know, special, retarded. . . . It was just highly enforced that she had a learning disability. Everybody was really set on that, whether she had one or not. It was like they wanted her to have a problem."

"How did Amber treat you when y'all were growing up?"

"Kind of like I was the one that was going to get somewhere. She kind of treated me almost like a caretaker, like I was always the better one, you know."

"When is the last time before today that you've seen your dad?"

"June of 1997."

"And how do you feel about being here today to testify, Tiffany?"

"Apprehensive, anxious, kind of sick to my stomach, and nervous." Tiffany appeared calm despite her words.

"Tell the jury how old you were when your parents got divorced and you ended up living with your dad."

"I don't really remember. I guess I was pretty normal when I moved in with my dad. Just in school. I was in advanced-learning classes in school. I did all right. I had friends," Tiffany responded, but she apparently misunderstood the question.

"Did there come a time when you and your sister went to stay with your grandmother in 1997, that you told your aunt Gina something for the first time?"

"Yes."

"And is she the first grown-up, the first person, that you told this to?"

"Yes, she is."

"What did you tell her, Tiffany?"

"I told her I was being molested by my father and that I was afraid to live with him anymore."

"Tell the jury what was about to happen that made you be afraid to come back to Houston," Siegler requested.

"My sister was going to go live with my aunt Gina for a year for school purposes and I would be living alone with him," Tiffany answered.

"And why were you afraid to live alone with him?"

"I was just afraid that being alone, there would be nobody around; that he would have more opportunities to do more things to me."

"How long had he been doing those things to you?"

"Honestly, I don't know. As far as I can recall, between the ages of ten and twelve. I have reason to believe that things went on when I was a child, but I don't know. I don't really remember any of my childhood at all."

"We won't go into all the details of it, but what do you mean when you say 'the things he was doing to you'?"

"Just inappropriate touching."

"On your private part?"

"Uh-huh."

"Was there a time when you were eleven years old and you were washing up in a bathtub?"

"Yes."

"And what was your dad doing to you this time you remember from the bathtub?"

"He was touching me inappropriately."

"Can you tell the jury what you remember about the hot chocolate, growing up?"

"If we had friends over when I was between the ages of, like, ten and twelve, he would always have us drink hot chocolate. And I always remember just falling asleep shortly after that."

"Would the friends drink the hot chocolate too?" Siegler wondered.

"Yes. There was a certain point where my sister and I became suspicious of it and didn't want to drink it anymore. It tasted funny too."

"Did your dad ever do anything to you when you were little that had to do with the sheets of the bed?"

"Uh-huh."

"Tell us about that."

"When we got in trouble and we would cry about

something, he would tie us up in our sheets and smother our face with a pillow and tell us we were not allowed to cry in his household."

"Was there a place where your dad threatened to send Amber when he got upset with her?"

Tiffany nodded. "He would threaten to send her to an institution."

"And when your dad would leave the house, how would he keep y'all in the house?"

"All the doors in the house had dead bolts on them and he locked all the dead bolts. And all the windows were either glued or nailed shut so that they didn't open."

"And when you were little, did you think that was unusual?"

"No."

"When you told your aunt Gina and your grandma in '97 in California about what was going on, you also talked to some police officers back then, did you not?"

"Uh-huh."

"And you were videotaped by that lady from the Children's Protective Services?"

"Uh-huh."

"And you were asked to go see a doctor about a sexual assault exam?"

"Uh-huh."

"Did you want to do that?"

"No."

"Why not?"

"Because I was uncomfortable with my body and being exposed to the people."

"And what do you mean by that, you were 'uncomfortable being exposed'?"

"Just uncomfortable being undressed."

"How about when it was just you, all by yourself, undressed?" Siegler probed.

"I was just uncomfortable being undressed by myself," Tiffany declared, "around other people, just at all."

"Did you wear a lot of clothes back then?"

"Yes, I did."

"Why?"

"Because I was ashamed of my body, and if I was covered in layers of clothes, nobody could see it. Just kind of, like, hiding."

"Besides just how you felt about your body, how did you feel about yourself back then?" the prosecutor asked.

"I hated myself. I had very little self-esteem. I basically just wanted to die."

"Are you seeing a counselor?"

"Yes, I am."

"And have you been seeing a counselor for a while?"

"When I moved to California, I went to counseling for three-and-a-half years. I was released from counseling and therapy, and recently, about a month ago, I started counseling again."

"And tell us, Tiffany, how you're doing in your life now?"

"I'm doing well for myself now. I have a good job. I have a good boyfriend. I'm in a good relationship. I like where I live. I have a decent roommate. I can pretty much trust the people that are in my life right now."

"And how do you feel about your father now?"

"He's dead to me. He's my biological father. I have people in my life that have been a part of my life for the past seven years that are just like parents to me and I see those people as my parents, not my biological parents, as my parents. They're just flesh and blood to me. That's all."

"Pass the witness." Kelly Siegler had concluded her questioning of both of Tony Shore's daughters.

Once again, Shore's defense team elected not to cross-examine the witness. "No questions," stated Gerald Bourque.

Judge Cosper excused Tiffany Shore from the witness stand.

CHAPTER 61

Wednesday, October 27, 2004,
Harris County Courthouse,
1201 Franklin Street,
Courtroom #337,
Houston, Texas.

The prosecution wanted to make sure the jury heard a clinical psychiatric evaluation of Anthony Allen Shore and what may have driven him to rape and kill young girls. Assistant District Attorney Terese Buess interviewed Dr. Sharon Burns, a registered sex offender treatment provider, and a professional counselor for Burns, Crimson & Associates, located in Houston, Texas.

Dr. Burns was a specialist in the field of "sex offender treatment." To receive such a distinction, she had to conduct nearly four hundred hours of sex offender–specific training with various authorities, such as FBI agents, a psychopathy specialist, and renowned sex offender–treatment therapist, Dr. Robert Hare.

Dr. Burns was also a veteran of courtroom testimony.

Buess asked the distinguished witness to "tell the jury, please, what sex offender treatment is."

"Sex offender treatment is a cognitive behavioral program," Dr. Burns asserted. "By cognitive, I mean the thoughts, thinking patterns. Behavior actually stems from how we perceive a situation and what we think about it.

"So, when we work with sex offenders," she continued, "we work on helping them understand the offense and the victim's point of view and what they're really doing so that they can learn to control the behavior, because once the thoughts change about an action, our actions change, or the thoughts change about a situation or an individual, our actions change."

"A lot of people that come for sex offender treatment," Buess asked, "what kind of people are they? How is it they come to be in your program?"

"They're all kinds of people," Dr. Burns answered. "We do have both men and women. We have people as young as eleven years of age through their eighties. There's no specific background as far as age, race, sex, kind of job, level of education, how much money they earn, or what part of the country they've lived in. It's a behavior that crosses a lot of different boundaries."

The doctor continued, "Many of them are incest offenses where they might have someone who, for whatever reason, became close with a child and used that child to meet needs that they weren't meeting appropriately in other ways."

"The people who come, who sign up for your course, do they do that just voluntarily on their own, come and pay their fee and take your course?" Buess asked. "Why are they there?"

"Actually, the vast majority—I've only had one voluntary client—the vast majority are court-ordered once they've been identified as having committed some type of sexual offense, anywhere from exposure to rape to

incest. But the most we see have female victims, children
and adults."

"Incest and rape?"

"Primarily."

"Is it about sex?" prosecutor Buess asked in regard to
rape.

The doctor shook her head and said, "It's about
power and control. Most of the individuals don't feel as
though they have self-control and so they try to control
others in their environment and they use others to meet
their needs, however inappropriate that may be."

"And is that even more so when it's a child that's the
victim."

"Yes, it is."

Buess then had Dr. Burns lay out the normal testing
procedure for a new patient. Dr. Burns informed the
jury that she administers four tests to each patient. She
tests intelligence levels, tolerance for drugs and alcohol,
a personality test, and a social-functioning test. For sex
offenders, Dr. Burns also includes a multiphasic sexual
inventory, which helps her determine what may drive a
sexual offender to commit such an act.

"Did you score and review the test results for Anthony
Shore?" Terese Buess queried.

"Yes, ma'am, I did," Dr. Burns answered.

"What year did he take that battery of tests?"

"I believe it was '98."

"Did he complete all of the tests that you asked?"

"He completed them all."

"And tell the jury what level his intellectual functioning was at."

"Superior range," replied Dr. Burns. Shore briefly
glanced up at the doctor and then glanced back down
at the defense table. "Oddly enough, when you got

somebody that's on either end of the intellectual functioning range, you run into more problems.

"There are obvious problems whenever they're in the mentally challenged range," Dr. Burns declared, "because you have to repeat and repeat and repeat. And they may not understand things.

"On the other hand, the superior side, we run into problems because they think, 'Well, I know more than anybody else. I know more than you, and I can play games with what you give me.'"

"What was the level of abstract reasoning that you saw for Anthony Shore?" Buess asked.

"Again, superior, extremely high."

"Any evidence of any kind of biological brain damage?"

"There was no organic brain damage indicated at all."

"Let's talk a little bit about his emotional functioning," Buess suggested. "Was that evaluated as part of the battery of tests?"

"That is in the personality assessment," Dr. Burns confirmed.

"And what was the result on that?"

"That Mr. Shore liked to be in control, that he liked to align himself with—actually, it said that he would adopt a cotherapist's role."

"What does that mean?"

"Anthony is good at hearing information and saying it back," Dr. Burns replied. "And what he would do is, if you align yourself with the therapist and you focus on the other members of the group—but if you put yourself in the therapist's role and are pointing out other people's problems, you can sound like you have a lot of knowledge and you can sound like you know the right material."

"When you do that, does it elevate you away from the group of sex offenders that are there for treatment?"

"It does."

"Talk to the jury, please, very briefly, about his personality functioning. What features were you seeing there?"

"Grandiosity."

"What is that? What is grandiosity?"

"Which is, 'I count more than you do. You don't really matter. I'm what's important.' Most people realize . . . there's a balance in that. Of course I want to elevate myself, but not to the extent that I think my needs are greater than yours. What I want matters to me and nothing about what you want matters."

"What else did you see?"

"Narcissism. Narcissism is self-love taken to the extreme. That person—you put those two together and they know everything about everything and it's about them. 'I'm wonderful.'"

"Is there an example of behavior that you could give the jury of someone who's narcissistic?"

"For the narcissist, it's just about them. They don't care about anybody else. They just want their life to be easy. And other people are really not people. There's not enough importance attached to other people. They have trouble with relationships because it's not 'Well, honey, you don't feel well today? Why aren't you up taking care of me?'

"And when he would come into treatment," Dr. Burns expounded on Shore, "the narcissist wants to be noticed. That's part of it, too, wanting to adopt that role because he wanted to be seen as 'Look how important I am. Look how much I know, and I'm in a much better place than you guys because I don't have the problems that y'all have.'"

"Is part of that also that superficially charming demeanor that he's got?" the assistant district attorney asked.

"He also had repressed anger," Dr. Burns added. "So, if he got angry, you wouldn't see it unless you just saw minute clinching of the jaw and different facial features, like a tic or something, you can see when somebody is angry and they say they're not. A clinched jaw, little things like that.

"If he didn't want to deal with an issue, he would shut down and become very complimentary. He was always very complimentary."

"When he is complimentary, what is he doing?" Buess wondered.

"The term that we use is called 'grooming.' Grooming is something we all engage in," the doctor began to explain. "I'm sure you've all been involved in a job interview or you want to go out with someone, and so what you did was presented your best side and you presented what that person wanted to hear. If you didn't like the painting on the wall and you're in a job interview, you don't say, 'That's an ugly painting.' If they like it, probably, 'Oh, that's very nice. And I like this about you and I like that.' You would present yourself to be what they want."

"Personality functioning," Terese Buess changed test categories. "Was it very clear from the test results that Anthony Shore knew what was socially acceptable and what was not?"

"He definitely showed awareness of that, not only in the testing but throughout the time in treatment," Dr. Burns responded.

"Let's talk a little bit about criminal characteristics. Is that something that typically is evaluated as part of the admissions process?"

"Yes, it is."

"Tell the jury what a criminal characteristic is."

"A criminal characteristic is something that you would see. Like, we see characteristics that might be similar among teachers or among coaches or among rock players. Criminals often have characteristics that are similar among each other," Dr. Burns explained. "For instance, they're interested in what they can get. They may be opportunistic, that when an opportunity for whatever crime is their choice occurs, that they are able to jump right in there and take advantage of it. That's a real strong criminal characteristic."

"And did Anthony Shore test high in that area?"

"He did."

"The ability to break a law when you think you can get away with it?"

"Right. And on that particular test, I think one of the statements is that as long as he thought he would get away with it, that he would be willing to engage in a criminal behavior."

"Was it clearly determined that he was going to be a manipulator?"

"Yes."

"Is part of that degree of intelligence that you are dealing with here," Buess asked, "and part of the personality quirks that you were looking at, the narcissism that 'I'm more important than anybody else,' did Anthony Shore perceive himself as being treated unjustly?"

"He did," Dr. Burns agreed. "There was an entire page that he wrote in 1999 in drug treatment that talks about how unfairly the criminal justice system had treated him, how they made lots of promises that he would not be subjected to the same kind of standard of supervision that the other sex offenders were, that he would be treated differently.

"And he was. In the page he wrote, he was quite distressed. He finally kind of just blew the whole thing off with anger, because it was something that he was seeing he wasn't getting out of.

"He actually spent three weeks in jail for not complying, for not getting with the program."

"Let's talk a little bit about how he tested in the area of sexual functioning. Are there questions about rape in that?"

"There are."

"And how did he respond to those?"

"He denied having any characteristics."

"Is he given an opportunity to provide you with a picture of him as a sexual being or as a nonsexual being?"

"Most people would admit to having sexual desires and would admit attraction to age-appropriate adults of the sex that they preferred to be with. When someone is trying to fake on that test, they present themselves as what's known as asexual. All it means is without sexual interest."

"In other words, 'I'm here for sex offender treatment because my probation has made me be here, but I'm really not a sexual person and, therefore, I don't need this'?" Buess asked.

"'How could I need this if I'm not sexual?'" Dr. Burns responded, as if speaking about Shore.

"Do you believe that test score?"

"No. I usually tell people maybe we need to call the coroner," which elicited chuckles from the gallery and some members of the jury.

"As a result of all these tests that were administered, was there a warning that was noted in Anthony Shore's file for your purposes for the therapist?"

"Yes. It warned us to be careful with him because he was of superior intelligence and that he would try to use his reasoning and verbal and social skills to—or, criminal is actually what they were—to manipulate our perception of him and how he was doing in treatment."

"Once he's accepted for sex offender treatment, is there a contract that is signed?"

"There is."

"And did Anthony Shore sign a contract?"

"Yes, he did."

"Are there a set of rules that are in writing as part of that contract that he's supposed to be abiding by?"

"Most definitely."

"And part of it is in conjunction with the conditions of probation he's not allowed to use any alcohol or drugs?"

"Correct."

"The rules that were given to him in writing, is he required to keep them in a workbook?" Buess questioned.

"Yes, he is."

"And is he ordered, as part of the treatment program, not to have contact with any minors, any children?"

"Yes, without therapist approval, and that was never given in this case."

"So, Anthony Shore never had therapist approval to live with a minor?"

"No, he did not."

"Part of the contract agreement for sex offender treatment, was it that he has to be honest and candid and truthful as he goes through his therapy?"

"That's a requirement for successful intervention."

"Because without that, the whole thing is kind of pointless, isn't it?"

"It is."

"If no progress is noted," Buess asked, "if someone's just sitting there and not admitting to anything and not working within the group, what happens?"

"We give them time to work through it," Dr. Burns responded. "But then there comes a time that they're unsatisfactorily discharged. Now, a requirement of sex offender probation is that they successfully participate . . . and so, they must talk. Otherwise, I don't know what they're thinking and cannot successfully work with them. So, they run the risk of being unsatisfactorily discharged, which is a technical violation, which sets them up for possible revocation of their probation."

"Revocation on a felony case, meaning they're going to prison?" the ADA clarified.

"Exactly."

"In Anthony Shore's case, were there frequent times when he was hitting that point where there was no progress and he was informed that a report was going to be sent to his probation officer that he was not in compliance with his treatment program?"

"Absolutely. We try to encourage them. And one of the ways that we do that is to say, 'Look, we're going to have to send this. These are the risks you run. So, you need to get honest. You need to start talking.'"

Terese Buess took a good long look at the jury, and then she turned to Dr. Burns.

"I want to talk with the jury and with you very briefly about your observations of Anthony Shore's participation and progress in sex offender treatment throughout the years that he was there. That would be 1998 up to 2003. Did he ever properly disclose? And that's important, is it not?"

"Yes."

"Just like an alcoholic standing up and saying, 'I am an alcoholic' as the first step. Do you require full disclosure of the offense that brought them to your treatment?"

"Yes. And it is extremely important that they do," Dr. Burns agreed.

"When things would get a little hot in your sessions, in other words, he's about to get kicked out, what would Anthony Shore do?"

"Anthony was taking a lot of time in what I call coming out of denial. At that time . . . we weren't always given all the details of the original offense. We kind of had to pull it out piece by piece." Dr. Burns paused and looked at her former client. "And in this process, after long periods of denial, Anthony finally admitted that his daughters had been drinking, had snuck out of the house, they came home drunk, that he was trying to help them sober up. And for his older daughter, he got her in the shower. She had been sick on herself and so he said he took her clothes off of her and that in the process he noticed that she was developing and she passed out and he did touch her breast and her vagina. And finally, even longer after that, that perhaps he did digitally penetrate her vagina."

"From total denial," Buess began, "which is where he was when he started, to getting to that point, how many years did that take?"

"It varied because what would happen is he would come to a point where he would admit it and then he would start working on it and then he would go back in denial."

"Did he blame others for what had happened?"

"Mostly, he minimized. It's like saying that you've only drank and drove one time when you've done it a thousand [times], or that you only touched the breasts when you actually had full intercourse."

"So, he was minimizing?"

"All the way through."

"Did he blame others for what he had done, for other things?"

"He blamed the courts for the situation that he was in. It was their fault because he really didn't do anything. He blamed his ex-wife because he said that she put his daughters up to saying that, just because she was angry at him and that he really didn't do anything. So, he was always the victim."

"You mentioned that there was a warning that Anthony Shore could become a cotherapist, controlling. Did that actually happen?" Buess asked.

"Yes, yes," Dr. Burns answered, along with a nod of her head. "Some of the guys say they got things from what Anthony Shore said to them. They would learn because he was good at saying the right things. Like, it's wrong to rape."

"Tell the jury, please, what Anthony Shore's response was to any attempts to get him to show empathy for his victims."

"He would say things like, 'They're not going to be able to have their dad around.' He envisioned having his daughters become rock stars and now the fact that he had done what he had done, they weren't able to be around him, so they lost out on that opportunity to become rock stars, and they were really wonderful kids."

"Tell the jury what's wrong with that."

"What's wrong with that is that that's the least of their concerns, that they lost out on an opportunity to become a rock star," Dr. Burns stated incredulously. "They lost out on an opportunity to have a life in which they could raise their children and love their husband and be loved by their husband and even others." The gallery looked appalled as they shot daggers into Shore's skull. "Victims . . . always question why others want to be around them. 'What do they want from me?' Especially if the perpetrator's a male and they're a female and they're heterosexual."

Terese Buess pulled out a leather-bound notebook. "Ms. Burns, I'm showing you what's been admitted into evidence as State's Exhibit 211. What is that?"

"That's Anthony Shore's treatment book."

"On October 21, 2003, did you come into possession of that?"

"Yes, I did."

"How did you come to have it?"

"Mr. Shore left it at his last treatment session before he was arrested."

"And was that book opened up to try and figure out who it belonged to?"

"Yes. My associate and I opened the book and went through it, recognized it was Anthony's and went through it a little bit more."

"Tell the jury, please, aside from the assignments that you found in there, what else was in there"

"There were images of nude females with shaved pubic hair and a conversational Spanish/English translation book."

Terese Buess held up the pictures of the naked women found in Shore's treatment book. "Tell me about these. Are these within your rules and regulations?"

"They are a definite violation."

"And, specifically, you mentioned the shaving of the pubic hair. Was that important to you?"

"In my training, that indicates someone who has an interest in children will ask that their partner shave their pubic hair. Many pornographers will use shaved pubic hair in the images for that reason, so they look younger." (This, despite the fact that many young men and women prefer themselves and/or their partners to be shaven so there is less interference when performing cunnilingus or fellatio.)

"As a result of finding those images in Anthony Shore's book, was a decision made at your program concerning his attendance and participation?"

"This to me said—him writing in his treatment manual—[that] he didn't have any interest in the program or what we were teaching."

"Was it significant to you that those images were actually in that binder?"

"It was significant to me," Dr. Burns replied.

"What did that say to you?"

"There's another part that we haven't talked about Mr. Anthony Shore, and that's the nature of his personality disorder. The narcissism, the grandiosity. 'See how I can carry this. And I'm sitting in group and you don't even know I have it.'"

"'So, I can get away with it?'" Buess added.

"'I can get away with it. I can do what I want to do.' And this book gets pulled open many times and papers are pulled out. So, it could have fallen out, but he had no concern about that. He would just sit there with it in his lap. The whole time he's sitting in group, he knew that was there. It was kind of thumbing his nose at everything we were doing, because he's sitting there going, 'Look, I've got this.'"

"Is it a violation of the contract to possess pornography?"

"It certainly is."

Buess then referred to the large box of porn that was discovered in Lynda White's garage when Shore was arrested. Buess mentioned the fact that not all of the magazines in the large box were pornographic.

"The magazines that were not porn did seem to be all of Hispanic origin," Dr. Burns informed.

"The pornography that's in here, was there a type of pornography that seems to be mostly?"

"It's mostly nude females and many of them do have shaved pubic hair. Some of them had physical damage to particularly the breast area."

Prosecutor Buess then directed Dr. Burns toward some of Tony Shore's collages, which the police discovered in Lynda White's garage. "Did we look at a variety of things that Anthony Shore has cut and worked on?"

"Yes, ma'am, we did."

Buess pointed to one of Shore's naked-women collages that was discovered in his box of porn. "They're all women, are they not?"

"They are all that we saw."

The prosecutor asked her to describe one of Shore's collages.

"It looks like he cut each image as if you would a paper doll—paper doll clothes. You know how you have to cut out exactly the edge of it. They're cut, just the image itself, and then he pieced the images together side by side so they're all interlocking with just this collage. All you see are women and their bodies."

"Is that easy to do?" Buess pondered.

"It doesn't look very easy, and I've done some collages."

"Tell the jury, please, what does that indicate to you, the amount of time and effort and the amount—we went through all those items and the envelopes of pictures and thousands of women that have been cut out. What does that tell you about Anthony Shore?" Buess wanted to know.

"Where you spend your time and your energy is where your interests are, and he spent a lot of time and energy on those pictures," Dr. Burns answered.

"Is this art?"

"I guess it depends on the person's individual perception."

"There were a few items that you and I separated from the massive cut pictures." She pointed to one of the pieces of evidence. "What does that contain?"

"These are varying young-looking girls," Dr. Burns responded in regard to a photograph from a magazine of a nude woman. "Again, the shaved pubic hair. She looks fourteen. They are very young and there's the word 'fresh.'"

"I'm going to show you now what's inside the envelope marked State's Exhibit 215. What is that?"

"This is hard-core pornography showing intercourse

between a man and a female. She's got on ankle socks and that is associated with young girls. Young girls frequently go to gyms. They might have on shorts. They've got their sneakers on. They might wear socks. So, certainly, things like pleated skirts, bobby socks, are associated with young females."

"And finally I'm going to show you what's inside State's Exhibit 217. What are those?"

"These are pictures of breasts that have been harmed. There are bruise marks."

"Why would someone keep pictures like that?"

"Because, again, of an interest in that particular behavior that's associated with that. That would be appealing to someone into inflicting pain on other individuals."

"We talked about rape not being about sex. Where does the pain come in to all this stuff?" Buess inquired.

"It's about power and control and it goes even further, because the sadomasochistic individual likes the infliction of pain. It brings them pleasure."

"So, it's all about them?"

"Yes. Them."

"During the time that you had Tony Shore involved with treatment, did he appear to know everything about everything?"

"He did. He's an interesting individual to converse with."

"On October 29, 2003, was Anthony Shore terminated from the program?"

"Yes, ma'am, he was."

"Now, since that time, have you reviewed the offense reports that you didn't have at that time of his offense against his own daughter?" Buess asked.

"Yes, I did."

"Now that you know all of that information, did Anthony Shore ever fully disclose or even get close to it?"

"He never even got close," Dr. Burns responded.

"You've read the statements of his girlfriend and his wife about the drugging and the choking and the sexual acts."

"Yes, ma'am, I did."

"Tell the jury what's important about that to you. What's going on there?"

"It seems like because he was being monitored, what he did was use the drugs to put these women and girls into a state simulating death. If someone is unconscious then and they're drugged unconscious, you can move their body and you can do what you want with them and they have no awareness of it, much like a dead person.

"The statements also indicated," Dr. Burns continued, "that the women would sometimes wake up with their throats and necks being sore and having a sore throat. Some would wake up with his hands around their throats. That was simulating the crimes he had committed."

"Did you learn that the defendant killed an animal, a cat, when he was a very young age, four or five or six?"

"Yes, I did," Dr. Burns answered.

"Is that significant to you?"

"Yes, it is in terms of the other aspects of psychopathy."

"So, when we talk about a psychopath, we're talking about someone who's aware of society's rules?"

"Yes."

"But is above all of that?"

"Yes," the doctor replied.

"And will do anything that they can, or want to, as long as they can get away with it?"

"Yes, yes."

"Tell the jury, please, how do you become a psychopath?" the ADA posed.

"From all we can determine, it's something that seems

to be more of what they are than what they've become. And it's not anything that's short-term."

"I want to go through the checklist of characteristics that are looked at [to determine whether or not a person is a psychopath]. Number one, glibness, superficial charm. There's something that's looked at?"

"That's somebody who's able to kind of sense what it is that you like and talk about the things that you like, a very charming individual. A lot of salesmen score high on that one."

"Grandiose sense of self-worth," Buess continued.

"That's when the individual feels like they're the king or queen and entitled to all sorts of things that the rest of us aren't entitled to by the very fact that we don't matter like they do."

"Cunning or manipulative?"

"Using whatever means they can to kind of set the situation up so that it's in their favor."

"Lack of remorse or guilt?"

"That enables the person to continue engaging in a behavior that even just a little bit of guilt could stop somebody from doing it. The person who doesn't have any remorse will go to the extreme that most people would stop way before ever getting there," Dr. Burns elaborated.

"Where does Anthony Shore fall on this particular scale?"

"As far as I've been able to determine . . . he's in the highest level."

"Let's talk a little bit about religion here. During the time that Anthony Shore was involved with treatment, was religion used as a crutch or as a topic of discussion for him or by him?"

"Anthony Shore talked about finding God several years back," Dr. Burns recalled. "It is not unusual, in sex offender treatment or in basically any kind of offense, for people to find God. One of the people I trained under, Dr. Anna Salter, did a study and called it the 'double life.' How the sex offender would pretend to be one person in front of other people and then when no one was around was this entirely different person. And so they would just use the manipulation and cunning to present who they thought you wanted them to be. And that's what he would do."

"So, if Anthony Shore is now claiming that he's found God since he's been incarcerated for the last year, that's nothing new to you, is it?" Buess wondered.

"No, he found God a while back."

"Based on what you know about Anthony Shore's behavior patterns, was it a surprise to find out that he asked this jury to give him the death penalty?"

"No, it wasn't. That's consistent with a psychopath."

"Which part of that?"

"He would be in control if he asked for the death sentence and was awarded it on his behalf. It also could be a manipulation when, 'If I ask for the death sentence and later I change my mind, I have a lot more ground to stand on than if you dictated for me.'

"Another thing is," the doctor continued, "that's a media catcher. His name would be dragged out in the limelight even more because it could catch people off guard. They would think, 'Wow!'"

Dr. Sharon Burns then added, "It's also a ploy for sympathy."

"What does killing young girls—raping them and killing them—do for someone like Anthony Shore?"

"It's an adrenaline rush. It's a thrill. That's the ultimate control—to have power over life and death—for an individual to have that power."

"Do you have an opinion about whether Tony Shore

presents a danger of committing violent acts in the future?"

"Yes, ma'am, I have. I do believe that he would. Everything that I've seen, he didn't stop. He continued to engage in behaviors that were on the fringes of it. He drugged his girlfriends to simulate victims that he had murdered in the past. He carried pornography in his treatment notebook. It looks like he was just biding his time until there weren't so many eyes watching him in order to act out again."

"Even in a controlled environment like the Texas Department of Criminal Justice, do you think he's a danger?" Buess inquired.

"Yes, I do."

"Are women employees at TDCJ, in the prison system?"

"In the male system, yes, there are."

"In your opinion, does Anthony Shore present a danger to these women that work in that system?"

"I believe that he is."

"Pass the witness." Prosecutor Buess was done with Dr. Burns.

CHAPTER 62

Wednesday, October 27, 2004,
Harris County Courthouse,
1201 Franklin Street,
Courtroom #337,
Houston, Texas.

There would be no more witnesses in the case against Anthony Shore. The jury was ready to hear closing arguments.

Up first was the defense. Alvin Nunnery announced, "Your Honor, at this time the defense waives any argument in this case at the request of Mr. Shore, but against the very strong advice of Mr. Bourque and myself."

Next up was Terese Buess for the state. She began her final closing argument by empathizing with the jurors. She let them know that she "agonized with you this entire punishment half of the trial." She talked about the evidence, the crime scene photos, the tearful testimony of Selma Janske, and the surviving family members of Tony Shore's multiple victims.

"Every one of us in this courtroom has been touched

by evil," Buess lamented. "All of us. Whatever it was he did to them, we are as marked as they were."

Buess then addressed Tony Shore's request for the death penalty. "Anthony Shore doesn't get it yet. He doesn't understand that this is not all about him. Even this trial. This is who it's about," Buess stated as she pointed at photographs of Maria del Carmen Estrada, Diana Rebollar, Dana Sanchez, Laurie Tremblay, Selma Janske, Lizz Martin, Amy Lynch, Pauline Cody, Amber Shore, and Tiffany Shore. "All of these women, four of them died at his hands. One of them he left alive after brutalizing her. His own children, the lives that he gave them, the way he sexually used them, that's what we're here about today."

In regard to Shore's request, Buess added, ". . . by trying to take that final decision away from you, which can't be done, it was just a poor attempt because now we're here and each of you have the power to make this end the way it should."

Assistant District Attorney Buess wanted the jurors to make sure that they were meeting the special issues against Tony Shore. She brought up his potential for future violence and how he had drugged and choked and raped the women he supposedly loved.

"You know what's scary about this?" Buess asked. "We all know he's got the intelligence to make it happen. If the opportunity arises, he will be out and he will be back in your community. And we all know what a dangerous situation that's going to be."

Buess then addressed the second special issue in regard to any mitigating factors that may have negatively contributed to Shore's actions.

"Let's take a look at him," Buess surmised. "Superior intelligence. And what does he choose? He plans. He fantasizes. Fantasies about the sick things that he's going to do and then he plans them and he executes them. Then he disposes of the bodies in ways that evidence can't be recovered from them.

"That's what he chose to do with his intelligence. That's not mitigating. That's damning."

Buess talked about his musical savant status. "You heard about him being a wonderful musician. A great artist. Can pick up an instrument and play it in fifteen minutes. Anything. He chose not to work with that. He chose not to be the professional musician he could have been.

"What did he choose to do with his hands instead? What did he choose to spend his time with? He broke pieces of wood. He got a toothbrush. He got the items together that he needed to commit his crimes. He took yellow nylon rope and singed the end so that the rope wouldn't come apart. That's what he chose to do with his artistic hands.

"Those are choices that Anthony Shore made. They're not mitigating. They're damning."

Buess closed with evocations of screams. "He talks about nine-year-old Diana Rebollar fighting the hardest of them all. That's because he was engaged with her fighting, fighting, fighting. What he didn't tell you about is all the screams because you know all four girls—Carmen, Dana, Laurie, and Diana—you know they all screamed like hell. But he can't tell you about that, because, you see, that's not about him."

Buess addressed the jury in closing. "You have the power. Not him. You have it. You have the power to do justice. You have the power to tell him we're going to hold you responsible for what you are and for what you have done. You're a horrible monster. You're a serial killer. You're a child rapist.

"Despicable isn't even a good enough word for what he is."

Kelly Siegler reiterated Buess's closing point that Tony Shore was still trying to control things by demanding to receive the death penalty. Siegler also wanted to make sure that the jury understood that Shore was truly a bad man.

"As much as we don't want to believe it, and as much as Sharon Burns still tries to figure it out, there are people who are just born mean and bad and sick and evil. And all the shrinks in the world can't fix them and can't figure it out."

Siegler continued, "And what's even more scary about that in a case like this is that sometimes those sick, evil, mean, bad people look just like him. Look just like us. Look normal. All-American. No one would ever suspect it. No one would have a clue. Look how many people he fooled.

"And now he wants you to think . . . that he's deserving of fame and recognition because he's special and he's to be analyzed and figured out, and people are going to use him as a case study for some reason.

"Now he's flipped all this into making you think he's special. Anthony Shore, you're not special. You're nothing."

Siegler ended her closing with "even the defendants on death row would give him the death penalty."

Less than one hour later the jury had returned with a sentence.

"We, the jury, find the defendant, Anthony Allen Shore, guilty of capital murder, as charged in the indictment.

"'Special Issue Number One—Do you find from the evidence beyond a reasonable doubt that there is a probability that the defendant, Anthony Allen Shore, would commit criminal acts of violence that would constitute a continuing threat to society?'

"Answer—We, the jury, unanimously find and determine beyond a reasonable doubt that the answer to this special issue is 'Yes.'

"'Special Issue Number Two—Do you find from the evidence, taking into consideration all of the evidence, including the circumstances of the offense, the defendant's character and background and the personal moral culpability of the defendant, Anthony Allen Shore, that there is a sufficient mitigating circumstance or circumstances to warrant that a sentence of life imprisonment rather than a death sentence be imposed?'

"Answer—We, the jury, unanimously find and determine beyond a reasonable doubt that the answer to this special issue is 'No.'"

After Anthony Shore received his death sentence, he requested that his attorneys forgo the filing of his appeal. He informed the judge that he wanted to be executed as soon as possible.

Tony Shore currently awaits his fate on death row at the Polunsky Unit in Livingston, Texas.

EPILOGUE

Some random discussions, thoughts, and quotes on Anthony Allen "Tony" Shore:

<u>Gina Worley Shore</u>

"I wish I knew where that person was and how I missed it. He was charismatic, not like in a Cary Grant kind of way, but he was always courteous and thoughtful and had a good sense of humor and [was] intelligent," Gina recalled. "He liked things to be neat and he liked his music. He used to be an avid reader, but as he got more into writing music, I'd say, 'Why don't you read a book?' He'd say, 'I read music.'

"He was like a kid that would throw temper tantrums."

In describing his temper tantrums, Gina recalled, "I saw him get really, really mad once. We were in Weingartens. I was pregnant with Amber and we were just doing regular shopping when a kid ran past me. I was eight months pregnant. This kid was a big kid and he hit me really hard in the shoulder and it was hard for me to catch my balance. I looked over at Tony and he turned the whitest shade of green. You know they say most people get flushed and turn red or they get pale?

He was green. It was weird. He wanted to go hurt that kid and I told him to calm down because I wasn't hurt. But that was the angriest I ever saw him."

According to Gina, Tony never directed his anger toward her. "We would have these little arguments, but it would always be about finances. "I'd say, 'Ha, ha, you spent way too much money on musical instruments.' He'd say, 'But, it was a helluva deal.' I'd ask him how many 'helluva deals' can you have in one day, Tony?"

When asked if she believed her ex-husband killed more than four girls, Gina replied, "I don't know. I have heard from his sister that he has since recanted his confessions and he wants another trial. Now he's saying he confessed under duress. 'Oh, just kidding,'" Gina joked as if she were acting like her ex-husband.

"And then he wrote his sister and he wanted to know *my* address. Frightening. I flirted with the idea for a while. But then I thought, I don't really know who he knows. Just because he's in jail doesn't mean he doesn't have people outside of jail.

"I'd be intrigued to hear what he has to say, but it's not worth the long-term risk."

Gina mentioned that Tony uses the Internet from prison to find pen pals. She spoke of a letter he wrote that is posted on a German Web site. "It's such a nice letter. That's the kind of person he is. He does have a way of sounding nice and not horrible."

As for Tony's current belief in religion, Gina had her doubts. "I don't know if he is sincere about anything. It's really hard to tell. Maybe this is really him and he's finally just come out of the closet and is saying, 'Okay, here I am, I'm horrible, I don't need to keep on pretending anymore.'"

Gina believed Tony's desperate need for attention and stardom simply boiled down to the fact that "he wanted to be a famous musician. He wanted to be famous. He was very gregarious; he liked parties; he liked being in large groups of people performing. If he had to choose between being rich or being famous, I think he would have chosen fame."

Rob Shore

"You wonder how it happened. Inevitably you're curious about that. Certainly you don't want to blame. I'm sure a lot of people sit and ponder what went wrong. If I did something wrong, it was unintentional. And I'm not sure I did."

Rob Shore spoke about his own upbringing. "I didn't have abusive parents. As a matter of fact, I was very lucky. My stepfather, more so than my mother, treated me as if I was his kid. He made no differentiation between me and his true kids. My mother kind of differentiated, probably hoping that she was pleasing, I don't know why. My real dad, he spanked me just like he spanked the rest of them. My stepmother stood up for me just like I was her very own. And all of my grandparents were the same way.

"All of my life I had friends here in the summer and I had friends here in the winter. But I was never tightly knit to someone with whom I played in the summer *and* someone with whom I went to school with in the winter. I think it made me unable to tightly associate myself, even with my own kids. I don't know that's a fact, but it's possible. I gave thought to that years before Tony's problems."

Were there drugs involved? Rob asked rhetorically. "I can only speculate. I know that a lot of people get into a lot of trouble with the drug stuff. You wonder on things like that and certainly over in that part of town that's an area that's more prone to that type of stuff, I think."

Rob Shore was doubtful whether he would get an honest answer from his son as to why he was the way he was. "I'm sure when I visit him, he's not going to give me great enlightenment as to how or why it started, or anything like that."

He's not your typical backwoods serial killer like most of them are.
                    —Detective Bob King, on Tony Shore

Bob King

"I guess when I realized the same guy had done Estrada, I knew the potential for him to strike again. The clock was ticking. And it's on my shoulders to find the guy. And, if I don't, a girl is going to be killed, and I've failed. And then, of course, eleven months later when Dana Sanchez was killed . . ." King paused to reflect.

"Wayne Wendel took the call from County Homicide, and when he told me that they found a girl strangled with a tourniquet, I just stormed around the room, and I was really beside myself, because here it is, proof that I failed. But even then, we couldn't prove that they were connected. I caught some flack from my supervisor because they didn't believe we could tie these murders together. So, then detectives who are supposed to be working on murder cases are out of the call-up and they're on this task force and you've got several guys tied up from county and city, and we don't even know if these murders are related and we're acting like they are."

King took the criticism hard. "I became miserable, but there was nothing I could do about it. It wasn't until nine years after Rebollar was killed, and eight years after Sanchez was killed, that it was proven by Shore's admission that those three were related. And, of course, he gave

John Swaim Laurie Tremblay. Then, of course, the question arises, did he do more? He also gave us Selma Janske. When she testified, the whole courtroom was riveted. I was standing outside. They could have given the death penalty for what he did to her and he didn't even kill her."

King continued to believe that Tony Shore might be responsible for even more killings. "John Swaim, Todd Miller, Allen Brown, and Eric Price, from the Friendswood Police Department, went back and talked to him about the Laura Smithers case [a thirteen-year-old girl from Friendswood, Texas, who went missing and was later discovered dead]. He would not fess up about any other murders.

"But it didn't hit on anything else. John Swaim, Todd Miller, Alan Brown, and Eric Price, they all think he's good for that [the Laura Smithers case]."

King spoke of the frustration of working with the local media on a serial killer case. "The tourniquet was a secret that we kept from the news, but I know who blurted it out. It wasn't someone with the Houston Police. The tourniquet was a secret until '95.

"The *Chronicle*, in an article about all these I-45 murders, printed that these three girls were killed with tourniquets. I couldn't believe it. It was done. We didn't mention it again. And I don't think the *Chronicle* mentioned it again. I think that person [the leaker] just made kind of an offhand comment. But it just threw me for a loop. Then, if you have murders subsequent to that where tourniquets are involved, you wonder, *Did the killers get the idea from the newspapers or are they connected to the original three murders?* It turned out it had no bearing, because there were no subsequent murders with tourniquets, and it turned out it didn't hurt us like I thought it might. But I was furious."

King's first thought when Tony Shore's name came

up as the killer was "I was surprised he wasn't a blond-headed guy. I was looking for this fair blond guy. Amy Lynch went to the police substation on Westheimer and filed a police report. She claimed that Tony 'choked me while we had sex' and we looked at that and said, 'All right.' And then we started looking at all of his addresses: where he worked, his proximity to the murder scene, and it put him right in the middle of all of it."

When asked about Laurie Tremblay, King mentioned how Shore claimed that he took her to school and picked her up at the bus stop. "'She was my girlfriend. She wanted to bum a cigarette off of me.' He says he has these relationships with these girls, but Diana Rebollar, no way.

"He tried to have an excuse for anything, but he knew he didn't have an excuse for everything."

King spoke of the pressure of working on such a high-profile case.

"There are guys up there who have solved several serial murder cases and will continue to solve serial murder cases and, here it is, I work on one case and we all solved it. Actually, DNA does and Katherine Long and Orchid Cellmark.

"But I think I feel better. I tell you what, they are really getting hammered up there now and I don't care to do multiple homicides anymore. When you're in Investigations, it could be robbery, burglary, theft, forgery, homicide. You've always got the cases hanging over your head, so even when you're off-duty, you're constantly planning how to attack the case. What am I gonna do tomorrow to work this case and keep my head above water on the new cases? I don't have to worry about that anymore. At the end of the shift that's the end of my problems, and that's another big [reason for] leaving Homicide and going back to Patrol."

<u>Kelly Siegler</u>

"Anthony is smart. He outplayed every woman he ever met. His sister said his IQ was 150, right?" Nonetheless, the prosecutor was shocked that so many women fell for his ruse. "Those eyes are horrible. Horrible eyes. But he gave good bullshit and he is very, very smart."

Siegler still had nothing but admiration for Bob King. "For ten years he had those boxes. The guys laughed at him because he had those boxes down there under his desk all that time. The other guys are like macho Homicide cops. Bob is not like that. He's just more eager, just kind of a good . . . you just want to hug Bob.

"I can tell you what got the cops fired up," she continued. "It was the way that the victims were tied up. And then when they found the little girl, Diana Rebollar, like that, you could feel the anger in them at the scene.

"Those guys, they're the heroes of the story. Not me and Terese and the trial.

"Tony was very subdued in the trial," Siegler continued. "He never looked at us. He pretty much just looked down or looked at the jury in a nonintimidating way. He never did anything to ratchet it up. He knew he was done."

As far as her thoughts on the trial, Siegler said, "It was too bad that those people had to go through the trial, testify, and endure it all. He's an animal. I haven't done that many cases where I think we shouldn't have to waste our time. He's one of them."

Kelly Siegler believed that Tony Shore was responsible for more deaths than just those he had confessed to. "I don't think we are done with this story. It's been long enough now for him to miss the attention. And like the guys told him, 'You aren't gonna be famous, five [including the rape of Selma Janske] doesn't do it. Five ain't shit.' At some point he's gonna realize that."

* * *

*I always said if this case gets solved, I'd go back to Patrol.
Case is solved and one month later I went back to Patrol.*

—Bob King, who currently works the grave-
yard shift as a patrol officer, by choice

*The rest of the family and I all believe that he should have
the death penalty.*

—Regina Shore Belt, on her
brother, Tony Shore

If Anthony Shore's not on death row, who the heck is?
—Kelly Siegler

*It has occurred to me more than once that I may have the
divine misfortune of being the reincarnation or in possession of his spirit (Rasputin, that is).*

—Tony Shore

*There is no Enlightenment, no evolutionary entrance into
the truly Spiritual Condition of human existence, without
ego-death, or transcendence of the mind.*

—Adi Da, "Scientific Proof of the
Existence of God Will Soon Be
Announced by the White House!"

*I believe that when I die I shall rot, and nothing of my ego
will survive.*

—Bertrand Russell

IN MEMORIAM

Laurie Tremblay
Maria del Carmen Estrada
Diana Rebollar
Dana Sanchez

Corey Mitchell will donate a portion of his royalties
for *Strangler* to the Parents of Murdered Children—
Heights Chapter (Houston, Texas).

Feel free to visit their site and consider donating:
http://www.pomc.com/heights/index.html

For *Strangler* updates and extras, please visit:
www.coreymitchell.com
www.myspace.com/coreymitchell

For Corey Mitchell's blog, please visit:
In Cold Blog
http://incoldbloggers.com

Join Corey Mitchell's MySpace TrueCrime Group:
http://groups.myspace.com/truecrime

Acknowledgments

It was my pleasure to be able to work with so many wonderful, funny, and inspiring people. I truly am lucky to have spent time with the following people in person or via modern communications: Diane Messimer, Kristi Thomsen, Kurt Wenz, Kelly Siegler, Terese Buess, Gina Worley Shore, Bob King, John Swaim, Lynda White, Rob Shore, Rose Shore, Dea Shore, Regina Shore Belt, Tiffany Shore, Terry Janske (pseudonym), Gerald Bourque, Andy Kahan, Gabe Vasquez, Ogoretta Worley, Jamie LaChance, Michaela Hamilton, Justin Hocking, He Who Shall Not Be Named, Adam Korn, Irma Rios, the fine folks at C & F Drive Inn, the tire guy, and many more, who wish to remain anonymous.

Sonic salutations go out to Divine Pustulence (check out my video for "Blowtorch Lobotomy"), The Wiggles, Cannibal Corpse, Isis, Pelican, Cult of Luna, Glass Casket, Between the Buried and Me, Cusp, Vapourspace, Intermix, Machine Head, Plastikman (Richie Hawtin is a genius), Phylr, Celtic Frost, Slayer, Strapping Young Lad, Winnie the Pooh, Necrophagist, Aix Em Klemm, The Dead Texan, Astonishing Sod Ape, Boards of

Canada, Neurosis, Carpet Musics, Jesu, Scorn, Dysrhythmia, These Arms Are Snakes, Aphex Twin, Labradford, Low, The Timeout Drawer, Stars of the Lid, Walls of Jericho, Ministry, Red Sparowes, Revolting Cocks, Loscil, Watchtower, Mouth of the Architect, Dread, A Life Once Lost, Autechre, Michael Haaga, Into the Moat, Zombi, Explosions in the Sky, Global Communication, and, as always, P. J. Harvey.

For my friends Ray Seggern and Kelly Nugent, Peter Soria, Lupe Garcia, Mike and Lynette Sheppard, Knox and Heather Williams, Ricky and Shirin Butler, Trey and Missy Chase, Clint and Cathy Stephen, Phil and Karen Savoie, Kevin and Shana Fowler, Chris and Beverly Goldrup, Dennis McDougal, Aphrodite Jones, Poppy Z. Brite, Kirk and Teresa Morris, Drew and Sarah Stride, Mike and Sarah Stinski (aka "Necrolagnia" and "Luna C").

To the Yahoo! True Crime Group for the enlightening book discussions for *Evil Eyes* and *Murdered Innocents*.

To my MySpace friends—thanks for your enthusiasm and keep checking out the site for more contests, freebies, etc. Be sure and join up with my MySpace True Crime group. I am your humble mod.

Thanks to Dave Prewitt and CapZeyeZ. You fawkin' rawk!

Thanks to the Chill Villain.

Thanks to Phyllis Coblentz and Will Robertson at E! Entertainment Television for the special on Hollywood homicides. Let's bring back *Mysteries and Scandals* with me as your host.

To all of the bookstores, radio and television stations, newspapers and magazines, Web sites and podcasts that have let me sign books, taken the time to review my work, or had me on for a discussion, I always enjoy getting to talk about my books and getting close to my readers. Thanks for your help in spreading the disease.

I have the greatest in-laws in the world, Dennis and Margaret Burke. Thank you for watching Emma on Fridays for me. You have helped keep me sane. Also, my sister-in-law Denise Burke ain't half-bad either. Of course I have the coolest Chi-niece in the world, Leah Burke. Lots of love to the Burke family.

I have been blessed with two of the most wonderful parents on the planet, Don and Carol Mitchell. Thank you, as always, for your unending support. I am blessed to get to say, "I love you both." Much love to my brother Kyle and sister-in-law Ramona, my brother Darrin, and all of my beautiful, funny, and intelligent nieces—Julie, Kaylee, and Madison—and my brilliant nephew, Ronnie. Also to Bill and Renee Runyan, Todd Solomon, and Jeremy Frey. Lucas, Dallas, and Max, of course, I would not forget y'all. I couldn't function without each one of you.

For my late wife, Lisa, who always supported my writing career. Thank you again. No matter what, I will always love you.

For my daughter, Emma. Welcome to this crazy world. I am always here for you, but promise not to be the overbearing father. Please know that I will love you forever and will be here for you whenever you need me.

For my wife, Audra, the most sensational bride a man could ask for. You are a wonderful mother, an incredible friend, and the perfect wife. I am completely amazed by you every day. You are an inspiration and my heart is yours forever. All my life and love.

Don't miss Corey Mitchell's true-crime classic

PURE MURDER

Available from Kensington Publishing Corp.

Keep reading to enjoy a compelling excerpt . . .

PROLOGUE

Monday, June 28, 1993—5:00 p.m.
T. C. Jester Park
T. C. Jester Boulevard
Houston, Texas

"Where are the kids at?" the large man, with shoulder-length blond hair, asked the Texas state trooper as he walked along the side of the railroad tracks.

"Sir, you can't go over there," the trooper informed the man, who had already bounded over the side down a steep gravel incline.

"I came for my daughter, goddamn it!" the man screamed, barely glancing back over his shoulder as he quickly scooted toward the trodden circle in the grass where several Houston police officers had gathered. "No, man. Fuck you!" he screamed. The trooper slowly took off after the man, but he did not press the issue.

The large man picked up his pace as he darted toward the cluster of officers. "Does she have blond hair?" the livid father screamed at the top of his lungs. The sound carried through T. C. Jester Park like the crack of a shotgun blast.

"Is she blond? Is one of them blond?"

Randy Ertman had been looking for his fourteen-year-old daughter, Jennifer, since the previous Friday. Jennifer had gone with her best friend, sixteen-year-old Elizabeth Pena, and other friends to an apartment located on the northwest side of Houston.

Two officers stepped forward to cut Ertman off. One officer placed his hand up to prevent the angry man from advancing. The other officer told him he could not go any farther.

"I want to know if that's my daughter, goddamn it!" he screamed at the police officers.

"Sir, I'm sorry, but you cannot go any farther," one of the officers informed him again. "This is a crime scene and you cannot be here."

"I want to know if that's my goddamned daughter in there!" he screamed again, but to no avail. The officers were not budging. They would not let him through.

Ertman stared over the shoulder of one of the officers into the gaping maw of the nearby green forest. Towering pine trees hovered over the enclosed area, where even more police officers were located.

Word had leaked out that the bodies of two teenage girls were discovered in that enclosed space. Randy Ertman believed his daughter, Jennifer Ertman, may have been one of the two girls.

Randy Ertman had exerted a lot of effort to find his daughter over the prior four days. He contacted all of Jennifer's friends to see if they had any clue where she might be. He printed up thousands of flyers and posted them from Galveston to Cypress-Fairbanks. He attended an anti–death penalty rally for convicted killer Gary

Graham in hopes of getting the media's attention to focus on his little girl.

When the call came in that there were two bodies found in the brush near the end of the tree line of T. C. Jester Park, Randy was speaking with newspaper and television reporters at his home in the Heights. He overheard the call on one of the reporters' walkie-talkies. The semihysterical father looked at a cameraman from the local ABC-affiliate channel 13 news division, grabbed his news van keys, and shouted out, "C'mon! Let's go." Randy jumped into the van and made the cameraman drive. They tore out of there like a scorpion shuttling over scorching asphalt.

The news van pulled up to the scene, skidded to a halt in the asphalt, and Randy leapt out of the passenger door. He noticed a large crowd of onlookers had gathered behind the invisible barrier. He was disgusted by the people. They reminded him of hungry, circling vultures eyeing rotted carrion on a deserted highway.

Randy ran from the van, jumped over the police barrier, and made a mad dash for the cluster of police officers.

"Is it my daughter?" he screamed. "Is my daughter back there?" he yelled as he advanced forward.

Sean O'Brien, an eighteen-year-old African-American male, watched the insanity unfold. He saw the van pull up to the scene and witnessed the hysterical father jump out and practically tackle one of the police officers. When O'Brien heard the man ask if one of the victims was blond, he realized it had to be one of the girls' fathers.

O'Brien sheepishly grinned. He slowly turned around and walked away.

Conne

Visit us online at
KensingtonBooks.com
to read more from your favorite authors, see books
by series, view reading group guides, and more.

for sneak peeks, chances to win books and prize packs,
and to share your thoughts with other readers.

facebook.com/kensingtonpublishing
twitter.com/kensingtonbooks

Tell us what you think!

To share your thoughts, submit a review,
or sign up for our eNewsletters, please visit:
KensingtonBooks.com/TellUs.